Global Legal Insights
Employment & Labour Law

First Edition
Contributing Editors: Charles Wynn-Evans & Georgina Rowley
Published by Global Legal Group

GLOBAL LEGAL INSIGHTS - EMPLOYMENT & LABOUR LAW
FIRST EDITION

Contributing Editors
Charles Wynn-Evans & Georgina Rowley, Dechert LLP

Marketing Managers
Suzanne Millar
Andrea Rubino

Production Editor
Andrew Schofield

Editor
Suzie Kidd

Senior Editor
Penny Smale

Managing Editor
Alan Falach

Publisher
George Archer

Group Publisher
Richard Firth

We are extremely grateful for all contributions to this edition.
Special thanks are reserved for Charles Wynn-Evans & Georgina Rowley for all their assistance.

Published by Global Legal Group Ltd.
59 Tanner Street, London SE1 3PL, United Kingdom
Tel: +44 207 367 0720 / URL: www.glgroup.co.uk

ISBN 978-1-908070-35-7
ISSN 2050-2117

Printed and bound by CPI Group (UK) Ltd, Croydon, CR0 4YY
September 2012

CONTENTS

PREFACE

We are delighted both to have been asked to act as Editors of *Global Legal Insights – Employment & Labour Law* and to present the first edition of this book, which addresses developments in labour and employment law across 24 countries worldwide. As can be seen from the variety and detail contained in this book, labour and employment law issues never stand still, and an appreciation of current trends and future changes to the employment law regimes in which they operate is important to any business which operates internationally.

The objective in compiling this book is to provide general counsel, human resource practitioners, lawyers, advisers and managers with an overview of the developments in employment and labour law across a variety of jurisdictions across the world. The authors were asked to provide their personal perspectives on those current and forthcoming changes to the labour and employment law regime in their respective jurisdictions which they considered to be particularly important in practice.

We are very grateful to all the authors for their contributions and hope that this book provides a useful and interesting snapshot of important issues in the employment field in the jurisdictions which it covers.

Charles Wynn-Evans & Georgina Rowley
Dechert LLP

Belgium

Koen De Bisschop
Advocatenkantoor Reliance BVBA

General labour market trends and latest/likely trends in employment litigation

For many years, the Belgian labour market has been known for the high charges that apply to labour. Indeed, repeated studies show that the (para-) fiscal pressure on labour income ranks among the highest in the EU. As the OECD puts it in its country note for Belgium, "*Belgium is the OECD country that levies the highest tax and social security burden on the labour income of single taxpayers regardless of the earnings level. In 2011 single taxpayers at average earnings took home less than 45% of what they cost to their employer (the "total labour costs"); taxpayers at high earnings took home even less than 40%. The average tax wedge (income taxes plus employee and employer social security contributions minus cash transfers as a percentage of total labour costs) faced by two-earner married couples was also the highest in the OECD in 2011. The tax wedge for average one-earner couples with 2 children was the second highest with 15 percentage points above the OECD average.*" (www.oecd.org).

It has also been documented that Belgium seems unable to reduce labour taxes significantly and move to more growth-friendly taxes instead.

Over the years, these high charges on labour have led to employees and employers looking for means to avoid or reduce them, such as for example the payment of significant lump sum cost reimbursements and the qualification of the professional relationship as a self-employed relationship instead of an employment relationship. These "alternatives" have become the subject of increased scrutiny by the authorities and are now very much in the public eye.

The advantages of qualifying a professional relationship as self-employed are self-explanatory from the employer's side. First of all, the fee of a self-employed contractor does not give rise to the high social security contributions that apply to an employee, i.e. 13.07% employee contributions to be deducted from gross salary and ±35% employer contributions to be paid on top of the gross salary. Moreover, there is no cap on the salary on the basis of which the contributions are calculated. Self-employed income, on the other hand, only gives rise to social security contributions at charge of (i.e. to be deducted from the fee of) the self-employed contractor. These contributions generally amount to 22% on a professional income (minus costs) up to €54,398.06 and to 14.16% on a professional income (minus costs) between €54,398.06 and €80,165.52 (figures valid for 2012).

On the part of the professional income (minus costs) that exceeds €80,165.52, no social contributions are due. Not only does the co-contracting party of the self-employed contractor not bear any social insurance cost, it can also determine most of the contractual terms and conditions without restrictions (unless a specific legal regime would apply, as is for example the case for sales agents). This is again a significant advantage compared to an employee relationship, to which a strong regulatory framework applies with mandatory rules on minimum salary levels, working time, vacation, termination, sick pay etc. This contractual freedom, combined with the significant cost advantage because of the absence of employer social security contributions, has led to a self-employed structure becoming common practice for both management positions (where the salary cost is significant) and certain labour-intensive sectors, such as the building sector.

The legal framework did not really prevent the setup of self-employed structures. Belgian law stipulates that the difference between a self-employed and an employee relationship resides in the absence (or the existence) of a subordinate relationship. A clear definition of the term "subordination" is however not provided for, leaving room for interpretation. As a starting point, the law provides that the parties may freely choose the qualification of their contract, provided that such qualification is not contrary to public order, mandatory legislation or morality. It also mentions a number of general criteria that should be analysed in order to establish the absence (or the existence) of a subordinate relationship, i.e. the freedom to organise the working time (or the absence thereof), the freedom to organise the work to be performed (or the absence thereof), and the absence (or the existence) of the possibility to perform hierarchical control. These general criteria may however be deviated from on the basis of particular circumstances. Finally, the law stipulates that if the terms of the self-employed contract conflict with the way in which the contract is performed in practice, the self-employed relationship may be re-qualified into an employee relationship. This is, however, a quite difficult test in practice if the contract has been well-drafted and the parties avoid clear (demonstrable) violations of its terms.

Requalification of a self-employed person into an employee relationship may, however, have serious negative consequences for the party who contracted with the (fake) self-employed contractor, in the sense that it may lead to a claim by the social security agency for (both employee and employer) social security contributions in arrears over the last 3 years, increased by a penalty equal to 10% of the contributions in arrears, and with interest on overdue payments at a rate of 7% per year. Moreover, the requalified employee may claim for labour law adjustments (salary indexations, 13th month, holiday pay etc.) in arrears, and additionally, in case of termination, may claim for termination indemnities as applicable to employees.

The tax authorities may claim professional withholding taxes in arrears, increased with a penalty (generally varying around 20%) and interests on overdue payment at the rate of 7% per year. Depending on the circumstances, they might also impose a so-called 'secret commissions' tax at a rate of 309%. Although these sanctions are severe, daily practice shows that the risks of requalification are often considered as rather low because of the absence of clear rules on subordination and the starting point that parties may freely qualify their relationship. When looking at recent case law in this respect, it should be noted that the courts generally continue to uphold the self-employed qualification to the extent that it can be shown that the self-employed contractor has indeed certain skills that allow him to perform task autonomously. The government on the other hand considers self-employment as a potential social fraud mechanism in the sense that it is a means of avoiding social charges and therefore potentially leads to unfair competition.

Consequently, it is proposing new legislation aimed at introducing a refutable presumption of employment or self-employment on the basis of criteria which may differ from business sector to business sector. The business sectors that would most likely be impacted are the building sector, the cleaning sector, the sector of the security services and the transport sector. Although this is still draft legislation, it clearly shows the government's intention to reduce the use of self-employed agreements. This may also result in more stringent government inspections and hence an increase in legal disputes in this respect.

The lump-sum reimbursement of costs proper to the employer is another illustration of a widespread tool used by employers to increase the employees' net remuneration without having to pay income tax and social security contributions. Indeed, employers are often tempted to overestimate the costs proper to the employer that are difficult to prove by means of supporting evidence. By acting in this way, they attribute a net payment to employees that does not correspond to real professional expenses. The government seems determined to tackle this point and it has instructed the tax and social security administration to pay more attention to this abuse mechanism. In order to strengthen the position of these administrations, it has included a provision in the social security legislation providing that in case of discussion about the reality of the costs proper to the employer, it is up to the employer (and no longer up to the social security administration) to prove the reality of these costs. Moreover, in an internal instruction of the central tax authorities, it has been specified that the tax inspectors should apply the special secret commissions tax of 309% in case of abuse, the (much softer) disallowance of business expenses no longer being a valid alternative.

As with the increased attention on self-employment, this increased scrutiny of the lump-sum reimbursement of costs proper to the employer show the government's intention to submit payments in the framework of a professional relationship to the largest extent possible in respect of employee / employer social security contributions and professional income tax. Budgetary constraints are obviously an important driver in this respect.

Another feature of the Belgian labour market that regularly comes under scrutiny when reviewing factors that affect its competitiveness, and which is again very much the subject of public debate today, relates to the so-called automatic wage indexation mechanism. This mechanism is often criticised because it allows for wage increases without any link to performance and productivity. Recent reports of both the OECD and the EU only illustrate this point. The chances of the automatic wage indexation mechanism being changed or abolished in the near future seem extremely remote, however, because of strong union opposition against any attempts to touch it.

The power of the unions in this respect is linked to an important feature of the wage indexation mechanism that is often overlooked, not only by these reports but also by employers. There is indeed no such thing as a wage indexation mechanism applying to all employees occupied in Belgium. First of all, the wage index mechanism differs from sector to sector. Belgian labour law is not only regulated by federal and regional legislation, but also by collective bargaining that is organised at both national, sector and company level. Wage indexation has always been regulated at the level of the "joint committees", which are sector-level bodies composed of employee (unions) and employer representatives who have the power to conclude collective bargaining agreements that apply to the entire sector. Not all joint committees have been able to reach an agreement on wage indexation, implying that there are sectors where there is no wage indexation mechanism. Secondly, a number of sectors, such as the chemical sector, only impose wage indexation for non-management employees. These points are often overlooked in practice, implying that employers might offer indexation to employees who are not entitled to it on the basis of sector-level rules. Employers should therefore always review sector-level rules before committing to wage indexation, as they might belong to a sector that does indeed allow for wage increases that are based solely on merit.

Key case law affecting employers' decision making over dismissals, redundancies dismissals etc.

There has been recent key case law affecting the dismissal of blue-collar workers and employees benefiting from a career interruption system. Whereas the former is to the employer's detriment, the latter is to the employer's benefit.

1. Belgian law has rather low notice periods for manual workers (so-called "blue-collars"). On average they vary between 35 and 112 days, depending on the blue-collar's seniority (there may be deviations at sector level). These notice periods do not, however, imply that the dismissal of a blue-collar worker should be considered as being cheap. Indeed, if the dismissal of the blue-collar worker is not related to his aptitude, his behaviour or (the requirements of) the functioning of the company, it is considered by law as being arbitrary. An arbitrary dismissal entitles the blue-collar worker to an additional indemnity of 6 months' salary on top of the notice / severance *in lieu* of notice.

According to a certain tendency in case law and legal doctrine, any reason related to the blue-collar's behaviour was sufficient to avoid the payment of this additional indemnity. This position obviously made it quite difficult for a blue-collar worker to succeed in his claim, because even an unfair, far-sought or insignificant reason related to the blue-collar's behaviour could suffice to avoid the payment of this indemnity.

In 2008, the Brussels Labour Court of Appeal held that the dismissal of a blue-collar worker, who was dismissed for having refused to clean up snow without proper gloves, was arbitrary and hence it ordered the employer to pay the additional indemnity of 6 months' salary. The employer did not agree with this decision and argued, as could have been expected on the basis of the aforementioned case law and legal doctrine, that as soon as the dismissal was related to the behaviour of the blue-collar worker, which was the case here, the additional indemnity was not due. The employer stated that the question whether or not the blue-collar's refusal to comply with the employer's instructions was justified or proportionate, was irrelevant and not required by law. Consequently, it felt that the Labour

Court had added a condition to the legal provisions and hence violated the law in this respect. The Supreme Court did not agree with this position. It stated that the additional indemnity was intended to avoid dismissals that were clearly unreasonable. Consequently, a dismissal based on the behaviour of the blue-collar worker may still give rise to the payment of the additional indemnity if the grounds for the dismissal are indeed clearly unreasonable. The courts are therefore entitled to analyse whether the blue-collar worker's behaviour can be considered as a valid reason for the dismissal.

This Supreme Court decision, which is in line with recommendations from the International Labour Organisation stating that a dismissal requires a valid reason, should end the discussion in case law and legal doctrine as to whether a dismissal based on the behaviour of the blue-collar worker should be considered as a reasonable reaction from the employer. If this would not be the case, the employer faces the risk of the dismissal being held arbitrary and hence having to pay an additional indemnity of 6 months' salary to the blue-collar worker.

2. Belgian law knows several legal entitlements for employees to temporarily reduce their working time from a full-time to a part-time occupation, e.g. in the framework of parental leave or career interruption. These systems led to a discussion in case law as to the computation basis that should be taken into account when determining the severance indemnity of a full-time worker who had temporarily reduced his working time in the framework of the aforementioned systems. Should one take into account the real (i.e. part-time) salary at the time of the dismissal or should one take into account a hypothetical full-time salary, considering among others that the part-time employment is *per* definition exceptional and temporary?

Although the Supreme Court already held in 2006 that the real (i.e. part-time) salary should be taken into account for determining the severance indemnity, it recognised in 2010 that for employees benefiting from part-time parental leave, the severance indemnity should be computed on the basis of a hypothetical full-time salary. The latter decision was based on the European framework agreement on parental leave of 14 December 1995 that opposed to a severance indemnity being calculated on the basis of the reduced salary that applied at the time of the dismissal. This decision did not, however, say anything about the other forms of career interruption. Subsequently, the government also enacted legislation that stated that specifically in the case of parental leave, the severance indemnity should be calculated on the basis of a (hypothetical) full-time salary.

The lower courts were however uncertain about the impact of the Supreme Court's 2010 decision on the severance entitlements of employees benefiting from career interruption systems other than parental leave. As a consequence, the Constitutional Court was requested to look into the question whether a different treatment between employees benefiting from parental leave on the one hand, and employees benefiting from other career-interruption systems on the other, is allowed. The Constitutional Court has now confirmed this point, implying that employees working part-time in the framework of career-interruption systems other than parental leave are in principle entitled to a severance indemnity computed on their real salary at the time of the dismissal. In other words, if they work part-time at the time of the dismissal, they will be entitled to a severance indemnity computed on the basis of a part-time salary.

Recent statutory or legislative changes

As of 1 January 2012, the legal provisions in relation to the dismissal of white-collar employees have been amended significantly. These amendments (the "new" termination rules) only apply to employees entering into service as of 1 January 2012. They do not apply to employees who were already in service prior to that date, nor to employees who were bound by an employment agreement before 2012 and who enter into a new employment contract with the same employer as of 1 January 2012, but without the interruption between the initial employment agreement and the agreement taking effect as of 1 January 2012 exceeding 7 days. To the latter categories of employees, the "old" termination rules continue to apply.

Both under the old and the new termination rules, the employer is entitled to terminate the employment contract either by giving notice or by paying a severance indemnity *in lieu* of notice (both options may also be combined). Although some legal authors have recently defended the introduction of a general obligation to motivate the dismissal, which was not required under the old termination rules with the exception of a few cases (e.g. the dismissal of employee representatives), the new termination rules did not introduce any additional requirements in this respect. They only impact the notice to be given by employer and employee respectively in case of dismissal or resignation.

Under the old termination rules, the notice to be respected by the employer is determined as follows. For employees earning up to €31,467.00 gross per year at the time notice is given (figure valid for 2012), the notice amounts to 3 months per commenced 5-year period of continuous employment with the employer. For employees earning more than €31,467.00 gross per year, the aforementioned notice is a minimum. The law does not provide any further guidance as to how the appropriate notice for these employees should be determined, stating merely that the employer and the employee should reach an agreement in this respect at the earliest at the time when notice of termination is given (for employees earning more than €62,934.00 (figure valid for 2012), the agreement on the notice may also be agreed upon in writing prior to the employee's entry into service, without however being inferior to 3 months per commenced 5-year period of continuous employment).

If they are unable to reach an agreement, it is up to the labour tribunal to determine the appropriate notice. The Supreme Court has given some guidance to the tribunals in this respect, by stating that the appropriate notice should be determined by reference to the time required to find comparable employment. In doing so, the employee's age, seniority, salary and function should be taken into account. In most cases, a statistical formula (the so-called "Claeys formula") reflecting case law makes it possible to determine the appropriate notice / severance compensation that a labour tribunal is likely to award. The formula reads as follows: $(0.87 \text{ x seniority}) + (0.055 \text{ x age}) + (0.000038 \text{ x annual salary x } 117.2 / \text{ current index}) - 1.95$. For employees with a gross annual salary that amounts to at least €120,000.00, it was documented that the formula gave a result that overestimated the court decisions. A separate formula has therefore been developed for these employees in which the salary has become a negative factor: $(0.87 \text{ x seniority}) + (0.055 \text{ x age}) + 2.96 - (0.0000029 \text{ x annual salary x } 117.2 / \text{ current index})$.

The notice to be respected by the employee under the old termination rules differs depending on the employee's gross annual salary at the time notice is given. For employees earning up to €31,467.00 gross per year (figure valid for 2012), the notice amounts to 1.5 and 3 months respectively, depending on whether the employee's seniority is less than or greater than 5 years. If the gross annual salary is higher than €31,467.00 but does not exceed €62,934.00, the law only sets a maximum notice of 4.5 months. It is up to the employee to propose a notice in his resignation letter, which then becomes the subject of negotiation or court review if the employer does not agree with the proposal. The same applies to employees earning more than €62,934.00 per year, the sole difference being that the maximum set by law amounts to 6 months.

Under the new termination rules, the notice to be respected by both employer and employee remains unchanged for employees earning up to €31,467.00 gross per year at the time of termination (figure valid for 2012). For employees earning more than €31,467.00 gross per year, the notice to be respected by the employer amounts to 91 days if the employee's seniority is less than 3 years, 120 days for a seniority between 3 and 4 years, 150 days for a seniority between 4 and 5 years and 182 days for a seniority between 5 and 6 years. If the employee's seniority amounts to at least 6 years, the employee will be entitled to 30 days' notice per started year of seniority. The aforementioned notice periods will change again slightly for dismissals as of 2014, to the extent that the notice to be respected by the employer will amount to: 91 days if the employee's seniority is less than 3 years; 116 days for a seniority between 3 and 4 years; 145 days for a seniority between 4 and 5 years; and 182 days for a seniority between 5 and 6 years. If the employee's seniority amounts to at least 6 years, the employee will be entitled to 29 days' notice per started year of seniority. As was the case under the old rules, it remains possible to determine an alternative (lower) notice period (with a minimum of 3 months' notice per started period of 5 years' seniority) at the latest upon the employee's entry into service, provided that he/she has a gross annual salary of more than €62,934.00.

The notice to be respected under the new termination rules by an employee earning more than €31,467.00 gross per year (figure valid for 2012), amounts to 45 days if his seniority is lower than 5 years, 90 days if his seniority is between 5 and 10 years, or 135 days if it amounts to at least 10 years. If the employee has an annual gross salary that exceeds €62,934 and a seniority of 15 years or more, the notice to be respected amounts to 180 days.

These new termination rules imply that for employees starting work as of 1 January 2012, there should no longer be any debate as to the appropriate notice, which was one of the main discussion points under the old rules.

Likely or impending reforms to employment legislation and enforcement procedures

Belgian employment law is characterised by the difference between white-collar and blue-collar workers. The difference between the two resides in the fact that a blue-collar worker is considered as performing manual labour, whereas a white-collar worker is considered as performing intellectual labour. Although this distinction used to make sense at the time of its introduction many years ago, changing production processes that have become increasingly technical and require specific skills from production workers, imply that there are only few jobs left that can be qualified as truly "manual".

Already in 1993, the Constitutional Court held that the distinction between white-collar and blue-collar workers was based on a distinction that it was hard to consider as reasonable and objective. At that time, however, the Constitutional Court did not impose a strict deadline on the government to abolish it. It merely constituted a firm recommendation for the government to take the necessary steps to harmonise both regimes.

The differences between these regimes are however considerable, implying that any harmonisation exercise is extremely difficult and sensitive. Indeed, the differences are spread across the legal framework, and touch on subjects such as the trial period, the appropriate notice (and the concept of arbitrary dismissal as discussed above), the way (timing) in which the salary should be paid out, the guaranteed salary in case of work incapacity, vacation pay and the applicable social security contributions. Moreover, because of the substantial differences between both regimes, the unions have also set up different sections for white-collar and blue-collar workers. This subdivision also implied that the unions were not really in favour of harmonising both regimes because of the substantial impact this would have on their organisation.

In 2011, the Constitutional Court was again asked to review the distinction between white-collar and blue-collar workers by the Brussels Labour Court, specifically in relation to the appropriate notice and the unpaid first day of sick leave, which only applies to blue-collar workers. The Labour Court wanted to know whether these different provisions for white-collar and blue-collar workers constituted a violation of the principle of equal treatment provided for in the Belgian constitution. The Constitutional Court explicitly held that these principles indeed violate the constitutional principle of equal treatment and non-discrimination, but that the distinctions could be maintained until new legislation was enacted to abolish them, with a final deadline of 8 July 2013. In other words, the legislator has until 8 July 2013 to abolish the differences between white-collar and blue-collar workers that were the subject of the decision of the Constitutional Court.

This decision of the Constitutional Court raises the question whether legislative action is only required in relation to the matters that were the subject of the decision, or whether it is time to harmonise / unify the white-collar and blue-collar systems altogether. One could indeed raise the question whether it is not time to go for a harmonisation exercise that exceeds the two items that were looked at by the Constitutional Court (i.e. the notice periods and the unpaid first day of sick leave). It can indeed be expected that if the Constitutional Court would be asked to look at other differences that exist between the two regimes, it would come to the same conclusion. In other words, it might not make a lot of sense to only address the matters that were the subject of the decision, as this only looks like postponing what seems unavoidable in the long run.

Another question raised by this debate is what would happen if the legislator does not succeed in harmonising the two regimes in general, or the two matters that were the subject of the decision of the Constitutional Court in particular. Taking into account that the legislator failed to harmonise the two regimes over a period of 18 years (between 1993 and 2011), it is difficult to imagine that it will succeed now over a time period of 2 years (2011-2013). Judging from the progress (or the absence hereof) made in this respect, it does not seem that unlikely that there will not be any harmonisation by 8 July 2013. According to some legal authors, the absence of any harmonisation does not create an entitlement for blue-collar workers to claim the more advantageous rules that apply to white-collar workers, especially in relation to the applicable notice. They would only be entitled to claim compensation from the Belgian State for failing to harmonise the regimes as required by the Constitutional Court, but could not be able to turn to their employer to claim the same benefits as those applicable to white-collar workers. However, others take the view that the only possible outcome in case of a failure to harmonise would be the levelling-up of benefits, i.e. awarding to blue-collar workers the benefits that currently apply to white-collar workers. Although both points of view can be criticised, it is in any event clear that the absence of harmonisation will lead to considerable uncertainty. To be continued…

Koen De Bisschop
Tel: +32 15 63 66 43 / Email: koen.debisschop@reliancelaw.be

Koen De Bisschop is a partner at Belgian HR niche law firm Reliance. From 2001 to 2009, he worked in the employment law departments of two magic circle firms. In 2009, he set up Reliance. Throughout his career, Koen has dealt with a wide range of employment law issues. He has advised companies on the (national and international) appointment and dismissal of executives, the setup of competitive salary structures and negotiations with unions. Koen also has a significant experience in company restructurings. He assists companies in the implementation of measures aiming at avoiding or limiting redundancies. He has also implemented numerous collective dismissals and closures, including in the framework of corporate transactions. Furthermore, Koen is a specialist in labour-related litigation and has built up an extensive experience in assisting clients before the labour courts. Koen is recommended in the 2010, 2011 and 2012 editions of the Legal 500.

Advocatenkantoor Reliance BVBA

Conventstraat 2, 2800 Mechelen, Belgium
Tel: +32 15 63 66 43 / Fax: +32 15 63 66 54 / URL: http://www.reliancelaw.be

Brazil

Fabio Medeiros
Machado Associados Advogados e Consultores

General labour market trends and latest/likely trends in employment litigation

Numbers are possibly the most illustrative and effective way of better understanding Brazil in terms of employment litigation. More than 2.1 million new labour lawsuits were filed in Brazil during 2011 according to the Superior Labour Court (TST), the highest labour court in the country. This alarming figure is equivalent to 1,073.71 labour lawsuits per 100,000 inhabitants, which undoubtedly spots Brazil as the leading country when it comes to labour lawsuits.

Labour lawsuits per year in Brazil

Year	Lawsuits
2011	2,110,718
2010	1,987,948
2009	2,107,449
2008	1,904,718
2007	1,824,661
2006	1,767,280
2005	1,739,242

Source: TST

There are many reasons for such a chaotic environment, but maybe the old labour and employment legislation is the most emblematic. In Brazil, rights and obligations regarding employment and the ruling of the relevant judicial system are substantially ruled by an old Decree, the Consolidation of Labour Laws, the so-called CLT, which will be 80 years old in 2013 and was issued when Brazil was mostly rural and industries were just starting up across the country.

Therefore Brazilian labour law nowadays is unsafe due to several major gaps in the rulings on contemporary and new employment relationships, a situation that pushes workers and employers to solve disputes in the labour courts. As result, it is the case law formed by a collapsing judicial system that eventually rules on numerous employment conflicts.

It is also important to point out that Brazilian legislation grants workers full access to labour courts. In spite of a legal provision stating that the employees should submit their claims to conciliation commissions formed by employees' unions and companies to settle private employment disputes prior to filing judicial lawsuits for such purpose, most are directly submitted to, and accepted by, labour courts.

Labour courts do not accept private arbitration as valid to settle individual employment disputes, but only for the resolution of disputes arising from collective bargaining between employees and employers' unions, as provisioned by the Federal Constitution.

The acknowledgment of employee status is probably employers' most feared workers' claim in Brazil due to all the statutory rights and costs triggered by an employment agreement. That set of rights and obligations generates hiring costs up to 103.46% over the salaries, including taxes, some studies say.

According to the Consolidation of Labour Laws, employees are specific individuals who are compensated for recurring rendering of services developed under subordination to the employer, who has the power of conducting the business and the employment relationship – power to control, inspect and sanction employees.

Independent contractors, in turn, are solely responsible for their business and they do not render services under such subordination to the engaging party, as the latter just aims at the outcome of the contract. Independent contractors may also allocate other professionals to comply with their contract, which does not apply to employees, so most of the rights and obligations are agreed between the parties and are not statutory by law.

Consequently, parties of an employment relationship are not allowed to choose between these types of worker status in Brazil. Neither employees' status, nor labour rights, except for salaries being above the lower limits, are negotiable. Brazilian labour law protects employees' rights grounded on two main principles: (i) the prevalence of substance over form (that is, preponderance of the facts over formal arrangements); and (ii) the assumption that the employee is the weakest party in the negotiation of terms and conditions of the employment agreement.

These principles are strictly respected by the labour courts in order to qualify independent contractors as employees. Once this happens, the employer is condemned to pay the employment rights prescribed by law to the claimant, which are mainly the following:
- national minimum wage, currently BRL 622.00;
- overtime payment of at least 50% over the normal compensation;
- in a work shift from 10pm to 5am, 52 minutes and 30 seconds are considered as one regular working hour (so-called reduced night shift hour), which is paid with an additional compensation of 20% over the regular hourly salary;
- a weekly rest, preferably on Sundays;
- Christmas bonus, also referred to as 13th salary, which is equivalent to 1/12 of the salary multiplied by the months of work during the year, paid in two instalments, one up to November 30 and the other up to December 20;
- 30 vacation days per year of work, with salary paid with an additional 1/3 bonus;
- profit or results-sharing programmes if negotiated with the relevant employees' union;
- justified work absences;
- 120-day maternity leave with salary paid by the employer which is then reimbursed by the social security, counted from birth or from 28 days before it;
- five-day paternity leave with salary;
- risk compensation of 30% over the base salary in case of work under some risky activities: (i) that imply contact with flammable or explosive substances under an strong risk condition; (ii) that imply contact with radioactive substances or ionising radiation; (iii) in the electric power segment; and (iv) subject to risky conditions in a permanent or intermittent manner;
- additional compensation in case of unhealthy working conditions equivalent to 10%, 20% or 40% of the national minimum wage;
- unemployment severance fund equivalent to 8% of the monthly compensation, which is deposited in an official individual bank account for each employee, who can withdraw the accrued funds in certain circumstances established by law, such as in case of retirement or dismissal without just cause;
- minimum prior notice period for employment agreement termination by the employer of at least 30 days plus three days per year for work, limited to the maximum of 90 days, or the employer may pay it *in lieu* of notice;
- fine paid by the employer of 50% over the balance of the unemployment severance fund deposited during the employment agreement in case of dismissal without cause (40% fine

reverting to the employee and 10% fine paid as an extraordinary social contribution);
*   family bonus, per child under 14, of BRL 31.22 (for employees with monthly salary up to BRL 608.80), and of BRL 22.00 (for employees with monthly salary between BRL 608.81 to BRL 915.05); the payment is made by the employer, which is then reimbursed by the social security system; and/or
*   public transportation vouchers for the employee's commuting to work and home paid by the employer, which must discount up to 6% of the relevant cost from the employee's monthly salary.

Other benefits may be mandatory by the application of collective agreements (between employees' unions and employers) or collective bargaining agreements (between employees and employers' unions).

Besides, the statute of limitations for labour lawsuits is two years from the termination of the employment relationship, provided that the labour claims comprise rights related to: (i) the past five years counted from the filing date; or (ii) 30 years in case of lawsuits regarding unemployment severance fund deposits counted from the filing date.

Foreign work in Brazil

This challenging scenario has been under the spotlight for foreign companies and workers due to the intensification of international mobility during the financial crises. Brazil has been appointed as the world's sixth-largest economy by nominal gross domestic product (GDP) and the country has been enjoying a modest, but continuing growth. The imminent FIFA World Cup 2014 and the Rio de Janeiro 2016 Olympic Games are also driving investments in the country, including those from international groups of companies, a situation that also attracts expats to take on job positions in Brazil.

A report organised by the Labour and Employment Ministry (Ministério do Trabalho e Emprego – MTE), that is the primary government agency responsible for the enforcement of labour and employment statutes and regulations, shows that the rate of work permits issued to foreigners in Brazil grew 177.22% between 2006 and 2011, a 25.92% rise in 2011 alone.

Work permits for foreigners in Brazil

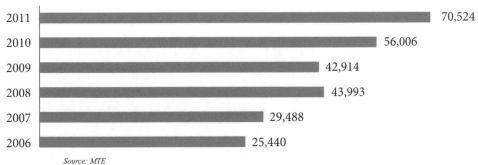

Source: MTE

From the total of 70,524, most of the work permits issued in 2011 were for: U.S. nationals (10,049) that were followed by workers from the Philippines (7,784); United Kingdom (4,817); India (4,235); Germany (3,142); Indonesia (2,679); Italy (2,406); France (2,240); Japan (2,062); and China (2,062).

Among many types of visas and work permits, the one most applied for is the temporary visa for foreign employees sponsored by a Brazilian company. It is valid for two years (non-renewable after a decision by the Ministry of Justice in November, 2011) upon the execution of an employment contract between the Brazilian company and the foreign professional, which shall be submitted to the Labour and Employment Ministry's analysis. This visa is available for employees who are transferred from one corporate entity in one jurisdiction to a related party in Brazil.

Work permits per nationality in Brazil – 2011

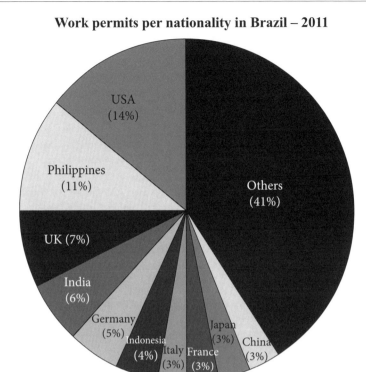

Source: MTE

Among the main requirements for the temporary visa and relevant work permit are the rules for compensation. On one hand, the compensation paid to the foreign employee may not be lower than the higher compensation paid in Brazil for those on the same positions in the company. On the other hand, the sponsor company shall provide evidence that the compensation paid to the foreigner abroad will be at least the same in Brazil.

The so-called "one third rule" is another restrictive rule with which the Brazilian company must comply with in order for a foreigner to be authorised to work in Brazil. According to the Consolidation of Labour Laws, for each foreign employee the employer must hire two Brazilian employees, a rule that is also inspected in relation to the proportional compensation to be paid to foreign and Brazilian employees.

Key case law affecting employers' decision making over dismissal, redundancies dismissals etc.

Prior notice period for termination proportional to the work period

The House of Representatives finally approved Bill 3,941/1989 from the Federal Senate to make effective the proportional prior notice for termination without cause. Thus, more than 23 years after being stated as a social right in the Federal Constitution of 1988, the "new" prior notice now follows the guidelines of Law 12,506/2011, published last October 13.

In its three very brief provisions, the new law added to the standard 30-day prior notice for termination without cause a proportional prior notice period: three days per year of work in the same company up to the maximum of 60 days. Therefore, the prior notice period may now be up to a maximum of 90 days.

It is important to note that before the new law, the rules for the prior notice were extracted from Article 487 and following of the Consolidation of Labour Laws. Thus, in case there is no stipulated term, the party (employee or employer) intending to terminate the employment agreement should give notice to the other at least 30 days in advance, under the penalty of having to indemnify the party not notified.

Notwithstanding, the changes to the prior notice provision have already started to generate significant doubts, such as:

(a) if the additional three days of prior notice per year of work should also protect the employer in case the employee resigns; or

(b) if the additional three days of prior notice should be counted from the first year of work to the same company or only from the second year.

Due to these and other uncertainties the Labour and Employment Ministry is studying to regulate the application of the proportional prior notice as to matters where the provision was unclear.

In our opinion, the "new" prior notice is still far from being applied with full legal assurance. Therefore, the controversies created by the new legislation will probably be solved on a case-by-case basis by the labour courts, unless a clear and legal regulation is enacted shortly.

<u>Mass layoffs</u>

Mass layoffs is another topic that has become much debated since the beginning of the current global financial crisis, mainly because of many lawsuits filed by labour unions against companies that dismissed groups of employees, in an attempt to reverse the dismissals in court.

Brazil has no specific legislation to regulate situations where the employer fires several employees on the grounds of financial hardship. Although the Federal Constitution provides that the employment relationship is protected against arbitrary dismissal or without cause, it delegates the regulation of these principles to a supplementary law that still does not exist.

Once again, disputes between employers and employees have been submitted to labour courts for settlement.

Perhaps the most emblematic case that has been influencing not only the case law, but mainly employers' decisions regarding mass layoffs is *Embraer's (Empresa Brasileira de Aeronáutica)*. The company is one of the world's largest aircraft manufacturers, focusing on regional, military, and corporate aviation, the country's third-largest exporter, and the world's third-largest manufacturer of commercial jets, after Boeing and Airbus.

In February 2009, *Embraer* announced the layoff of 4,000 employees of the total 21,362 employees, stating that such critical situation was a result of the crisis affecting the global economy, particularly the airline industry, so according to the company a review of its base cost and, consequently, its headcount became inevitable.

The employees' union quickly began protests and even contacts with the mayor of São José dos Campos, a city located in the State of São Paulo, where the Company is established and creates many direct and indirect jobs for the region. From the standpoint of the union the company should first have sought alternatives to avoid layoffs, such as reducing working hours without reducing wages and job tenure. The company was also notified by the Labour Prosecutor to provide justifications for the terminations that were denounced by the employees' union as unfair and that if any of *Embraer*'s problems were real, they were actually resulting from speculation by the company with risky investments in the stock market.

Trying to reduce damage to the dismissed employees, as well as to raise awareness of the employees' union, *Embraer* guaranteed benefits not provided by law, such as the extension of health insurance for workers for one year from the date of dismissal and an additional indemnity according to the seniority of each employee.

Given the irreversible position of the company, the employees' union also in February 2009 filed a lawsuit against *Embraer* in an attempt to reinstate the dismissed employees, arguing that before firing, the company should have negotiated with the union. It is worth mentioning that the labour court system in Brazil is basically divided into three levels:

(a) the labour courts (*Varas do Trabalho*) within cities, which are the lower courts for judgment of individual lawsuits by single judges;

(b) the Regional Labour Courts (TRT) in the states' capitals, which are appellate courts or for judgement of collective lawsuits, such as those filed by unions, as happened in the *Embraer* case; in these courts the lawsuits are generally judged by panels of judges;

(c) the Superior Labour Court (TST) in Brasilia (Federal Capital), which is the ultimate appellate court, where just very specific appeals are accepted to be judged, also by a panel of judges. It is also the appellate level in the case of collective lawsuits.

Although the Regional Labour Court has granted an injunction to interrupt the layoffs and *Embraer* was forced to reinstate the dismissed employees, the case was eventually decided by the Superior Labour Court, which did not accept the reinstatement of the employees, but kept the obligation to pay an additional indemnity for dismissal calculated proportionally to length of service of each employee. The majority of judges considered that the mass layoff of employees of *Embraer* was not improper; however, the judicial interpretation came to be that companies need to negotiate with the employees' unions before the execution of mass layoffs.

From that final judgment taking place in August 2009, according to the labour courts a mass dismissal is a collective fact that must be governed by principles and rules of the collective labour law. Therefore although the mass layoffs are not prohibited, they are subject to the procedure of a collective bargaining.

Thus, currently in Brazil, layoffs should be effectively supported by reasons based on technical and financial evidence, preceded by a collective bargaining with the employees' unions.

Recent statutory or legislative changes

Reduction of taxation on payroll for some sectors

Besides the mentioned long list of labour rights triggered by the employee status in Brazil, the employer is also liable for the following employment-related taxes:

*   20% social security contribution on the monthly compensation;

*   1% to 3% variable social security contribution to fund work-related accident benefits and special retirement on the monthly compensation, according to the activities performed by the company, which can be reduced to half or doubled according to the social security benefits related to work-related accidents;

*   6%, 9% or 12% variable social security contribution on the monthly compensation earned by the employees entitled to accelerated retirement due to work under harmful conditions;

*   contributions levied at variable rates of up to 5.8% for social services provided by associations representing the rural, industrial, services and trade sectors; and

*   8% unemployment severance fund on the monthly compensation.

Aiming to generate more jobs and investments, the Federal Government decided in 2011 to reduce taxes on the payroll of various economy sectors by replacing the 20% social security contributions on salaries mentioned above by rates of 2.5% and 1.5% on gross revenues of some service providers and product manufacturers, respectively. These rates are reduced to 2% and 1%, respectively, from August 2012 on, after the sanction of an amendment to the law.

The system is part of a government programme referred to as *"Brasil Maior"* (Greater Brazil) that is intended to be valid from December 2011 to December 2014. The first affected were the sectors of outsourcing of information technology (IT) and call centre services. Such a programme to cut down taxes on the payroll of the companies will also reach the hotel industry from August 2012 to encourage Brazil's preparation for the FIFA World Cup 2014 and the Rio de Janeiro 2016 Olympic Games.

The system to cut down the payroll burden is also mandatory for a list of specific products mainly in the following sectors: textile; leather and footwear; plastic; electrical equipment; capital goods; buses; auto parts; shipping and airline; and furniture.

The Federal Government has announced a gradual expansion of the programme to other sectors of the economy, but it is still too soon to know whether the State goals of increasing the number of jobs will work.

Work performed out of the employer's establishment

In 2011 Article 6 of the Consolidation of Labour Laws was amended by Law 12,551/2011 just to make clear something that has long been defined by case law: employees working at home or remotely are not distinguished from employees who work in the employer's establishment, provided that the conditions of employment are detected, mainly subordination and personal involvement.

The legislation also has just made clearer that the telematics and computerised command, control and supervision methods are equivalent to personal and direct command, control and supervision methods, for purposes of hierarchical subordination. These changes in the law, however, were already amply adopted as rules by case law.

Some lawyers, and even some judges boasted that these changes actually represent a radical change in labour law in Brazil, because from now on employees who work remotely and using mobile phones and internet paid by the employer, in fact, would have their full time available to their employer, co-workers and customers. Thus, these employees would have to be paid for all time available for work.

This is an interpretation that is totally distorted in our opinion. Brazil already has a specific rule governing the situation where the employee is prevented from leaving their home or city of residence to wait to be called to work by the employer, colleagues or customers. In this case, if the fact that the employee cannot move due to employer's orders is proven, the employee is entitled to receive one third of their salary for the period referred to as "on-call duty" (Article 244, paragraph 2 of the Consolidation of Labour Laws).

On the other hand, if the employee is free to leave their home city, only the hours actually worked should be compensated as overtime hours, with an additional of at least 50% of the regular hourly salary. This interpretation was also consolidated by the Superior Labour Court case law in May 2011:

> Ruling 428 – On call-duty – The use of communications devices, like BIP, pager or mobile device by employee, by itself, does not characterise on-call duty, since the employee does not remain at home, at any time, waiting for a work call.

Therefore, although there are already some lawsuits filed by employees involving the matter, none of the known precedents has been against the case law interpretation, according to which the mere use of corporate mobile phones by employees does not give rise to the payment of additional remuneration for on-call duty or overtime.

Likely or impending reforms to employment legislation and enforcement procedures

Outsourcing – Definition of what is possible and what is prohibited in Brazil

The outsourcing of services in Brazil is seen as a risk for various sectors, because there is no law regulating when such employment is permitted or prohibited. There is a normative statement of the Labour and Employment Ministry about the oversight of outsourcing, but its rules are much more related to the types of documents that companies must make available to the inspectors, rather than necessarily what types of activities can or cannot be outsourced.

The difficulty due to the legal gaps is to determine what activities the company may or may not outsource. As a consequence many outsourcing contracts are challenged before the courts by the allocated employees, by the unions or even by Labour Prosecutors. The most frequent allegation by them is that outsourcing contracts are illicit because professionals working in the same place, but for different companies (some for the outsourcing company and others for the service contracting party), have different labour rights, such as salaries, additional for overtime, meal vouchers and collective bargaining agreements, among others. These inconsistencies are making labour relations more precarious, they believe.

Nowadays the main parameter for companies that hire third-party services is Ruling 331 of the Superior Labour Court:

> SERVICE AGREEMENT. LEGALITY
>
> I – The hiring of workers through an intermediary company is illegal, forming the employment directly with the party engaging the services, except in the case of temporary work (Law 6,019/1974).
>
> II – The irregular hiring of workers through an intermediary company does not create an employment relationship with the governmental entities (Article 37, item II of the Federal Constitution).

III – No employment relationship arises with the company that hires surveillance services (Law 7,102 /1983) and services of repair and cleanliness, as well as specialised services not connected to the core activity of the service contracting party, provided that no work on a personal basis and direct subordination exists.

IV – The non-compliance with labour obligations by the employer involves the liability of the service contracting party in relation to those obligations, provided that the service contracting party has been included in the lawsuit and in the judicial enforcement.

...

VI - The liability of the service contracting party shall cover all amounts arising from the award concerning to the period of employment."

In this sense, according to case law, companies may outsource activities that are ancillary or which are just means to achieve the core business. Classic examples of such type of hiring are cleaning services for the industries and security services for offices. In such situations the case law interprets that the outsourced services are not related to the manufactured products or to the services provided by the offices. Thus, the hiring of companies specialised in these ancillary services is perceived as lawful by the courts.

The Society urges for a specific law on outsourcing soon. Currently the main bill related to outsourcing has been awaiting a Congress vote since 2004 (Bill 4,330) and it has been discussed in forums organised by various sectors, including the Superior Labour Court.

Social media and employment

There are no specific restrictions on background checking of applicants, provided that intimacy, private life, honour and image of people are respected. For instance, lawsuits may be filed by applicants for indemnification due to alleged moral or material damages, regardless of the fact if the background check is conducted by the future employer or by a third party.

With regard to the use of social networks in the workplace, Brazil has no specific regulations on the subject. In a poll conducted in March this year by our firm, 47.7% of the 155 professionals who answered questions about the social media and employment matter said that the companies they work for have been using social networks for corporate purposes, especially Facebook (73%), LinkedIn (52.7%) and Twitter (58.1%).

The most curious and important results of the poll are that although 62.6% of professionals said they had permission to use social networks at work, 25.2% said they did not know if their employers have policies to regulate employees' use of social networks, and a further 42.6% said their employers do not have such policies.

In other words, on the one hand, most workers are allowed to use social networks at work without rules or guidance given by the employer. On the other hand:

- 36.2% of the professionals who answered the poll said their employers monitor the use of social networks during the work shift;

- 19.4% said that their employers have already dealt with situations caused by employees misusing social networks; and

- 18.7% answered that their employers have already taken disciplinary actions against employees due to such misuse.

As the number of lawsuits involving the limits for employers on their employees' use of social networks has increased, much has been said about the need for separate legislation on the subject. Again, cases where employees post pictures of the work environment or complain about bosses and co-workers, for example, have been discussed in lawsuits.

In short, employers in Brazil are still only beginning to evaluate ways to protect them against the risks of their employees' use of social networks. Timidly, some companies have been inserting clauses on rules related to the topic in labour contracts, collecting written authorisation of the employees to perform the monitoring. But the path to a specific legislation still seems to be long and uncertain, even though crucial to protect businesses and employees.

Fabio Medeiros
Tel: +55 11 3093 4855 / Email: fbm@machadoassociados.com.br
Partner of the labour, employment and social security practice, focusing on legal advising, which includes audit and mergers and acquisitions projects (due diligences) and legal opinions on compensation and benefits for professionals – rendering of services. Graduate from Universidade Católica de Santos (1996), postgraduate studies in Labour and Employment (2004) and LL.M. in Social Security Law (2009), both in Pontifícia Universidade Católica de São Paulo – PUC. Author of several articles published in local and foreign publications. Member of associations such as the International Bar Association – IBA – part of the Employment and Industrial Relations Law Committee, the Discrimination Law Committee and the IBA Global Employment Institute, and of the American Bar Association – ABA – part of the Section of Labour and Employment Law. Member of the Brazilian Institute of Social Law Cesarino Júnior – IBDSCJ – Brazilian Section of the "Société Internationale de Droit du Travail et de la Sécurité Sociale", part of the International Labour Organization – ILO. Member of the Legal Committee of the British Chamber in Brazil.

Machado Associados Advogados e Consultores

Av. Brig. Faria Lima, 1656 – 11º andar – São Paulo-SP, Brazil
Tel: +55 11 3093 4855 / Fax: +55 11 3819 5322 / URL: http://www.machadoassociados.com.br

Bulgaria

Violeta Kirova
Boyanov & Co.

General labour market trends and latest/likely trends in employment litigation

The latest trends in employment litigation have developed in four main areas:

1. Non-compete clauses in employment contracts

Whilst the Bulgarian labour legislation and the court practice undisputedly agree that employers may impose certain non-compete obligations on the employees for the duration of their employment, until recently there was no established or consistent court practice on whether such non-compete obligations could be validly imposed by employers for a period after the termination of employment.

The validity of a general non-compete clause to be applied following the termination of the employment relationship was, until recently, highly disputable for the reason that there was material risk that they could be declared null and void by the competent courts as violating basic individual rights guaranteed under the Constitution of the Republic of Bulgaria. Also until recently the generally accepted understanding (however not supported by a consistent court practice) was that if the non-compete clause was tailored in a way that the employee was obliged to refrain from undertaking such activities against a certain consideration to be paid by the previous employer for a certain period of time following the termination of the employment, such a non-compete clause could be viewed as an agreement for the provision of negative services under the Bulgarian VAT Act, thus accepted as valid and binding by the Bulgarian courts.

In mid 2010 the Supreme Court of Cassation of the Republic of Bulgaria issued a milestone decision on this issue. The Supreme Court of Cassation expressly ruled that a post termination non-compete clause is invalid as violating the law. Under the Constitution of the Republic of Bulgaria, each citizen has the right to freely choose his profession and place of work, therefore this constitutional right may not be validly waived or restricted through a private agreement (either through a separate agreement or through a clause in an employment contract). It is inadmissible to waive one's personal right to labour guaranteed by the Constitution of the Republic of Bulgaria.

In 2011 and 2012 the lower ranking courts developed steady and consistent court practice on the issue of post termination non-compete clauses fully in line with the 2010 decision of the Supreme Court of Cassation of the Republic of Bulgaria.

It is now clear that any non-compete clause which prohibits the employee to work for a competitive employer after the termination of his employment is null and void, irrespective of the duration of the non-compete period and irrespective whether the employer pays non-compete consideration or not. Any penalty agreed between the employer and the employee for violation of a post termination non-compete clause will also be invalid.

2. Delegation of powers in the area of employment relations

Under the Bulgarian legislation, the employer's functions in the area of employment relations (i.e., conclusion, amendment and termination of employment contracts, seeking disciplinary / financial liability of the employee, etc.) have to be exercised by the statutory representatives of the employer. As statutory representatives are considered the persons entitled to manage and represent the employer, they are entered in the Commercial Registry with the Registrations Agency as such.

It has always been a critical issue to multinational companies, having registered as statutory representatives of their Bulgarian subsidiary expatriates residing outside Bulgaria, whether such statutory representatives could validly empower a local resident to exercise their day-to-day functions in the area of employment relations.

Undoubtedly such an approach has a tremendous practical value and ensures a higher level of flexibility of employers. However, from a legal standpoint, such an approach proves to be extremely risky. Over recent years, the Bulgarian courts adopted a constant court practice that the employer's responsibilities in the area of employment relations could be assigned (by way of a power of attorney) from the statutory representatives to other officers/employees only in cases explicitly established in the Bulgarian Labour Code. And the only case where the Bulgarian Labour Code allows such assignment is in the case of imposition of disciplinary sanctions. The Supreme Court of Cassation of the Republic of Bulgaria has accepted that the specific nature of the employment contract and the employment relationship requires extremely limited possibilities of the employer to assign its powers (exercised by its statutory representatives) to other officers/employees. In this respect, the Supreme Court of Cassation of the Republic of Bulgaria accepts that the employer cannot refer to the general civil law provisions and principles regarding the issue of powers of attorney. This means that the general civil law rule that a person can authorise another to undertake any and all actions unless such authorisation is expressly prohibited, is inapplicable in the case of employers' responsibilities.

For this reason, the lower ranking courts have ruled in a number of cases that a termination order signed by a proxy of the statutory representative of the employer is illegal. Furthermore, if the statutory representatives of the employer are more than one and they represent the company jointly, a termination order signed by one of the representatives (even if he has a power of attorney from the other representative) shall also be illegal.

Conclusion, amendment and termination of employment contracts should be performed only by the statutory representative of the employer. However, from a purely practical point of view, we consider that when it comes to the conclusion of employment contracts, administration of the internal documentation of the employer (meaning authorisation of paid leave, increase of the salary, etc.), which bear more or less lower risk of being challenged before the court, the statutory representative could issue an express power of attorney to another officer/employee to handle such issues. In the case of the conclusion of an employment contract on the basis of such a power of attorney, the risk is that this contract could be viewed as invalid, however if there is a court dispute over the validity, the statutory manager could always confirm (countersign) the employment contract, which will remedy the violation and the employment contract shall become valid.

In all other cases, especially in the cases of termination of employment on different grounds (except disciplinary dismissal), it is strongly recommended to avoid issuing powers of attorney in order to limit the risk of successful challenge of the dismissals before the court.

3. Contracts with the members of the management of a company

It has always been an interesting issue for multinational companies, having registered a subsidiary in Bulgaria, what type of contract they should offer their management bodies (statutory managers, executive directors, members of the management board or the board of directors) and the other key/management employees – a management contract or an employment contract and what the basic differences are between the regimes of these contracts (if any).

As a first step, it should be made extremely clear that the regime of the management contract differs completely from the regime of the employment contract:

• Employment contracts are governed by the Bulgarian Labour Code, which gives the parties extremely low flexibility to freely negotiate the clauses of the employment contract. The majority of the provisions of the Bulgarian Labour Code (i.e., regarding working hours, breaks, leave, labour discipline, information and consultation, duration, termination of the employment, etc.) are mandatory in nature and may not be waived even with the consent of the employee. Any mutual understanding to that effect (in the employment contract) would be null and void because of violation of the Bulgarian Labour Code and could lead to the imposition of sanctions for the employer. Management contracts, on the other hand, are governed by the Bulgarian

Commerce Act and the Obligations and Contracts Act. The Commerce Act only provides that the manager shall organise and direct the activities of the company in accordance with the law and the resolutions of the general meeting/single shareholder. Relations between the company and the manager shall be regulated under a management contract, executed in writing on behalf of the company by a person authorised by the general meeting/single shareholder. The parties are free to negotiate the contents of such contracts.

- Employment contracts have minimum required contents defined by the Bulgarian Labour Code. Management contracts do not have such minimum required contents, therefore the parties would need to agree on the so-called "*essentialia negotii*", the basic elements of the contract.
- Employment contracts need to be concluded for indefinite duration (fixed-term employment contracts are concluded only as an exception in cases exhaustively listed in the Labour Code). Management contracts are typically concluded for the manager's term of office (indicated in the Deed of Incorporation or in the Resolution of the Single Owner/general meeting of the shareholders). There is no express rule in the Commerce Act on the duration of the management contract.
- Employment contracts need to strictly observe the mandatory limits set by the Labour Code regarding maximum duration of the working hours, minimum breaks, extra work, leaves, etc. There are no statutory limitations/standards with respect to the management contracts - the parties are free to agree on how the manager is going to organise his/her own working process, in conformity with the corporate policies.
- Employees are financially liable for damages caused due to negligence upon or in connection with the performance of their employment duties. The Labour Code sets limitations towards the financial liability of employees to 1-3 monthly salaries. Liability for damages caused intentionally or as a result of a criminal offence or caused not upon or in connection with the performance of their employment duties is determined by the civil laws. Managers are liable to the company for any damages caused (both as a result of negligence or intentionally). The Commerce Act sets no limitations towards the amount of the liability.
- Employment contracts may be terminated only on the grounds exhaustively listed in the Labour Code. Additional grounds cannot be validly agreed upon in the employment contract. The Labour Code also sets forth the duration of the notice period (parties have only limited power to deviate), which is equal for both parties. Management contracts may be terminated on the grounds agreed between the parties in the contract. The Commerce Act expressly provides that the manager could be discharged by the sole owner of the capital at any time upon adopting of a written resolution to that effect. Further and more detailed termination options need to be agreed in the contract. Parties are also free to negotiate (and even change) the notice periods in the contract.
- The Labour Code provides for mandatory compensation packages to employees depending on the grounds for termination of the employment contract. The Commerce Act provides for no mandatory packages to managers in case of termination of the management contract. All elements of the compensation are to be negotiated between the parties.
- The only area where employees and managers are treated equally is in the area of social and medical security coverage and taxation.

In conclusion it should be emphasised that statutory managers working under management contracts are not employees and they do not enjoy the general protection provided by the Labour Code.

As a second step, it should be made extremely clear that the Commerce Act expressly provides that commercial companies should enter into management contracts with their statutory managers (i.e., the persons appointed to manage and represent the company and who are entered in the commercial registry as such), therefore it is, in our view, highly disputable whether such persons could work under employment contracts. Even though the Bulgarian market is aware of such cases, our recommendation is to avoid hiring managers under employment contracts.

As a third step, it should be made clear that all other key/management employees need to work under employment contracts, despite their place in the company/group hierarchy.

4. Independent contractors

Similar to the case of the employment and the management contract, the Bulgarian legislation sets forth some principal differences between an employment contract and a civil contract (for the provision of various services, etc.).

The employment contract is a contract by virtue of which an individual provides his work force (i.e., physical/mental exertion, professional expertise and skills) to perform a certain type of work defined in the job description in return for salary. This type of contract is governed by the mandatory provisions of the Labour Code and a large number of regulations. As indicated above, the majority of its provisions are mandatory in nature and may not be waived even with the consent of the employee.

The civil contract covers the provision of various services (i.e., consultancy, technical, advisory, etc.), fulfillment of certain assignments, accomplishment of certain tasks, etc., and the salary received is tied up with the delivery of a certain result. However, apart from the delivery of such result, the contractor is free to determine the remaining parameters himself (i.e. how to work, when to work, what materials to use, etc.). These contracts are governed by Bulgarian civil law, in particular the Contracts and Obligations Act, defining them as agreements between two or more persons aiming to create, settle or terminate a legal relation between them. As a main rule, the parties are free to negotiate the contents of such contracts. Individuals working under civil contracts, i.e. contractors, are not subject to employment legislation, and the rules of the Labour Code do not apply.

However, the Labour Code expressly stipulates that all relations between parties in connection with the giving of the individual's labour are regulated solely as employment relationships, to which the Labour Code applies. This provision aims to prevent the concealment of employment relationships by the conclusion of civil contracts for the purpose of evasion of constraints imposed by the labour legislation. It is considered that such concealment leads to the abuse of employees' rights guaranteed by the Labour Code (i.e. specified working hours, annual paid leave, breaks, salary, protection against termination of the contract, etc.). The Labour Code explicitly requires an employment contract where the relationship between the parties features the characteristics of an employment relationship (as indicated above, these are the relations requiring the provision of an individual work force). The Executive Agency General Labour Inspection is empowered to exercise control over the observance of employment legislation in Bulgaria and it can declare the existence of an employment relationship between the parties, even when they have entered into a civil contract.

In view of the above, companies should carefully consider the nature of the work to be performed in order to enter in the correct type of contract and avoid future complications.

Key case law affecting employers' decision making over dismissal, redundancies dismissals etc.

We have chosen to present two aspects that might interest employers when taking decisions on making dismissals.

As an introduction, we need to outline that the procedure and grounds for the termination of an employment contract are not freely negotiable between the parties. The employer may terminate (with or without notice) an employment contract only on certain grounds exhaustively listed in the Labour Code and following a specific procedure. The non-observance of such grounds and such procedure may result in a court dispute whereby the termination is found unlawful, involving the reinstatement of the employee to his previous position and the obligation of the employer to pay compensation to the employee for the period of unemployment but for not more than 6 months. An employee may terminate the employment contract at any time without stating any reasons but following a special procedure.

1. Dismissals due to closure of the entire enterprise

One of the grounds for unilateral termination by the employer, which is explicitly provided by the Labour Code, is the closure of the entire enterprise of the employer.

Despite the clear wording, in reality the termination of employment on these grounds is a somewhat grey area. In practice, employers struggle to identify which is the exact moment of closure of the enterprise, which could allow the termination of employment on these grounds. As such moment could be considered:

- the date on which the competent body adopts a decision to shut down the entire activity of the company (irrespective of whether there will be subsequent termination of the legal entity as a result of liquidation or bankruptcy proceedings);
- the date on which the decision of the competent body is entered in the Commercial Register (i.e., in this case the shutting down of the company's activity is linked to the subsequent termination of the legal entity as a result of either liquidation or bankruptcy proceedings). For different reasons which we shall not outline in details, the technological time to make that entry in the Commercial Register is approx. 2/3 months later than the date of the decision; or
- the date of the actual de-registration of the company from the Commercial Register, which depends on the period of the liquidation/bankruptcy proceedings but cannot be less than 6 months as of the date under the second bullet point.

Most recent court practice seems to support the first opinion (under the first bullet point), which in practice means that employers could adopt decisions to shut down their activity and terminate their employees without taking any decision on the actual termination/de-registration of the legal entity. We also strongly support this opinion and understanding.

However, there are also older court cases, where the courts have adopted the second opinion (under the second bullet point).

The least likely opinion the courts might adopt in a court dispute is the third one (under the third bullet point).

2. Selection of the employer in cases of unilateral (by the employer) termination of employment on certain grounds

The Labour Code provides that in cases of closure of part of the employer's enterprise, staff cuts (closure of positions) or reduction in the volume of work, the employer has the right to make a selection among the employees and, for the benefit of the production and the business, to terminate employees whose positions are not made redundant/closed in order to retain in employment those employees who possess higher qualifications and work better.

One of the most recent interpretative decisions of the Supreme Court of Cassation as of January 2012 ruled that the employer's judgment (on the issue of which of the employees have the higher qualification and work better) is subject to judiciary review. The court should investigate whether the assessment made by the employer on the criteria set by him correspond to the qualifications possessed in reality and the level of performance of the assigned tasks by the employees.

Recent statutory or legislative changes

In 2011 and 2012, the Bulgarian Parliament enacted a number of changes in the Bulgarian Labour Code:

1. New explicit regulation of the status of the outsourcing agencies

At the beginning of 2012, the Bulgarian Parliament finally provided some statutory rules regarding the activities of the enterprises providing temporary/leased staff ("outsourcing companies"). For the past 6-7 years, outsourcing companies (mainly HR agencies) had a presence and successfully offered services in Bulgaria, despite the lack of statutory rules in this aspect of their employment practices. Their existence and operations were recognised and tolerated in practice, but their activities took place in a legal vacuum.

However the newly introduced express rules seem to tie the hands of the business rather than effectively regulate the relations between the commissioned employees, the outsourcing companies and the employers using leased staff (user undertakings). It is not a secret that both outsourcing companies and user undertakings feel that they had a lot more business flexibility at the times of the legal vacuum. The main challenges before them are as follows:

- The total number of employees commissioned by an outsourcing company at a user undertaking may not exceed 30% of the employees employed by that user undertaking.
- User undertakings which have performed mass dismissals may not use leased personnel prior to

the lapse of 6 months as of such dismissals.

- Employment contracts between the employees and the outsourcing company could only be concluded as fixed-term contracts on 2 grounds: for the completion of a specific assignment; or for the replacement of an employee absent from work.
- The Labour Code did not establish a transition period during which the existing outsourcing companies and user undertakings had to comply with the new rules or procedure on how to handle the existing cases.

The outsourcing companies are now required to undergo a registration procedure with the Bulgarian Agency of Employment. The rights and obligations of the outsourcing companies and the user undertakings *vis-a-vis* the commissioned employees are explicitly listed in the Labour Code. They represent a split of the functions of the employer between the two entities. In fact they do not create additional burden to these entities.

The relations between the outsourcing company and the user undertaking need to be regulated in a written contract, further specifying a number of details, including but not limited to:

- the job positions and the nature of work for the performance of which employees are to be commissioned;
- the period for which employees are to be commissioned;
- the procedure applicable to the use of the leaves of absence;
- the procedure applicable to the exchange of information between the outsourcing company and the user undertaking concerning the salary structure and organisation, the types of additional salary and their amounts at the undertaking, as well as the collective employment contract concluded at the user undertaking, if any; and
- the liability in case of default.

Both entities are jointly liable to the employees for any obligations arising in the course of, on account of, or in relation to, the performance of the work assigned.

The employees commissioned to perform work at a user undertaking shall have the typical rights they would have under a permanent employment, namely: salary; leaves of absence; trade union association; participation in the general meeting of employees in the user undertaking; social, welfare and cultural services; healthy and safe working conditions; initial and continuing training in accordance with the position and the nature of work at the user undertaking; and compensations under the terms and in accordance with the procedure provided for in the Social Security Code; etc.

2. New explicit regulation of the telework

These changes have been enacted by the Bulgarian Parliament in view of the implementation of the European Framework Agreement on Telework as of 16 July 2002.

Similar to the issue with the outsourcing agencies, telework existed in reality for the past several years even though it was not expressly regulated.

Telework is defined by the Labour Code as a form of organised work outsourced from the employers' premises and performed under an employment contract through the use of information technology, which was, or could have been, performed on the employers' premises before it was outsourced. Telework is only voluntary. An employer may propose to an employee to switch from working on the employers' premises to telework, but the employee's refusal to do so may not lead to adverse consequences for him. Likewise, the employee may propose to his employer to switch from working on the employers' premises to telework.

An employee-teleworker needs to designate a specific area in his home or in other premises chosen by him outside the enterprise to serve as a workplace. The issues related to the operational, technical and other equipment at the workplace, the obligations and costs pertaining to its maintenance, other conditions relating to the supply, replacement and maintenance of the equipment, as well as clauses relating to the acquisition of separate items of the equipment by an employee-teleworker need to be regulated in the individual employment contract.

The employer in this case needs to ensure the following at its own expense:

- the equipment needed to perform telework, as well as the supplies needed for its operation;

- the software needed;
- preventive maintenance and technical support;
- devices intended for communication with the employee, including Internet connectivity;
- data protection;
- information on and requirements for operating the equipment and keeping it in good repair, and the legal requirements and rules, including those of the enterprise in the field of data protection for data to be used in the course of the telework; and
- a surveillance system, where it is necessary to install one at the workplace and the employee's written consent thereto has been obtained.

The employee-teleworker is responsible for the proper storage and operation of the equipment provided to him. In case of a failure of the equipment or a breakdown of the information and/or communication systems used, he needs to immediately alert the employer thereto in accordance with a procedure and in a manner agreed upon in advance.

Employee-teleworkers enjoy the same rights related to the organisation of work and the health and safety at work as stipulated by Bulgarian law as those enjoyed by the employees working on the employers' premises. The employer shall ensure that the remote workplaces satisfy the minimum requirements for health and safety at work under the Health and Safety at Work Act. The employer is responsible for the safe and healthy conditions at the workplaces of the employee-teleworkers. The latter have the right to request a visit at their workplace by the Labour Inspection authorities. Likewise the employer, the trade union representatives, the employees' representatives and the Labour Inspection authorities have the right to access the workplace within the limits stipulated in the individual employment contract, subject to advance notification given to the employee-teleworker and subject to his consent. Employee-teleworkers shall not have the right to deny access to the workplace without reason, within the established working time and/or within the limits stipulated in the individual employment contract.

Employee-teleworkers are subject to the standard rules imposed by the Bulgarian Labour Code in terms of working hours and reporting of the working hours, rests, and leaves of absence. Employee-teleworkers benefit from the enterprise's social programme on an equal footing and have labour and trade union rights equal to those of employees working on the employers' premises.

3. New explicit regulation of the work from home

Similar to the previous two issues, the work from home existed in reality for the past several years even though it was not expressly regulated.

The recent changes in the Labour Code now expressly provide that an employment contract may provide that work obligations related to the manufacture of products and/or provision of services may be performed at the employee's home or on other premises of his choice outside the employer's work location, the employee using his own and/or the employer's equipment, materials and other accessory means.

Employers need to keep records of each employee working at home. Upon request, employers need to submit this information to the General Labour Inspectorate Executive Agency.

Work-at-home employment contracts have to be concluded under the terms and in accordance with the general procedure under the Labour Code and need to regulate: the workplace location; the labour salary; the procedure of work assignment and reporting; the manner of materials supply and delivery of ready products; the consumer costs for the workplace and the payment thereof; other terms related to the specific requirements for work at home.

The employer needs to ensure, *inter alia*, the following:
- conditions for performing the work;
- payment and treatment equal to those which the employer has provided to employees working at the enterprise;
- healthy and safe working conditions;
- qualification, re-qualification and training;
- social and health insurance subject to conditions and in accordance with a procedure provided for by law; and

*   social, welfare and cultural services, etc.

Employees working at home are free to choose the start and end time and the distribution of their working time, subject to observing its statutory length. Employees working at home shall be free to choose the periods of rest within a working day, between working days, and within a week. Employers may not establish open-ended working hours or impose overtime work for employees working at home.

Likely or impending reforms to employment legislation and enforcement procedures

There are no material impending reforms to employment legislation and enforcement procedures.

Violeta Kirova
Tel: +359 2 8055 055 / Email: v.kirova@boyanov.com
Violeta Kirova is a qualified legal adviser and Senior Associate at Boyanov & Co. where she is currently in charge of the employment practice within the M&A Department. She focuses on labour law and commercial law (in particular, company law). She has advised a number of international companies and their subsidiaries on a day-to-day basis regarding employment issues including collective redundancies related to restructuring of the business and closing of operational units, negotiations and relations with trade unions and employee councils, employment litigation, social security, employee benefits, etc.

Violeta Kirova was educated at Sofia University St. Kliment Ochridsky, Legal Faculty and the Academy of American International Law, Dallas, USA (2003).

Membership in Professional Societies includes: Sofia Bar Association; and Centre for International Legal Studies.

Boyanov & Co.

82, Patriarch Evtimii Blvd., Sofia 1463, Bulgaria
Tel: +359 2 805 5055 / Fax: +359 2 805 5000 / URL: http://www.boyanov.com

France

Anne Le Quinquis & Anne Denisart
Fromont Briens

General Overview

French labour law is constantly evolving. Employment law has also undergone significant developments since 2008 when rules and regulations regarding collective negotiation and union representation were totally overhauled. Moreover, within the last few months, the financial and economic crisis has emphasised additional issues regarding the increase in restructurings and redundancies. Indeed, the number of redundancies has significantly grown with the unemployment rate reaching 9.2% in 2011, and is currently at 10%. It is also quite alarming if one considers that these figures do not take into account the unemployment situation of an increasingly greater segment of the younger population in France. They encounter significant difficulties in finding their first job, or are only able to enter into fixed-term contracts, and are, therefore, not entitled to unemployment benefits and may not rely on dismissal regulations.

In this context, one must keep in mind that the unemployment situation has been a constant concern in France since the 1970s, and there has been a constant debate regarding the efficiency of legislation (i.e. regulations and case law) to protect employees in cases of restructuring. There have also been heated discussions regarding the dichotomy between indefinite employment contracts and fixed-term contracts and the question as to whether or not indefinite employment contracts should remain the only French "model" for employment contracts.

In this quite gloomy atmosphere, having failed to reform French employment law, the French parliament and government finally, more or less officially, delegated additional authority to the French courts and the relevant social partners to carry out such reform.

1. In this regard, to reinforce the legitimacy of the latter, the French parliament renewed the rules regarding collective negotiations. Paradoxically, many issues remain unsettled, whereas this reform was meant to be revolutionary.
2. Restructuring rules also remain unclear.
3. In this rather complex legal environment, the French courts have established one strong and clear principle: the obligation for the employer to ensure the physical and mental health of its employees at work. This guideline helps to understand and anticipate the evolution of French case law.

1. Collective negotiations: a new uncertain landscape

Collective agreements have a crucial impact in France, because they are applicable to all employees even if they are not members of a signatory union. Regarding working time or profit-sharing schemes, for example, collective agreements are essential (for instance, in order to calculate the working time of employees on a daily/yearly basis, a collective agreement must be entered into). Furthermore as previously mentioned they are, nowadays, the favoured means used by the French government and parliament to reform employment law.

1.1 In this context, in 2008[1], the rules of the French Labour Code relating to union representation and collective negotiation were thoroughly reviewed with a view to increasing the legitimacy of the staff delegates and consequently the agreements negotiated. Indeed, please remember that France suffers from the fact that the vast majority of French employees are not affiliated to any of the five national traditional trade unions (CGT - CGT FO - CFTDT - CFTC - CFE CGC). It should also be noted that the said trade unions used to be very powerful since they could sign any type of collective agreements (with some limits regarding the CFE CGC dedicated to executives).

One of the most important measures is related to the rules regarding the validity of collective agreements. As a preliminary remark, it should be noted that French company collective agreements are entered into between the head of the company and the representatives of one or more trade union organisations represented within the company. Prior to 2008, collective agreements were valid even if only one union among the five national unions signed the agreement. As of 2008, the validity of the agreement is subject to it being signed by one or more trade union organisations (which can be an organisation other than one of the main five unions provided it has obtained at least 10% of the vote at the last professional elections) and who collectively obtain at least 30% of the vote at the last professional elections and who do not have any objection from one or more trade union organisations that obtained the majority of the casting vote at the same elections. The other collective agreements can also be concluded according to the same kind of rules. Clearly, results at the professional elections have become the key criteria, i.e. a proof of legitimacy. This reform has had a significant impact on the traditional practices of the relevant social partners, and on the day-to-day life of the company and the group companies.

However, since the amendment of the law regarding collective negotiations and union representation, there are still many grey areas. The situation is so problematic that the French Supreme Court does not hesitate to raise questions relating to crucial issues regarding French labour law be it at employment law conferences, symposia or on the website of the French Supreme Court which provides a list of issues yet to be resolved. These unclear areas are quite numerous and relate to important issues, for instance the conclusion and validity of collective agreements after a restructuring or the nature of the collective agreement which enables to determine whether or not an agreement is deemed to be an Economic and Social Unit (i.e. "UES") agreement. Surely to reach a unanimous agreement is the safest way to proceed but it is not always possible. In such cases and in the absence of clear case law, companies are more and more likely to reach an agreement in good faith by promoting a vision of the future of the company rather than trying to secure an agreement based on the French Labour Code. A good knowledge of European case law is often a valuable help in this regard.

1.2 At the same time, without any obvious coherence, according to a certain number of scholars, the French Supreme Court is currently questioning the validity of collective agreements which provide different treatment between employees. Historically, collective agreements and especially industry-wide collective agreements used to differentiate between blue-collar and white-collar workers. For instance, the majority of industry-wide collective agreements provide a different severance pay for blue-collar and white-collar employees, a different number of paid holidays, as well as separate retirement plans (i.e. DB or DC plans). However, in 2009, the French Supreme Court[2] ruled that employees could not be treated differently based only on their respective occupational groups (i.e. *catégories professionelles*). The French Supreme Court confirmed this ruling in several judgments issued in 2012[3].

The consequences would be risking the nullity of most pension and benefit plans and of at least a few sections of most collective bargaining agreements. However, the president and some judges of the French Supreme Court have recently expressed their concern regarding the repercussions of any precedent in terms of cost for companies (the state retirement scheme was implemented pursuant to a national collective agreement and is based on a difference of treatment between blue-collar and white-collar employees). The French Supreme Court has indeed organised several meetings to question, in particular, the social partners in view of assessing the possible impact of its precedents. Depending on the results of this kind of analysis, the French Supreme Court could decide to alter its case law. Should the French Supreme Court persist on this line, numerous measures of collective agreements (at the company or industry level) could be deemed to be null and void, and employees who are treated differently might request more favourable treatment from the French courts.

2. Restructuring: an area still uncertain

In France, restructurings involve mainly mass collective redundancies. However, as far as group companies are concerned, until now, restructurings principally involved voluntary departure plans. Mass collective redundancies entail dismissals based on economic grounds whereas voluntary departure plans involve mutual-consent termination agreements based on economic grounds. The legal obligations of the employer are, however, different in terms of proceedings and also regarding its obligations with regard to redeployment. The second option is preferred by the employers, if possible, because it remains the more secure way to implement a restructuring in France and the less traumatic for the company and the employees concerned. Both situations however still involve uncertainty.

2.1 Generally speaking, a collective redundancy must be based on real and serious grounds and the employer must, prior to making any of its employees redundant, define the criteria that shall govern the order of the contemplated redundancies. The criteria is defined based on the number of dependants, the employee's length of service, the employee's employability (notably for disabled and old employees) and the employee's skills assessed in light of his/her professional category. The employer must also do its utmost to redeploy the affected employees to other positions within the company and more importantly within the group, irrespective of the number of redundancies and the headcount.

The statutory and case-law framework regarding redundancies dates back to the 1980s. Until last year, it could be assumed that after much turmoil, the mass collective redundancies regime became quite firmly established. The main rules were the following:

- a specific procedure must be followed for all collective redundancies of more than 10 employees per month. The employer is required to implement a job protection plan, which provides, for instance, for specific allowances, additional severance pay and a redeployment plan. The validity of the job protection plan must be assessed based on the size and financial situation of the group and the redeployment opportunities available within the company and the group; and
- layoffs must be based on economic grounds provided by the French Labour Code and applicable case law, i.e.:
  - economic difficulties;
  - maintaining competitiveness;
  - technological developments; and
  - termination of operations.

Laid-off employees and/or works council committees may challenge the redundancies, be it the grounds for the lay-offs, or the validity of the job protection plan.

- Should the French Employment Tribunal rule that the layoff was unfair, damages may be awarded against the company, after the termination: for employees with at least two years of tenure, the amount of damages for unfair layoffs is at least six months' salary.
- Furthermore, should the job protection plan be deemed to be insufficient by the French Employment Tribunal, the layoffs would be ruled null and void. In this case, any employee who has been laid off is entitled to be reinstated and may claim damages corresponding to his/her previous salary during the period between his/her layoff and reinstatement. Should the employee refuse to be reinstated, the French Employment Tribunal may award the employee damages amounting to at least 12 months' salary.

However in 2011, certain appellate courts, and more particularly the Court of Appeal of Paris, sought to change the redundancies regime. The Court of Appeal of Paris[4] held that the lack of economic grounds should render layoffs null and void (and not only unfair). It was followed by a similar decision of the Court of Appeal of Reims[5]. Such case-law caused a real storm! There was not only a risk of increased damages but mainly the threat of group companies no longer being able to carry out certain necessary restructurings because the grounds would be challenged by, for instance, the works council during the information/consultation procedure i.e. before the termination of the employment contract. It cast uncertainty on all ongoing redundancy proceedings in addition to those which were not yet statute-barred.

The French Supreme Court quashed the judgement of the Court of Appeal of Paris and reasserted that a layoff can only be considered as null and void where the job protection plan is deemed to be insufficient. The uncertainty seemed to have been removed. However, the president of the French Supreme Court has not firmly closed the door regarding any developments in this area. Indeed, he publicly declared that the debate is totally legitimate. In other words, he deemed that the criticised decision had to be sanctioned but another decision with the same kind of reasoning, although differently grounded, could be upheld by the French Supreme Court. Furthermore, some French courts[6] have deliberately decided to resist the French Supreme Court's ruling. In the same way, some scholars continue to advocate against this "established" case law. Therefore, the outcome of redundancy proceedings must be deemed to still be uncertain.

Generally speaking, it is clear that in this current climate of financial crisis, courts in France seek to determine the best way to compensate damages of employees dismissed in the context of a restructuring plan. The more solvent company is then always required to offer the best possible compensation to employees. In this context, where redundancies are implemented in a group, after a run-off, the parent company may be held responsible under certain circumstances in place of its subsidiary, i.e. the actual employer. For this purpose, French courts have not hesitated in shifting away from the traditional concept of co-employment.

2.2 Voluntary departure plans seem to be a safer and clearer option.

In a nutshell, the French Labour Code provides two means[7] by which indefinite-term contracts may be terminated i.e. dismissal or resignation.

However, based on the French Civil Code, practitioners have been aware since the 1980s that it was possible to terminate employment contracts in a restructuring context by a mutual-consent termination of the employment contract based on economic grounds.

This practice has been widely developed alongside the French Labour Code. It presents some major advantages such as reduced trauma, mainly relieving the employer of the obligation to put in place an internal redeployment plan, to apply the order of the contemplated redundancies and preventing the employee from challenging the economic ground of the restructuring after the termination.

Some recent decisions have been issued securing this practice in defining the job departure plan regime. Indeed, the French Supreme Court has recently ruled that in cases of voluntary departure it is not a requirement to implement an internal redeployment plan[8] which is the key issue for multinational group companies which are generally unable to freeze world-wide vacant job positions for the duration of the information/consultation procedure in France (which could potentially last between six to nine months or sometimes longer). However, if dismissals are not excluded it is still necessary to provide for internal redeployment measures[9].

Paradoxically, it is important to highlight that the intrinsic validity of the termination concluded in application of this particular type of job protection plan has yet to be approved by the French courts. Indeed, since the creation by the French legislature of a new kind of mutual termination, known as a *rupture conventionnelle*, specifically established by the French Labour Court with a system of approval by the French administration, there is a strong debate regarding the validity of this mutual termination only concluded based on the French Civil Code.

3. Health and Safety: a new key notion under French case law

The underlying theme behind the recent ruling of the French Supreme Court is the concern regarding employees' health and safety. The French Supreme Court seeks to protect the health and safety of employees and examine each matter, be it a restructuring, redundancy, or a case of harassment from an employees' health and safety perspective, protecting employees from any psycho-social risks (i.e. *risque psycho-sociaux*).

- Generally speaking, should the employer infringe the rules governing health and safety in the workplace, it will be held liable unless it can be shown that the employee was entirely responsible for the accident. In such a case, sanctions may be imposed on the head of the company consisting of fines of up to €3,750 for each employee concerned. In the event of any further offence, fines of

up to €9,000 may be imposed and/or a sentence of up to one year's imprisonment may be ordered.
*   It is important to stress the significance of this notion in the most recent case-law and the fact that it will have an increasingly important place in the French employment law landscape beyond health and safety legislation, as shown below.

Bullying in the workplace

Article L.1152-1 of the French Labour Code and Article 222-33-2 of the French Criminal Code define moral harassment as follows: "*repeated conduct which is designed to or which leads to deterioration of [the employee's] conditions of work liable to harm his rights and his dignity, to damage his physical or mental health or compromise his career prospects*". Moral harassment is strictly prohibited as are any discriminatory measures (including dismissal) taken against a victim of moral harassment or an employee who has witnessed such an act. These actions are punishable by a maximum of one year's imprisonment and/or a maximum fine of €3,750. The misdemeanour of moral harassment is punishable in France under criminal law by a maximum sentence of one year's imprisonment and a maximum fine of €15,000. Moreover, any dismissal resulting from workplace bullying is considered null and void. In this case, the employee must be reinstated or receive damages in compensation.

In this context it is important to stress that over the last few years, the French Supreme Court increased the scope of the meaning of moral harassment with a view to protecting the health and safety of employees. Please note that:
*   moral harassment may be established even in the absence of malicious intent (i.e. *intention de nuire*)[10];
*   employers have an obligation to produce results, and any failure to prevent moral harassment results in their liability[11];
*   moral or sexual harassment may be committed by people outside of the company and the employer may be liable for such harassment[12]; and
*   the French Supreme Court has held that moral harassment can be "managerial", i.e. management methods performed by a manager resulting in the deterioration of work conditions which may harm the rights and dignity of an employee, causing physical or mental health damage or compromising career prospects shall constitute moral harassment.

Please note that at the same time, whereas the French Supreme Court remains very keen on protecting employees' physical and mental health, and whereas it had become very strict regarding bullying in the workplace, the French Constitutional Council[13] repealed the law sanctioning sexual harassment. Since 1 March 2010, the French Constitutional Council can indeed examine whether or not a specific law complies with the Constitution *a posteriori*, i.e. subsequent to its enactment. Prior to 2010, the French Constitutional Council could only examine the law after its adoption by the French parliament and before its enactment by the president, and only the president and some members of parliament or senators could refer the matter to the French Constitutional Council. As of 2010, any party to a proceeding may refer the matter to the French Constitutional Council (the French Supreme Court decides on whether or not it should be referred to the French Constitutional Council). The mandate of the French Constitutional Council is to rule on whether or not a law complies with constitutional principles.

In 2012, the law relating to the criminal offence of sexual harassment was challenged based on its ambiguity; indeed, according to constitutional principles, a criminal offence must be precisely and clearly defined. Article 222-33 of the French Criminal Code provided that: "*The harassment of another person for the purpose of obtaining favours of a sexual nature is punished by one year's imprisonment and a fine of €15,000*". However, the French Constitutional Council held that the definition of sexual harassment was not precise enough to be deemed a criminal offence. This article of the Criminal Code has now been repealed. Victims of sexual harassment were shocked as they feared that this change in the law would prejudice the outcome of ongoing proceedings based on a lack of legal grounds. However, new legislation relating to the criminal offence of sexual harassment should be adopted by the French parliament in the following weeks.

Suicide

The French Supreme Court has highlighted the responsibility of the employer in cases of suicide. Suicide committed in the workplace can be deemed by the French courts to be an occupational accident.

Moreover, in the event of reckless misconduct *(faute inexcusable)* by the employer, the victim or his/her estate may file a suit claiming damages over and above the compensation paid by the social security authorities. In addition, the annuity granted to the victim or his/her estate by the social security authorities may be increased. The company would then be required to pay a contribution to meet this increase.

The French Supreme Court[14] previously ruled that "*the employer was under the obligation to provide for employees' safety, in particular with regard to occupational illnesses contracted by an employee as a result of products used by the company*". The French Supreme Court considered that "*any failure to comply with this obligation qualifies as reckless misconduct/inexcusable negligence (...) when the employer was or should have been aware of the danger to which the employee was exposed and did not take the necessary preventive action*".

Similarly, the Court of Appeal of Versailles[15] held a company responsible when one of its employees committed suicide in his place of work, and the said company was deemed responsible for reckless misconduct. It should be noted that the Court of Appeal of Paris[16] has held that the death of an employee by infarction due to overwork to be an occupational accident.

Working time

Pursuant to the French Labour Code, working time of executives is calculated based on days worked per year (i.e. *forfait jour*) instead of hours worked per week, where provided for by both the relevant collective agreement and employment contract.

The French Supreme Court had previously restricted[17] the condition which allows for the provision of a *forfait jour* within the employment contract ruling that "*Fixed annual working time in days must be provided by a collective agreement ensuring compliance with maximal working time, and daily and weekly rest periods*".

The French Supreme Court based its decision on the applicable European rules and regulations regarding working time and the right to health, and on the constitutional principle relating to employees' right to health and rest. Henceforth, the French courts must determine whether the collective agreement providing for a *forfait jour* complies with the employee's right to health and rest.

On this basis, the French Supreme Court[18] ruled that the company-wide agreement of the chemical industry is not valid.

Recently, the French Supreme Court[19] also held that fixed annual working time in days must be provided by the employment contract. If the employer fails to do so, it may be sanctioned for undeclared work.

Health, safety and working conditions committee

In this legal environment, the health, safety and working conditions committee is vested with increased powers. As a reminder, all companies employing at least 50 employees are required to establish a health, safety and working conditions committee, whose role is to inform the staff regarding all measures taken to prevent occupational accidents and to improve working conditions. It is composed of the head of the company, staff representatives and other consultants (such as an occupational doctor).

The committee is traditionally informed and consulted on issues relating to health and safety in the company but increasingly on all decisions affecting working conditions (which is very wide).

It may be all the more restrictive where the committee requests an expert assessment regarding the matter it is informed and consulted on (to be paid by the employer). Furthermore, the most recent case-law has held that the works council can refuse to give its opinion as long as the health and safety committee has not issued its own opinion in due form[20].

Please note that, apart from the works council, there is no central health and safety committee. Each place of business with more than 50 employees must, however, have a health and safety committee and thus, in some French companies there are hundreds of such committees. It should be noted that each committee has the right to be specifically informed and consulted about projects which affect working conditions, and may also request an expert assessment. Certain scholars and practitioners have stressed the importance of amending the French Labour Code in this respect. However, there are no signs that show that this will occur within a short time period. Consequently, French companies will have to continue to work with their health and safety committee and keep in mind that the elimination of all psycho-social risks must become the key point of their employment policy.

Indeed, beyond all traditional concepts such as, for instance, the difference between any changes made to the employment contract which may not be carried out without the prior consent of the employee concerned (versus changes to working conditions which is the prerogative of the employer), any changes to working conditions may be deemed unlawful if they affect the balance between professional and family life. Any decision is furthermore *per se* unlawful if it may endanger the mental or physical health of the employee and risk incurring the civil and criminal liability of the employer.

To conclude, certain major areas of French employment law still remain uncertain which may surprise companies and mainly worldwide group companies. However in this moving context, the importance and the strength of the concept relating to the "security obligation" and its significant consequences on most traditional case-law must always be kept in mind. In our opinion, this is the most important trend of the last and possibly the coming years in the French employment law landscape. It must remain the key criteria assisting all companies in carrying out any proposed project without the risk of being too surprised by any forthcoming developments in French employment law.

* * *

Endnotes

1. Law n°2008-789 of 20 August 2008.
2. Employment Div. of the French Supreme Court, 1 July 2009, n°07-42.675.
3. Employment Div. of the Supreme Court, 28 March 2012, n°11-12.403; Employment Div. of the French Supreme Court, 30 May 2012, n°11-11.902; Employment Div. of the French Supreme Court, 8 March 2012, n°10-17.900; Employment Div. of the French Supreme Court, 6 June 2012, n°10-27.468.
4. Court of Appeal of Paris Pole 6 Ch2, 12 May 2011, n°11/01547.
5. Court of Appeal of Reims, Civ. Div. 1st, 3 January 2012, n°11/00337.
6. Court of First Instance of Créteil, 22 May 2012, n°12/01498.
7. The French Labour Code also provides for a specific contractual termination agreement since 2008 (i.e. *rupture conventionnelle*), but this specific system is clearly not applicable to termination based on economic grounds.
8. Employment Div. of the French Supreme Court, 26 October 2010, n°09-15187.
9. Employment Div. of the French Supreme Court, 25 January 2012, n°10-23516.
10. Employment div. of the French Supreme Court, 10 November 2009, n°08-41.497.
11. Employment div. of the French Supreme Court, 21 June 2006, n°05-43.914.
12. Employment div. of the French Supreme Court, 19 October 2011, n°09-68.272.
13. French Constitutional Council, 4 May 2012, Question n°2012-240.
14. Employment Div. of the French Supreme Court, 28 February 2002.
15. Court of Appeal of Versailles, 5th Div., 19 May 2011, n°10/00954.
16. Court of Appeal of Paris, 6th Div., 30 June 2011, n°10/05831.
17. Employment Div. of the French Supreme Court, 29 June 2011, n°09-71.107.
18. Employment Div. of the French Supreme Court, 31 January 2012, n°10-19.807.
19. French Supreme Court, Employment Div., 28 February 2012, n°10-27.839.
20. French Supreme Court, Employment Div., 4 July 2012, n°11-19.678.

Anne Le Quinquis
Tel: +33 1 44 51 63 80 / Email: anne.lequinquis@fromont-briens.com
Anne Le Quinquis is a partner at Fromont Briens. Anne has significant expertise in employment law, particularly in high-profile mergers & acquisitions and restructuring transactions.

Anne Denisart
Tel: +33 1 44 51 63 80 / Email: anne.denisart@fromont-briens.com
Anne Denisart is an associate at Fromont Briens. Anne is involved in employment law issues, notably in restructuring issues.

Fromont Briens

5, rue Boudreau 75 421 Paris Cedex 09, France
Tel: +33 1 4451 6380 / Fax: +33 1 4451 6389 / URL: http://www.fromont-briens.com

Germany

Michael Kuhnke & Holger Meyer
Schramm Meyer Kuhnke

General labour market trends

The increasing importance of small, specialised craft unions

For several years, it has been possible to observe the increasing importance of small craft unions, focussing on strategically relevant professions such as air traffic controllers, pilots, train drivers, doctors, etc. Traditionally, labour unions in Germany are organised according to the "branch principle", meaning that workers in the same industry belong to the same union, irrespective of their profession (e.g. chemical industry, logistics, etc.). This structure was reinforced by the established case law of the Federal Labour Court, which established the principle that only one tariff or collective bargaining agreement may apply to each enterprise, the so-called "single-tariff principle" (*"Grundsatz der Tarifeinheit"*).

However, in a decision from 2010, the Federal Labour Court abandoned this principle, resulting in employers facing the risk that certain highly qualified and strategically important groups of employees may leave industry-wide unions and use their structural power in order to negotiate higher than average tariff or pay increases. Furthermore, while the single-tariff principle ensured that the employer may only be confronted by a strike once every two or three years, depending on the duration of the relevant collective bargaining agreement, some employers have experienced in 2011 and 2012 several strikes by different groups of employees during the same time period (e.g. airlines may be affected by strikes by pilots, cabin crew and ground personnel). It goes without saying that traditional industry-wide labour unions are very critical *vis-à-vis* this new development as they fear the strategic loss of important groups of employees who, in the past, have ensured the negotiating power of the union from which less qualified employees have also benefitted. This poses a risk to the collective solidarity principle on which industry-wide unions are based.

It is not surprising then that industry-wide labour unions as well as employers' associations have called for the German legislator to re-establish the single-tariff principle. However, it is doubtful whether the government will engage in such a politically, and also legally, highly controversial legislative process. The reason being that such an act would obviously restrict the freedom of employees to establish labour unions and the right to strike. Both are fundamental rights protected by the German constitution (*Grundgesetz*) and, in fact, the Federal Labour Court justified its decision to give up the single-tariff principle by declaring its incompatibility with these rights. Therefore, we do not expect any activities by the legislator in this respect, at least not prior to the next federal elections in September 2013. Consequently, employers who are confronted with different labour unions operating within their enterprises will have to develop specific defence strategies in response to tariff conflicts.

Minimum wages

Another rather political discussion that has already been taking place for several years now relates to the introduction of a general, nationwide statutory minimum wage. Unlike most other EU-countries, there is no general statutory minimum wage applicable in Germany. This means that, in the absence of any binding collective bargaining agreement, employers are able to set the wages as long as their level is not considered to be immoral. The Social Democratic Party (SPD) and the labour unions in particular, want to maintain this topic on the political agenda whereas the parties of the government coalition (CDU/CSU and FDP) have been and remain traditionally opposed to a statutory approach. However, the debate has gained some momentum due to on-going discussions about the precarious working conditions of temporary agency workers as well as employees in other industry sectors where collective bargaining agreements traditionally do not apply on a larger scale.

As a consequence, minimum wages have been introduced by way of statutory ordinances in several areas such as construction, security and cleaning services, temporary agency workers and geriatric care. The particularity of these ordinances is that the minimum wage has in each case been negotiated by the competent labour union and the employers' association beforehand. Given that this approach still leaves a vast majority of workplaces uncovered, the labour unions and the opposition parties have maintained their claims for a nationwide general statutory minimum wage. In a very recent initiative, the governing party CDU has now reacted and developed an alternative model which aims to introduce minimum wages on a larger scale. We therefore expect that statutory minimum wages will also be implemented in Germany in the near future.

Key case law

Equal pay for temporary agency workers

Two decisions of the Federal Labour Court in 2010 and 2012 have had a great impact on the working conditions of many thousands of temporary agency workers in Germany and in particular on their remuneration entitlements. The German Temporary Agency Worker Act (*Arbeitnehmerüberlassung sgesetz*) establishes the "Equal Pay Principle" for temporary agency workers. According to this law, temporary workers have to be paid the same wages as comparable employees of the hiring company they are temporarily working for. An exception to this rule is only legally valid if a collective bargaining agreement applies to the employment relationship between the temporary worker and the temporary employment agency either by way of a reference clause in the worker's contract or by virtue of the membership of the temporary employment agency in an employers' association which has entered into a collective bargaining agreement. Therefore, in practice, although the German legislator has enacted the "Equal Pay Principle", the vast majority of "temps" in Germany are remunerated at hourly wages that are far below the rates applicable to comparable employees of the hiring company. To this end, temporary employment agencies generally apply collective bargaining agreements that have been agreed specifically for the temporary agency workers industry. The exception to the Equal Pay Principle therefore becomes the norm.

However, the exception to the Equal Pay Principle obviously only applies if the relevant collective bargaining agreement applied by the temporary employment agency is valid. This requires that the collective bargaining agreement is concluded by a labour union or an association of labour unions that is empowered to conclude those agreements. The above mentioned decisions of the Federal Labour Court clarified that the association of labour unions called "*Tarifgemeinschaft Christlicher Gewerkschaften für Zeitarbeit und Personalserviceagenturen*" (short "CGZP"), whose collective bargaining agreement for the temporary agency workers industry is applied by many agencies in Germany, had neither in the past nor in the present the power to conclude collective bargaining agreements. Consequently, all collective bargaining agreements the CGZP had signed are invalid, which has a significant financial impact for those temporary employment agencies, who had applied these collective bargaining agreements, as well as for the hiring companies, as the Equal Pay Principle has to be fully implemented, even retrospectively.

Temporary employment agencies are therefore currently confronted with a wave of law suits as many temporary workers are now claiming the higher wages they should have been paid during the last four years (it is estimated that some 1,500 equal pay claims have been brought before the German labour courts after the first of the two relevant decisions of the Federal Labour Court in December 2010). In addition, the social security authorities will claim the higher social security contributions that should have been paid, as well. In this respect, the social security authorities are entitled to the higher contributions, even if the relevant employee does not bring an equal pay claim. It is therefore expected that the retroactive claims for additional social security contributions will put many smaller temporary employment agencies into economic difficulties. In such a scenario, the social security authorities may also claim any outstanding social security contributions from the hiring company as the Temporary Agency Workers Act stipulates that the hiring company is severally liable for such outstanding contributions. Employers are therefore well advised to make sure that the temporary employment agency with which they are engaging applies valid collective bargaining agreements.

No overtime remuneration for executive staff?

Collective bargaining agreements and/or works council agreements generally provide comprehensive rules regarding the extent to which employees are obliged to work overtime and the remuneration of such overtime (in most cases either by additional paid leave or by additional salary payments). However, if no such collective agreements apply (for example, if the employer is not a member of an employers' association or in the case of more senior employees, whose remuneration exceeds the ceiling of the applicable tariff), the parties are free to agree in the employment contract how extra hours shall be compensated.

In the past, many employers have therefore included a clause in their standard employment contracts stipulating that any overtime is already compensated by the base salary (e.g.: "The above Salary shall be deemed to cover any and all of the Employee's claims for remuneration, including any overtime work."). However, in a decision from September 2010, the Federal Labour Court ruled that such a clause lacked transparency according to the provisions of the German Civil Code (*Bürgerliches Gesetzbuch*) on standard contract clauses and is therefore invalid. The Court criticised the fact that the clause did not specify the amount of extra hours the employee has to work without being entitled to any additional payments. According to the Court, the contract clause must be explicit enough to enable the employee to assess in advance how many hours he has to work in exchange for the agreed base salary. In the aftermath of this decision, legal commentators were unanimous that contract clauses which stipulate that any extra hours are deemed to be covered by any base salary should not be used anymore. Instead, the question was how many hours overtime per week could still be covered by the base salary?

It was therefore very surprising that the Federal Labour Court in a decision from August 2011 rejected a retroactive claim for payment of overtime pay by a lawyer working as an associate for a German law firm. It goes without saying that the decision received much attention from various sides. The lawyer, who was entitled to a fixed annual salary of EUR 80,000, claimed compensation for approximately 930 extra hours accrued during the preceding three years after his expectations to become a partner did not materialise and he was served notice of termination.

In line with its previous decision in 2010, the Federal Labour Court first stated that the contractual clause stipulating that any extra-hours are deemed to be compensated by the salary is invalid, meaning that the employer could not rely on this clause as a defence to the payment claim. Therefore, the question was whether statutory law supported the overtime payment? In this respect, the Court made reference to §612 German Civil Code, which applies in a situation in which the parties did not explicitly agree on a specific level of remuneration when entering into a service agreement. According to this provision, the employee shall be entitled to a remuneration in exchange for his services, if, given the circumstances, the employee could reasonably expect to be remunerated.

In the case of the lawyer claiming compensation for his extra hours, the Federal Labour Court found that there was no such reasonable expectation. The Court stated that employees, who are performing high level services and who receive remuneration that is significantly above average cannot expect to be paid for any extra hours worked. Although the outcome of this decision makes sense, the question remains, why the contract clause denying any overtime payment was non-transparent and therefore invalid, if the employee could not reasonably expect any such overtime payment anyway. Therefore, as a matter of precaution, it may still be advisable to include clauses in the contracts of executive staff excluding any overtime payment. Even if a labour court should come to the conclusion that the clause is invalid, it might help to prevent the employee from having an expectation that his extra hours will be remunerated separately.

In a further decision in February 2012, the Federal Labour Court had the opportunity to clarify its decision. In the case at hand, the Court had to decide whether an inventory surveyor in a warehouse with a salary of around EUR 22,000 p.a. could claim overtime payments. The Court granted such payment as, given his salary, the employee could reasonably expect to be paid for any extra hours worked.

Fixed-term employment contracts

An important and indeed surprising decision by the Federal Labour Court in April 2011 has made the interpretation of fixed-term contracts a lot easier. According to the Act on Part-Time Work and Fixed-Term Employment Contracts (*Teilzeit- und Befristungsgesetz*), the duration of an employment contract may be limited if this is justified by a legitimate reason. Such a legitimate reason can be the temporary substitution for a sick employee or for an employee on maternity leave, etc. Alternatively, if no such legitimate reason applies, a limitation of up to a maximum limit of two years is permitted. However, this rule does not apply if the employee has already been employed by the same employer in the past. The law itself is very specific on this requirement: any previous employment relationship with the same employer renders the agreement of a fixed-term null and void. Nevertheless, the Federal Labour Court has now ruled that only those employment relationships are able to impede the validity of a fixed term agreement, where they have been in force within the three years immediately preceding the date on which the fixed-term employment contract was entered into.

In our view, the Federal Labour Court was right to argue that the intention of the Act is to prevent "chains of fixed-term contracts" and that this risk does not exist if a significant amount of time has elapsed since the end of the last employment relationship. Considering that German labour laws guarantee very extensive protection against dismissals, it is crucial that employers have the option to first enter into a fixed-term contract before entering into an employment contract with an indefinite term. This recent decision of the Federal Labour Court will therefore prove quite helpful in practice. Although it is not fully comprehensible why a time span of three years between two contracts should be sufficient while one or two years is not, the definitive determination of the necessary time period between two contracts by the Court – whether it is two, three or four years – has brought legal certainty and such a transparent and practical solution offered by the Federal Labour Court is to be welcomed.

Formation of age groups for social selection does not violate the Anti-Discrimination Act

In December 2011, the Federal Labour Court ruled that the formation of age groups in order to simplify the social selection process required in the case of mass redundancies is permitted. According to the German Protection Against Unfair Dismissal Act (*Kündigungsschutzgesetz*), an employer can only dismiss an employee, who has been employed in the same establishment or the same company without interruption for more than six months, if the dismissal is justified by legitimate reasons. Such a reason could be a serious breach of contractual duties, personal reasons relating to the employee (e.g. long-term illness) or operational reasons (e.g. restructuring such as site closures or downsizing). In order to be valid, a dismissal for operational reasons has to be based on an entrepreneurial decision whose implementation results in the loss of existing jobs. In addition, there must not be a vacant yet reasonable position within the company in which the employee could continue to be employed. If those requirements are fulfilled, the employer has to undertake a so-called "social selection". This means that, rather than dismissing the employee whose position has become redundant, the employer may instead dismiss an employee who is comparable to the "redundant" employee but who is less in need of social protection. The decision of which employee from the group of comparable employees deserves social protection the least, and therefore has to be the first to be dismissed, is based on the following four social factors: length of service; age; number of dependants (such as children or spouses); and severe disability. It might sound surprising that – considering the European prohibition of discrimination on the grounds of age – the factor "age" should also be taken into account for the selection process. However, the Federal Labour Court has now clarified that this practice is not discriminatory as it is legitimate to consider age as a criteria for the selection process as long as this helps to reflect the employee's chance on the labour market.

Especially when a company intends to eliminate a large number of positions, the result of such social selection is that first and foremost younger employees are dismissed. Not only are they younger, but they usually have a shorter length of service, have fewer dependants and are less likely to be severely disabled than older employees. Therefore, in order to avoid a resultant ageing of the workforce, companies often set up age groups before carrying out the social selection. This means that, at the outset, the personnel who are affected by the restructuring project are divided into age groups and then the social selection is executed only within those groups. Even though this practice has its basis in the German Protection Against Unfair Dismissal Act itself, which explicitly allows companies to ensure a balanced personnel structure within the company, some legal commentators have considered this practice to be a violation of the prohibition against discrimination on the grounds of age as regulated by the German General Equal Treatment Act (*Allgemeines Gleichbehandlungsgesetz*). The earlier mentioned decision of the Federal Labour Court has now rejected this argument and has decided that the formation of age groups is permitted, as long as the age groups are reasonably constructed. The Court thereby finds an adequate balance between the goal to protect older employees on the one hand and the goal to promote the integration of younger employees on the other hand.

Payment *in lieu* of vacation not taken on account of incapacity for work

In the aftermath of the well-known decisions of the European Court of Justice *Schulz-Hoff* and *Schulte*, a variety of German labour court decisions have discussed the question if and for how long, employees that have been on long-term sick leave are, in cases of their recovery, still entitled to take accrued vacation, and, in cases where their employment ends, may claim compensation *in lieu* of paid leave.

According to the German Federal Vacation Act (*Bundesurlaubsgesetz*), vacation has to be granted and taken in the current calendar year, while the transfer of the vacation to the next calendar year is only permitted if justified by compelling operational reasons or personal reasons of the employee, e.g. sick leave. In case of a carry-over, the vacation must be granted and taken within the first three months of the succeeding calendar year. After that date the vacation is forfeited. The German Federal Vacation Act is absolute, which means that, according to the statutes, those rules apply without any exceptions even if the employee has been ill and therefore unable to work.

These rules, however, have been doubted ever since the European Court of Justice ruled on that matter. In its *Schultz-Hoff* decision, the European Court of Justice decided that national legislation may provide that an employee on sick leave is not entitled to take paid annual leave during that sick leave, provided however that the employee in question has the opportunity to exercise his right to vacation during another period. This means that an employee who has been absent on sick leave during the whole holiday year and the carry-over period, cannot be deprived of his right to holiday pay for that year. Instead, irrespective of the length of the sick leave, holiday will accrue while the employee is unable to work. Upon termination of the employment relationship, the employee is entitled to an allowance *in lieu* of paid annual leave accrued but not taken.

However, in the case of *Schulte*, in 2011 the European Court of Justice established some limits to its rules previously set in *Schultz-Hoff*: the purpose of the entitlement to paid annual leave is to enable the employee to rest and to enjoy a period of relaxation and leisure. However, an unlimited accumulation does not answer this purpose, since the relaxation effect diminishes as the time span between the holiday year and the year in which the vacation is actually taken, increases. Therefore, the laws of the European Union do not preclude national legislation which provides that the right to paid annual leave is extinguished at the end of a carry-over period as long as the carry-over period is significantly longer than the reference period. The European Court of Justice also decided that a carry-over period of 15 months is to be considered as "significantly longer" and therefore compatible with European Law.

German jurisprudence is now facing the following situation: although the European Court of Justice ruled that a carry-over period of 15 months should be sufficient, the German Federal Vacation Act only provides a carry-over period of 3 months and is therefore, even in the light of the *Schulte* decision, still void. Since German employers continue to demand an attenuation of the dramatic financial implications of the *Schultz-Hoff* ruling, it is not completely unlikely that German Courts decide to "interpret" the 3-month carry-over period as a 15-month carry-over period, so that any holiday claims are forfeited after that period. However, as long as the Federal Labour Court has not ruled on that issue, the legal situation remains uncertain.

The majority of German verdicts concern scenarios in which the employment relationship is terminated before the employee can recover, resulting in a claim for payment *in lieu* of annual leave. However, just as important is the question how to proceed after the recovery of an employee after long-term sickness absence. Assuming that the Vacation Act cannot be interpreted as providing for a 15-month carry-over period, a recovered employee could return to work claiming to be granted the accumulated vacation of the last few years. The Federal Labour Court has not finally decided whether it will follow this conclusion. However, until this question is answered, employers have to deal with the risk that an employee who has just returned to work will soon take his legitimate vacation.

Clauses providing for longer vacations for older employees can be discriminatory

Not only has the discussion about the forfeiture of paid annual leave and the allowance *in lieu* of occupied German Courts in the last few months but so has the question whether clauses providing for increased vacation days depending on the age of the employee are discriminatory on the grounds of age. The collective bargaining agreement that was the subject of a decision of the Federal Labour Court published in March 2012 contained the following provision: "Employees who are younger than 30 years are granted 26 holiday days per year, employees who are younger than 40 years are granted 29 holiday days per year and employees who are older than 40 years are granted 30 holiday days per year." The Federal Labour Court decided that the provision discriminates against younger employees and is therefore incompatible with the German General Equal Treatment Act. According to this Act, employees may not be treated adversely on the grounds of age, unless the differences in treatment are objectively and reasonably justified by a legitimate aim.

In the case at hand, the employer argued that the legitimate aim of that provision was the protection of older employees. Although the Court conceded that the protection of older employees can be qualified as a legitimate aim in general, it argued that in this particular case the provision under discussion could not be considered as protecting older employees. According to the Court it was not plausible that the parties of the collective bargaining agreement wanted to promote the older employees' increased need of relaxation. If they had followed that aim, they would have designed a different provision in which the amount of vacation days would continue to increase after the employee had reached the age of 40. Instead, the Court questioned why, under the relevant clause, a 30-year old employee should need three more holiday days per year than a 29-year old employee, while a 40-year old employee should deserve the same amount of holiday days as a 65-year old employee. According to the General Equal Treatment Act, a provision which violates the prohibition of adverse treatment shall be invalid. However, in this case the Federal Labour Court decided that it was not sufficient to declare the provision as invalid, but that the only way to eliminate the discrimination was to grant every employee the maximum amount of holiday days.

The resulting consequences are drastic. Employers who are bound to that very collective bargaining agreement or those whose employment contracts contain similar provisions will have to grant to all of their employees – even retrospectively – the maximum amount of holidays in the highest age-category. As it remains unclear which kind of clause would subsist the anti-discrimination test of the Equal Treatment Act, we would instead recommend complete avoidance of any clauses in the employment contract that provide for longer vacation according to the age of the employee.

Recent statutory or legislative changes

Reform of the Temporary Agency Workers Act

As already mentioned above, a very strong public debate has taken place in recent years regarding the working conditions of temporary agency workers, fuelled by some cases of abuse which have received broad media coverage. The most striking case related to a chain of chemists which had dismissed large numbers of its staff and hired these employees back from a temporary workers' agency immediately thereafter, but at much lower salaries. Although this practice was legal, the public uproar was strong and the legislator had to react.

The German Temporary Agency Workers Act has therefore been amended in several respects. The most important change relates to the heavily criticised "fire and hire back" practice. To the extent that an agency worker is hired by a company or a group of companies where s/he was employed within a period of six months prior to being re-hired, the temporary workers' agency has to now pay the same remuneration to that agency worker as a comparable employee of the hiring company is paid (Equal Pay Principle).

Another important modification of the relevant Act relates to the access to social facilities. Temporary agency workers shall now have the right of access to social facilities (e.g. a canteen, a company kindergarten, etc.) under the same conditions as the regular employees of the hiring company. Finally, the legislator has introduced a system of minimum wages for temporary agency workers. The modifications came into force on 30 April 2011 and 1 December 2011.

Likely or impending reforms to employment legislation and enforcement procedures

Proposal for a new Act on the Equality of Remuneration

According to statistics presented by the Social Democratic Party of Germany (SPD) there is a gap of 23% between the average salaries of men and women. In the party's opinion, this gap cannot be explained by different social or professional qualities but is the result of discrimination on the grounds of gender. Therefore, the SPD submitted a proposal for a new act to the German Federal Parliament, the Bundestag, that provides regulations, which are supposed to decrease this gap. The party argues that the current acts of discrimination cannot be prevented by the intervention of governmental institutions. Instead, employers, works councils and the parties of collective bargaining agreements should be obliged by law to promote the equality in payment.

The main feature of the proposed act is the introduction of an examination procedure, certified by the Federal Anti-Discrimination Agency. Employers, who regularly employ more than 15 employees, shall be obliged to examine their payment policy on a regular basis by using certified procedures. This means that a representative of the Federal Anti-Discrimination Agency or an investigator approved by this Agency has to carry out the procedure. If the result of the examination is that the payment policy in the company is indeed discriminatory, there are two possibilities for the way in which the procedure must be continued. Firstly, if a works council exists in the company, a conciliation board has to be formed. The board must review the examination procedure and then grant the employees against whom the employer has discriminated the same salary as the other employees receive. However, if there is no works council, the employer has to take measures to eliminate the discrimination, supervised by the Federal Anti-Discrimination Agency. The proposal was submitted in June 2012. This means that the parliamentary debate is still on-going. Due to the extensive administrative procedures this proposed Act would create, it is in our view rather unlikely that it will be ratified. However, the topic in general is quite popular and we expect that the legislator will adopt a law aiming to promote the equal pay principle after the general elections in September 2013.

Reform of the Data Protection Act

The German Data Protection Act (*Bundesdatenschutzgesetz*) only contains one rather generic clause (§ 32) regarding the use of employee data, leaving it to the courts, the legal commentators (and the employers) to deal with the manifold problems resulting from the increasing use of modern communication technologies in the workplace. The legislator is well aware of this problem and in 2010 presented a draft proposal for an act implementing comprehensive rules regarding the protection of employee data in a modern working environment. The draft Act contained, among others, rules on the use of biometric data, the use of internet and email, surveillance by using GPS systems and background-checks of applicants using social media networks. Although the different political parties still disagreed on two essential points (firstly, to what extent the employee may by explicit consent waive certain rules of the act and secondly, to what extent the employer and the works council may deviate in works council agreements from the level of protection in the act), it was expected that the parties would reach a compromise and that the act would enter into force in 2012. However, on 25 January 2012 the EU-Commission presented its proposal for a General Data Protection Regulation, which could render large parts of the German Data Protection Act obsolete, and given that the government is currently absorbed by other, more important projects such as the Euro-crisis, we do not expect that the reform on the protection of employee data will be implemented any time soon.

Dr Michael Kuhnke
Tel: +49 40 27 88 537 10 / Email: m.kuhnke@SchrammMeyerKuhnke.de
Michael Kuhnke completed his legal education at the University of Konstanz, Germany, and the McGill University Montreal, Canada. Prior to founding Schramm Meyer Kuhnke, he worked for many years in the Employment, Pensions and Benefits practice group of the leading international law firm Freshfields Bruckhaus Deringer LLP. Michael specialises in individual and collective employment law, particularly in the context of mergers and acquisitions, outsourcings and restructurings. His advice also focuses on all topics in relation to board level and senior executive service agreements and compensation structures. Michael is the author of several publications on employment law.

Dr Holger Meyer
Tel: +49 40 27 88 537 11 / Email: h.meyer@SchrammMeyerKuhnke.de
Holger Meyer completed his legal education at the Christian-Albrechts University Kiel. Before founding Schramm Meyer Kuhnke, Holger worked from 2001 until 2010 in the employment, pensions and benefits practice group of the leading international law firm White & Case LLP.
One of Holger's main areas of expertise is the legal and strategic preparation of restructuring and outsourcing projects and the negotiation of social compensation plans with works councils. Furthermore, he advises clients on labour law issues of M&A transactions, amongst others in crisis or insolvency. Holger Meyer is recommended in the JUVE handbook 2011/12 as an "experienced transaction employment lawyer".

Schramm Meyer Kuhnke

ABC-Str. 38, 20354 Hamburg, Germany
Tel: +49 40 27 88 537 10 / Fax: +49 40 27 88 537 20 / URL: http://www.SchrammMeyerKuhnke.de

Hungary

János Tamás Varga & Dóra Bocskov-Szabó
VJT & Partners

Overview

Owing to the severe impact of the economic crisis on the Hungarian economy, increasing the number of those in employment has been at the very heart of the Hungarian government's economic policy. The government has also declared the need to increase the level of flexibility in employment contracts to enable the Hungarian economy to respond more effectively to the changing economic climate.

To this end, the government launched a complete overhaul of current labour legislation, the result of which was the introduction of a Bill to the Hungarian Parliament on 26 October 2011. Although the new regulations have been criticised heavily by trade unions for diminishing employee rights and cutting back salaries, the government was determined to adopt this new approach. The Parliament finally passed the Bill without major amendments and Act I of 2012 on the Labour Code (**"New Labour Code"**) was adopted on 13 December 2011.

Although the Act on interim provisions has not yet been adopted by Parliament, it is anticipated that most of the provisions of the New Labour Code will come into force on 1 July 2012, introducing significant changes to most elements of the employment 'relationship' and replacing the currently effective Act XXII of 1992 on the Labour Code (**"Old Labour Code"**).

Below follows an introduction to general labour market trends in Hungary and the summary of the most noteworthy labour court decisions of last year. In addition, we highlight the most significant and interesting changes of the new labour legislation.

General labour market trends

In 2009-2010, the Hungarian economy went through severe crisis. In the first half of 2010, the recession slowed, then the declining trend reversed and by the second half of 2010 the rate of growth reached the level prior to the economic crisis. In 2011 however, both the international and the internal economic environment became unfavourable again, thus the growth of the Hungarian economy slowed down in the first three quarters of 2011.

The Institute for Economic and Enterprise Research, a non-profit economic research institute operated by the Hungarian Chamber of Commerce and Industry, conducted comprehensive research of managers in over 7,000 Hungarian companies about their short-term expectations for 2012 (**"Labour Market Forecast"**). The major findings were that for companies generally the economic crisis is expected to deepen instead of improve in the first half of 2012.

The Labour Market Forecast revealed that companies' business expectations for 2012 significantly declined compared to last year. However, a small majority of the companies still anticipate an improvement in their own business circumstances in 2012. The companies which produce or perform services mostly for export and are in foreign ownership have the most optimistic outlook. The Labour Market Forecast shows that companies involved in catering and/or industry are more likely to plan staff increases. By contrast, companies in the financial sector appear least likely to increase the number of their staff.

The Labour Market Forecast also illustrates that skilled physical employees are needed the most; which is the same as in 2011.

Based on the latest data from the National Employment Service, the *demand for manpower* has increased in the first four months of 2012. However, in comparison to data from April 2011, a 22.8% decrease can be observed in the number of open positions. The demand for manpower mostly came from the processing industry (especially food, beverages and tobacco manufacturing), vehicle repair and the building industry.

Based on the latest data of the Hungarian Central Statistical Office, the labour market opportunities for both men and women have improved in the first quarter of 2012. The number of employed people (i.e. those employees and self-employed persons who perform work legally) in the first three months of 2012 is up 1.6% compared to the first three months of 2011 despite the unemployment rate not changing significantly. The recently released data of the Hungarian Central Statistical Office indicates that the unemployment rate in Hungary in the first quarter of 2012 is 11.7%, which is 0.1% higher than in the first quarter of last year.

The *number of registered job seekers* (i.e. job seekers registered to the competent employment office cooperating with it to find a job) reduced over the last few months, even in comparison to the same month of last year. Among the registered job seekers, the number of long-term registered job seekers (i.e. unemployed for more than a year), as well as new entrants to labour market also reduced in the first four months of 2012. The average period of unemployment at the end of the first quarter of 2012 is 17.3 months.

The regional differences with respect to unemployment are still significant in Hungary. Job seekers in the north-eastern counties are in the most difficult situation, whereas the north-western regions and the capital are those parts of Hungary where the chances for job seekers are the most favourable. As a means of decreasing the regional differences, the government will be entitled to determine different levels of minimum salary with respect to the employees working in different regions of Hungary once the New Labour Code comes into force.

According to the latest data of the National Employment Service, the number of employees affected by *mass dismissal* (i.e. when an employer decides to terminate the employment relationship of a significant number of its employees within a short term due to any reason related to its operation) was considerably higher both in March and April 2012 than in the same months of the previous year. In April 2012, 19 companies notified the competent labour centres of their planned mass dismissals affecting altogether 2,129 employees, which is five times higher than in April 2011.

One of the recent largest mass dismissals affecting a total of 2,300 employees was announced by the Hungarian subsidiary of Nokia in February 2012. In line with the agreement reached between Nokia and its workers' council, the mass dismissal will take effect in three phases by the end of 2012.

Besides the increasing number of mass dismissals, however, some significant staff increases also took place in Hungary recently. For instance, Mercedes-Benz Manufacturing Hungary Ltd. (**"Mercedes-Benz"**) having started its manufacturing activity on 29 March 2012, decided to increase the number of its employees from 2,500 to 3,000 during 2012. To date Mercedes-Benz is working with 17 Hungarian suppliers, however this number may further increase in the near future. The number of people employed by the local service industry serving Mercedes-Benz was estimated at around 10,000, however, an increase in this regard is also anticipated. Another large staff increase took place at Audi Hungaria Motor Ltd. (**"Audi"**), which increased its staff numbers by 1,000 employees between October 2011 and April 2012. By expanding its factory, Audi plans to create 2,100 new jobs by the end of 2013.

Latest trends in employment litigation

Based on the statistics of the labour courts, the number of new employment lawsuits decreased by 15% in 2011 compared to 2010. With regards to the subject of the employment litigation cases, both in 2010 and in 2011 most lawsuits were initiated in connection with: (i) salaries and other emoluments; (ii) termination of an employment relationship; and (iii) liability for damages caused by the employer.

Key case law affecting employers' decision making over dismissal, redundancies dismissals etc.

Decisions of the Hungarian Supreme Court ("**Curia**") have always had significant impact on the interpretation of the regulations of labour legislation. Considering that the lower level courts cannot practically deviate from the fundamental decisions of the Curia, the Curia's decisions in many cases have not only interpreted certain ambiguous regulations but also developed the labour legislation by extending or narrowing the scope of certain provisions. Below, we highlight the most noteworthy decisions of the Curia from last year.

Clarifying the definition of executive employee

Following the definition set forth by the Old Labour Code, the employer's executive officer and his/ her deputy qualify as executive employees. The Old Labour Code provided (and the New Labour Code will also provide) special and more stringent provisions with respect to employees in executive positions than to employees belonging to the general workforce. For instance, the employer may terminate the employment relationship of an executive employee without having to give a reason for the termination. Thus, it has always been crucial whether a position in fact qualifies as an executive position under the Old Labour Code or not. As the definition provided by the Old Labour Code turned out to be rather brief, it has been up to the judiciary to clarify its content.

One of the recent decisions of the Curia further clarified the definition of executive employees. Under the Old Labour Code not only the executive officer but also his/her deputy qualify as an executive employee. It has therefore always been a question as to what kind of deputising right is necessary to qualify a position as 'executive'. The Curia extended the scope of executive employees as, according to its interpretation, not only employees being entitled to permanently deputise the executive officer with full competence in his/her absence fall under the definition of executive employees, but those ones unauthorised to have such full competence upon deputising may qualify as deputies of executive officers (i.e. as executive employees) as well under certain circumstances. The Curia stated that not the name but the content of the position shall be examined and the determining factor is whether the employee carries out tasks and has competences which allow him/her to influence by his/her own decisions the operation or management of the employer and to have a crucial role in managing the employer.

The New Labour Code provides a more precise definition of 'executive employees' than the Old Labour Code, which corresponds to the above interpretation of the Curia. Therefore, in our view the decision of the Curia, above, will continue to have relevance even after the New Labour Code comes into force.

Extending the content of waiver of rights

With respect to a lawsuit initiated by a former employee, the Curia had to decide on the employee's entitlement to a bonus. The employee's employment relationship was terminated by the mutual agreement of the parties. The mutual agreement contained that *the parties do not have any further claims arising from the employment relationship against each other*. After the signing of the mutual agreement, however, the employee commenced a lawsuit against the employer requesting his annual bonus. He claimed that he became entitled to the annual bonus on the basis of his annual performance, however, as the due date of bonus payment was a few days after the termination of his employment relationship, he did not get it.

When finally deciding the lawsuit, the Curia had to take into consideration two aspects. On the one hand, the Curia had to decide whether the employee's declaration in the mutual agreement on termination stating that he does not have any further claims arising from the employment relationship can be interpreted as a waiver of his right to the annual bonus or not. On the other hand, the Curia had to decide whether a waiver as such is valid or not considering that in line with the Old Labour Code an employee cannot waive his/her salary or other emoluments in advance.

The judicial practice has interpreted waivers of rights rather narrowly stating that the right being the subject of the waiver must be expressly defined and the waiver needs to be explicit in order to qualify as a valid waiver of right. However, the present decision of the Curia seems to extend the scope of such waivers. The Curia stated that the provision of the mutual agreement according to which *the parties do not have any further claims arising from the employment relationship against each other* entirely reflected the parties' will in the present case and it includes the employee's waiver of the eventual claim for the annual bonus. As the employee was aware of the conditions of his annual bonus entitlement (i.e. he knew that his entitlement thereto was based on his annual performance) when signing the mutual agreement, he could not lawfully claim that his declaration in the mutual agreement did not include the waiver of the bonus. The Curia also pointed out that as at the time of termination the employee must have been aware of having fulfilled the conditions of bonus entitlement, the annual bonus became due when terminating the employee's employment relationship, i.e. the employee's waiver cannot be interpreted as a prior waiver of salary or other emoluments, and thus it is valid.

Withholding information on additional work as a lawful reason for termination

Under the provisions of the Old Labour Code an employee is obliged to notify the employer of any additional legal relationship for performing work. In case such an additional legal relationship violates or jeopardises the employer's legitimate economic interests, the employer may prohibit the establishment of the additional legal relationship or oblige the employee to terminate it.

With respect to a lawsuit initiated by a former employee, the Curia had to decide whether the reason for termination provided by the employer was lawful or not. The employee alongside his primary employment relationship performed additional work under a civil law contract. He only informed the employer verbally that he had been offered additional work, however he did not reveal any further information on it, nor that he had in fact accepted the offer. The employer finally terminated his employment relationship giving the reason that the employee breached his cooperation and notification obligation with respect to the additional work.

When finally deciding the lawsuit, the Curia declared that the employee, pursuant to his information obligation under the Old Labour Code, should have provided sufficient and detailed information on his additional work covering all relevant circumstances and conditions. In the event of a lack of detailed and thorough information the employer is not in a position to be able to decide whether the additional legal relationship in fact jeopardises its economic interests or not. Thus the Curia pointed out on the one hand that an employee only fulfils its information obligation with respect to the additional legal relationship if he/she gives detailed and thorough information about all relevant circumstances relating to the additional legal relationship, whereas on the other hand, breaching this information obligation by the employee is a lawful reason for termination.

Considering that the New Labour Code only contains a general rule under which the employee must refrain from any activity during the term of the employment relationship which jeopardises the employer's rightful economic interests, however it does not contain the employee's special information obligation relating to additional legal relationships, we are of the opinion that the above decision of the Curia will be especially relevant once the New Labour Code comes into force.

Quality replacement as a reason for termination

Both under the Old Labour Code and the New Labour Code, if the employer terminates the employment relationship of an employee by ordinary or extraordinary notice, it must give a reason for it. According to uniform judicial practice the reason for termination must be clear, real and causal. In one of its recent decisions, the Curia confirmed and strengthened the consequent court practice relating to quality replacement as the reason for termination. Quality replacement covers those cases when the employer decides to replace its employee with a more qualified new employee. The Curia pointed out that quality replacement as reason for termination is not causal, i.e. the termination is unlawful if the given position in fact does not require a previously indicated ability or knowledge. For example, if the reason for termination is the lack of foreign language knowledge, however in the given position the employee in fact never has to use the foreign language when performing the daily tasks, the termination will be found unlawful.

Recent legislative changes – the New Labour Code

The New Labour Code will introduce significant changes to most elements of the employment relationship. Below we summarise those changes which we consider the most noteworthy:

Deviation from the rules of the New Labour Code

The new regulations will preserve the general rule that individual employment agreements may only deviate from the rules of the New Labour Code in favour of the employees. However, unlike the current system, collective bargaining agreements may also be able to deviate from the rules to the disadvantage of employees. This conceptual change is supposed, and is likely, to intensify the collaboration between employers and the trade unions.

Changing rules relating to exercising employers' rights

As a prevailing judicial practice developed under the Old Labour Code, in most cases the labour courts have found invalid (and consequently unlawful) those legal statements (e.g. terminations of employment) in which the employer was not represented by the person formally authorised to exercise the employer's rights (e.g. due to the authorised person's sudden illness). The legal statement and the decision implied therein must have been made by the person exercising employer's rights, and later approval of such decisions did not suffice. The New Labour Code introduces a more flexible regulation in this regard.

The new, rather more practical regulation, allows the person exercising employer's rights *to subsequently approve* the legal statement issued by the 'pseudo representative', i.e. by the person formally unauthorised to exercise employer's rights. The New Labour Code neither sets forth a specific deadline for the approval nor any special formal requirements, however the commentaries recommend to approve the statement in writing and within a reasonable time period.

Changing rules regarding non-compete obligations

Under a non-competition agreement the employee must refrain from engaging in any conduct jeopardising or violating the employer's rightful economic interests following the end of the employment relationship (e.g. he/she may have to refrain from performing work for the employer's competitor). As an offset, the employee shall be entitled to compensation.

Pursuant to the Old Labour Code, non-compete obligations may stand at a maximum of three years. The New Labour Code, however, reduces the previous time limit by providing that the term of non-compete agreements cannot exceed two years as from the date of termination of the employment relationship.

As the Old Labour Code did not determine the minimum compensation an employee shall be entitled to as an offset for keeping the non-compete obligations, it was up to the labour courts to set the amount. The prevailing judicial practice has fixed the eligible consideration in an amount equivalent to half of the employee's average salary for the term of the non-competition agreement.

The New Labour Code reduces the amount of minimum compensation determined by the judicial practice. Under the new rules, the minimum acceptable amount is one third of the employee's base salary to be paid during the term of the non-competition agreement.

As another new rule introduced by the New Labour Code, if the employee terminates his/her employment relationship by extraordinary notice, he/she shall be entitled to rescind from the non-competition agreement.

Notwithstanding that the New Labour Code sets forth the above special statutory rescission right of the employee, the new regulation does not exclude the right to stipulate in the non-competition agreement the rescission right of the employer and/or the employee as well as the penalty payment obligation in case of the breach of obligations.

Temporary exclusion of right to terminate by ordinary notice

Under the Old Labour Code any restriction relating to the right of termination set forth in the agreement of the parties was unlawful.

The New Labour Code, as a general conceptual change in the labour legislation, has placed a higher emphasis on the parties' agreement. This is manifested, *inter alia,* in one of the new provisions introduced by the New Labour Code allowing the parties to expressly agree in *the exclusion of the right to terminate the employment relationship by ordinary notice* for a period of one year following the establishment of the employment relationship. Under the new rule, the exclusion of this right shall be mutual, i.e. such exclusion must be binding for *both* parties, exclusion by only one party will be found invalid.

By the mutual waiver of ordinary termination right, the parties evidently express that they do wish to maintain the employment relationship for a longer period of time.

Restrictions to practising the right of termination by ordinary notice

Under the Old Labour Code the employer was not allowed to terminate the employment relationship of an employee during time periods related to: (i) the illness of the employee or his/her children or close relatives; (ii) military service; and/or (iii) childcare (e.g. pregnancy, maternity leave) (i.e. during 'protection periods'). In these cases the employer could only deliver the ordinary notice to the employee on the first day of his/her return to work with the proviso that the notice period would start 15 or 30 days later depending on the length of the protection period.

The New Labour Code has left unchanged the institution of 'protection period' with respect to time periods related to military service and childcare; i.e. the employer still cannot lawfully deliver an ordinary notice to the employee during the term of these protection periods. However, with regard to the protection periods related to pregnancy, it introduces a significant amendment corresponding to new judicial practice in this regard.

The Curia in many of its earlier decisions interpreted the protection periods set forth by the Old Labour Code as objective circumstances. Such interpretation had particular relevance in case of an employee's pregnancy, especially when the employer was not aware of the fact that its employee was pregnant when delivering the ordinary notice to her. The Curia consistently found the termination unlawful if the employer terminated the employment relationship of a pregnant employee by ordinary notice, even if neither the employee nor the employer were aware thereof or even if the employee did not inform the employer thereof. In its recent decisions the Curia changed its former, rather partial practice and declared that the employee cannot adduce her pregnancy if she intentionally withheld this information from the employer.

The New Labour Code, corresponding to the changing judicial practice, sets forth a supplementary rule with respect to protection periods related to pregnancy. The employee may only claim that she was under a protection period related to pregnancy if she informed the employer thereof prior to the delivery of the ordinary notice.

In contradiction with the prior legislation, time periods related to illness no longer belong to the category of protection periods. Nevertheless the New Labour Code preserves some kind of restriction in this regard as well. Under the new rules, during time periods related to illness, under the New Labour Code the employer is allowed to notify the employee on ordinary termination on condition that the notice period starts on the first day following the employee returns to work.

Changing conditions of eligibility regarding severance pay

Conditions on eligibility for severance pay are subject to amendment under the New Labour Code.

Under the Old Labour Code, if the employer terminated the employee's employment relationship by ordinary notice, regardless of the reason for termination, the employee became entitled to severance pay provided that he/she had spent at least three years at the employer. In this way, severance pay was payable even if the employee was dismissed due to his/her inappropriate behaviour or breach of his/her obligations, for instance, which has been considered unfair with respect to the employer.

As a new rule introduced by the New Labour Code, should the reason for termination by ordinary notice be in connection with the employee's abilities (provided that they are not connected to health conditions) or his/her inappropriate behaviour related to the employment relationship, severance pay shall not be payable.

Employee's right to terminate in case of business transfer

Unlike some European countries, the New Labour Code will still not require employees' consent for any change in employer owing to the transfer of the business.

However, under the new regulations, employees will have the right to terminate their employment relationship if the substantial and disadvantageous changes in employment conditions due to the business transfer cause 'excessive grievance' to them. In such cases they will be entitled to the same remuneration as if the employer had initiated the termination (e.g. severance pay and salary for release period). However, they must give a justifiable reason for termination when adducing such circumstances in the ordinary notice and the burden of proof is on them with respect to the reason provided, i.e. that the reason for termination is in fact clear, real and causal. The employees are entitled to terminate the employment relationship with reference to such circumstances within a 30-day deadline as from the change of the employer.

New way of terminating definite term employment relationships

Under the Old Labour Code, the employer could only terminate a definite term employment relationship: (i) with immediate effect under the trial period; (ii) by the mutual agreement of the parties; (iii) by extraordinary notice; or (iv) with immediate effect provided that the employer reimbursed the employee's average salary due for one year or for the remaining period if less than one year was left from the definite term. However, the employer was not allowed to terminate definite term employment relationships by ordinary notice.

The New Labour Code, as a new rule, entitles the employer to terminate the definite term employment relationship by a 'reasoned ordinary notice':
(i)   during liquidation or bankruptcy proceedings;
(ii) if the reason for termination is related to the employee's incapability; and/or
(iii) if the maintenance of the employment relationship becomes impossible on the part of the employer due to circumstances beyond its sphere of control.

Similarly to terminating indefinite term employment relationships by the employer, the burden of proof is on the employer with respect to the reason provided in the ordinary notice, i.e. that the reason for termination is in fact clear, real and causal.

Conceptual change relating to the consequences of unlawful termination

The New Labour Code amends the provisions relating to the consequences of unlawful termination with a conceptual edge.

As per the Old Labour Code, if the court found that the termination of the employment relationship had been unlawful, provided that the employee so requested, under certain circumstances, the court restored the employment relationship by placing back the employee to his/her original position (ordering the employer to reimburse the employee for his/her salary and other emoluments until the date of restoration). If the employee did not request the restoration of his/her employment relationship or if the court refused such request, the employment relationship was deemed terminated as of the date the court's decision on unlawful termination became final and binding. As a consequence, the employee became entitled to his/her lost salary and other emoluments (reduced by the employee's salary recovered elsewhere) until the date of the final and binding court decision and to damages for damage incurred by him/her; additionally, the employer was ordered to pay the employee 2-12 months' average salary as a lump sum compensation (i.e. as a penalty for the unlawful behaviour).

As a conceptual change, the New Labour Code on the one hand, restricts to apply the restoration of the employment relationship to a few special cases (e.g. when the unlawfulness of the termination lies in the discriminative behaviour of the employer), whereas on the other hand, it entirely eliminates the concept of 'lump sum compensation' to be paid by the employer as a penalty for its unlawful act. In this way the New Labour Code entirely limits the consequences of unlawful termination to a damages claim basis.

As a general rule, the New Labour Code sets forth that the employer shall reimburse the damage incurred by the employee in connection with the unlawful termination of his/her employment relationship. However, with regards to damages to be paid for lost salaries, the New Labour Code introduces a cap; under the title of 'lost salaries', the amount of damages shall not exceed the amount of the employee's 12 months' average remuneration (i.e. 12 months' 'absent fee' according to the terminology of the New Labour Code). The introduction of this new cap is supposed to result in much more foreseeable judicial practice relating to the amount to be paid by the employer as a consequence of unlawful termination. Considering that under the Old Labour Code the actual amount an employer was ordered to pay in practice depended on the length of the judicial procedure (which is significantly longer at the Metropolitan courts than at the country courts), the monetary cap introduced by the New Labour Code is a guarantee for a fairer and more foreseeable judicial practice.

If the employee did not incur any damage as a consequence of the unlawful termination (e.g. because he/she soon found a new job with higher salary), under the New Labour Code the employee may request the amount of his/her absent fee due for the notice period.

<u>Changing rules with respect to multiple-shift work schedule and shift allowances</u>

The New Labour Code also brings a major change in the system of shift allowances.

Under the Old Labour Code, employees were entitled to afternoon and night shift allowances for the work performed during afternoon and night periods provided that they were employed in a so-called 'multi-shift work schedule'.

Under the Old Labour Code the employee's work schedule qualified as a multi-shift work schedule if: (i) the employer's daily operation was longer than the normal daily working hours of the employee; *and* (ii) the employees performed the same tasks; *and* (iii) they regularly took over the work from each other within a day from time to time. In line with the Old Labour Code employees were only entitled to shift allowances if all of the above (i)-(iii) conditions were met. However, the court practice extended the scope of the multi-shift work schedule as a result of which a lot of employers were obliged to pay afternoon shift allowances to their employees, which was an unduly serious financial burden on them.

The New Labour Code is a breakthrough in this regard since on the one hand, it eliminates the afternoon shift allowance, whereas on the other hand, it notably simplifies the definition of a multi-shift work schedule minimising the ground of judiciary extension. Under the New Labour Code, if the employer's operation exceeds 80 hours per week (i.e. it qualifies as multi-shift operation) a *uniform* shift allowance shall be payable to the employees for the work performed between 6pm and 6am, provided that the starting time of their daily working hours varies on a regular basis.

<u>New definition of freely determined work schedule</u>

The Old Labour Code did not set forth a definition for 'freely determined working hours', only reference was made thereto, i.e. if the employee was entitled to determine his/her working hours on his/her own, he/she was not entitled to remuneration for extraordinary work and the employer was not obliged to register his/her working hours.

As per the prevailing judicial practice, the term 'freely determined working hours' has meant that the employee shall be authorised to *freely* and *completely* determine his/her working hours on his/her own. In the light of this, the labour courts only exceptionally accepted it as lawful conduct if the reason for the non-payment of extraordinary work allowances was that the employee was entitled to freely determine his/her working hours, even if such stipulation was incorporated into the employment agreement. In such cases, the labour courts thoroughly investigated whether the employee's position in fact made it possible to determine his/her working hours entirely on his/her own. The New Labour Code provides a new definition for freely determined work schedule changing the substance of the previous regulation by extending its confines. In terms of freely determined work schedule the employee still will not be entitled to remuneration for extraordinary work, and his/her working hours still will not have to be registered. Under the New Labour Code the employee's work schedule qualifies as 'freely determined work schedule' when the employer transfers the employee its right to schedule *at least half of the daily working hours* on his/her own. This will lawfully give rise to qualify work schedules as freely determined in a wider range of cases as opposed to the prevailing judiciary practice.

<u>Conceptual change regarding employer's liability for damages</u>

Under the Old Labour Code the employer was only relieved of liability with respect to any damage suffered by an employee in connection with his/her employment relationship, if the damage was caused either by *an unavoidable event beyond the employer's scope of operation* or *solely by the unavoidable conduct of the employee.*

The prevailing judicial practice has unreasonably extended the definition of 'scope of operation', practically excluding the chance for being relieved of liability. The Curia once had to decide on a case in which the employee had been walking down the stairs at the site of the employer when his attention was diverted from his steps causing him to fall from the stairs and get badly injured. The objective liability of the employer was declared by the Curia, as the accident had taken place at the workplace during working hours, and the employee's activity fell under the employer's scope of interest. In other cases, even if the employee performed work out of the workplace (e.g. in case of a postman delivering letters) the employer's liability was also declared for damage resulting from accidents (e.g. when the employee slipped over on the icy road and got badly injured).

It is a clear goal of the new regulations to narrow such extensive liability of employers. Under the new rules, employers will be liable for damage suffered by employees only if the damage was caused by (i) circumstances being within the employer's sphere of control, (ii) which are foreseeable, and (iii) the employer should be expected to avoid them or to avert the damage.

Based on the commentaries of the New Labour Code, under the new rules the employer shall be exempt from liability in case of events detailed above. For instance, the employer's activity shall be regarded as falling beyond the employer's sphere of control if the performance of work takes place on public roads or any other territories available for third persons (e.g. postmen, repairmen fixing on site) or the employee suffers an accident on a public road by a vehicle owned by the employer (provided that it is not the bad condition of the vehicle giving rise to the accident).

Employee's liability for damages

The New Labour Code raises the cap of employees' liability for any damage caused by breaching their obligations arising from the employment relationship to an amount equal to four months' average remuneration (i.e. four months' 'absent fee' according to the terminology of the New Labour Code).

Besides, under the new rules, employees shall reimburse the amount of the entire damage both in cases of damage caused wilfully and by gross negligence. In line with the Old Labour Code, gross negligence did not lead to the reimbursement of the entire damage.

Deadline of legal remedy

The New Labour Code maintains that the employer's written legal statement must contain information on *the employee's right to contest the employer's decision before court including the applicable time limit for filing the claim* provided that it is shorter than the general three-year limitation period (e.g. in case of termination).

In line with the prevailing judicial practice, if the employer failed to give the employee such information, the employee could file a claim within *the general three-year limitation period* instead of the shorter specific (e.g. 30-day) deadline.

The New Labour Code changes the above consequences developed by the judicial practice. Under the new rules, if the employer fails to give the required information to the employee regarding legal remedy, the employee may file his/her claim within a six-month limitation period (and not within the general three-year limitation period).

This article gives examples of the expected changes in Hungarian employment law. For more background, please contact the authors.

* * *

Sources

1.   EBH 2011. 2346 Court Decision of the Curia.
2.   EBH 2011. 2342 Court Decision of the Curia.
3.   EBH 2011. 2340 Court Decision of the Curia.
4.   EBH 2011. 2339 Court Decision of the Curia.
5.   Institute for Economic and Enterprise Research: *Short-term Labour Market Forecast 2012.*
6.   Hungarian Labour Inspectorate: *Development of the labour market based on the latest data of the National Employment Service in March 2012.*
7.   Hungarian Labour Inspectorate: *Development of the labour market based on the latest data of the*

National Employment Service in April 2012.

8. Hungarian Central Statistical Office: *First Release – Employment, January-March 2012, April number*, 27 April 2012.

9. Hungarian Central Statistical Office: *First Release – Unemployment, January-March 2012, April number*, 27 April 2012.

10. *The manufacturing has started at the Mercedes-factory in Kecskemét*, 29 March 2012; on 31 May 2012 it was available at: http://vallalkozoi.negyed.hu/vnegyed/20120329-autogyartas-megindult-a-termeles-a-mercedes-kecskemeti-uzemeben.html.

11. Audi Hungaria Motor Ltd.: *The 8,000th colleague at Audi Hungaria*, 5 April 2012; on 31 May 2012 it was available at: http://www.audi.hu/hu/profil/gyarbovites/hirek/reszletek/276_8_000_munkatars_az_audi_hungarianal/.

12. World Economics Online (in Hungarian: Világgazdaság Online): *Nokia: The national reduction starts in April*; on 29 May 2012 it was available at: http://www.vg.hu/vallalatok/infokommunikacio/nokia-aprilisban-indul-a-hazai-leepites-370708.

13. *Statistics of the labour courts, 2010*, on 31 May 2012 it was available at: http://www.birosag.hu/engine.aspx?page=Birosag_Statisztikak.

14. *Statistics of the labour courts, 2011*, on 31 May 2012 it was available at: http://www.birosag.hu/engine.aspx?page=Birosag_Statisztikak.

János Tamás Varga
Tel: +36 1 501 9900 / Email: VargaJT@vjt-partners.com
János Tamás Varga is Managing Partner of VJT & Partners, a leading Hungarian commercial law firm. With over 15 years' experience advising on contentious and non-contentious employment law matters for international and Hungarian companies, he is one of the most experienced employment lawyers in the Hungarian legal market. Recognised as a leader in employment law in Hungary by the EMEA Legal 500, Chambers Europe and Best Lawyers, his expertise includes employment litigation, due diligence, employee transfers, HR policy, terminations and immigration. János Tamás is also well-known as a leading corporate lawyer in Hungary, with experience of financing and regulatory matters. He also acts for clients in high-value civil litigation and arbitration matters.

Dóra Bocskov-Szabó
Tel: +36 1 501 9900 / Email: Bocskov-SzaboD@vjt-partners.com
Dóra joined VJT & Partners following her graduation and was made a partner in 2011. Her main focus is employment law. Her experience covers due diligence, employee transfers in outsourcing and M&A transactions, employment litigation, implementation of foreign employment agreement templates in the Hungarian legal environment, preparing internal HR policies and guidelines, advising on termination and immigration matters. Dóra has also been involved in a number of highly complex employment litigation matters. Dóra graduated from the Faculty of Law at the University of Szeged in 2006. She also graduated from the Faculty of Arts at the University of Szeged in both English and Hungarian.

VJT & Partners

Kernstok Károly tér 8., 1126 Budapest, Hungary
Tel: +36 1 501 9900 / Fax: +36 1 501 9901 / URL: http://www.vjt-partners.com

India

Akila Agrawal, Pooja Ramchandani & Devleena Bhattacharya
Amarchand & Mangaldas & Suresh A Shroff & Co.

This chapter provides an overview of the recent trends in the Indian labour market and employment litigation including significant case laws. It also summarises the latest changes on employment law and impending reforms to employment legislation and enforcement procedures.

General labour market trends and latest/likely trends in employment litigation

The recent trends in the Indian labour market are on the aspects of development of skilled labour, growing recognition of the women's workforce, growing need of quality employment and the need to rationalise and simplify the extant labour regulations commensurate with the expectations of both the employers and employees.

The demographic dividend of the Indian population makes India one of the youngest nations in the world. While the population bulge is advantageous from the viewpoint of availability of a large workforce, the increasing demand for skilled labour and declining demand for the unskilled ones, poses a challenge on gainful employment for all. Given the increasing demand for skilled labour and the larger Indian labour population being unskilled, the Government of India has taken steps towards enhancing employability by setting up skill development and training centres. Such initiatives have been undertaken with the objective to meet the demand for skilled labour and benefiting from the demographic dividend.

The Indian labour market has not been insulated from the global economic slow down of the recent past. The impact, albeit moderate, affected the profitability of industries which resulted in downsizing of the workforce across sectors. The Indian economy is now on the road to recovery and opportunities in the labour market have gained momentum. The Indian government has taken measures to counter job losses and plan employment generation in a futuristic approach. However the quality of employment continues to remain a concern. An employed status does not necessarily imply a reasonable standard of earning. To this end, the Ministry of Labour and Employment of the Government of India aims at promoting decent employment opportunities and conditions across the strata of employees.

The workforce in India is multifaceted. It comprises of full-time and part-time workers, seasonal workers, daily wagers, contract workers, workers with multiple jobs, low wage workers and women workers. Social and cultural factors restrict the women workers from participating in the labour market. In order to create a gender friendly labour market environment, there is an increasing realisation to broaden the definition of economic activities and to provide conducive working environment. The Indian Government has taken various initiatives to protect the interest of women workers and encourage their participation in the Indian labour market. These include amendment of several labour legislations to include provisions relating to establishment of day care facilities, guidelines on protection from sexual harassment in the workplace, setting up of centers for skill development and vocational training.

The labour market in India is divided into the organised sector and the unorganised sector. Such division is distinguished by significant differences in the conditions of work, remuneration and social security benefits available to the workers. Various kinds of social security schemes are already in operation for workers in the organised sector. These range from adequate paid leave, to health insurance and pension schemes. However, the unorganised sector workers lack the benefit of such schemes. Providing social security to workers is an important component of the social policy in India. Recognising the need to address this limitation, the Indian Government has taken several initiatives to safeguard the interest of the unorganised sector workers. Such initiatives include the introduction of insurance policies in the nature of life, accidental and health and social security for the unorganised sector workers.

In the new economic scenario, the need for changes in the archaic Indian labour laws has been emphasised. The views on the effect of the extant labour laws on the quality and quantity of employment in India are divergent from the employer and employee perspectives. From the employer's side, the contention is that the labour laws are restrictive to the extent of hiring and firing of employees and, as such, impose an impediment on the changing economic environment. The employers find such restrictions unreasonable as it forms a deterrent to new business modules. With the advancement of technology, it is more efficient to replace human capital with machine capital for certain industries. However, the current regulations discourage replacement of labour with capital intensive machines. On the other hand, from the labour force standpoint, leniency in the labour laws would lead to exploitation and deterioration in quality of employment.

Nonetheless there is a need to rationalise and simplify these laws, and at the same time to broaden the scope of laws to include all sections of the working population irrespective of the number of employees, wages, gender, and duration of employment. Further, the issue of enforcement of labour regulations is crucial for any meaningful reform of labour law. The complexity and multiplicity of the regulatory systems makes compliance of the regulations onerous. Simplification of procedural formalities by introduction of self certification or third party certification reduces the burden of inspection and enforcement. The need of the hour is to rationalise the application of labour laws by making it uniform so as to reduce the compliance cost amongst other things. A step towards this objective is the amendments with respect to filing of returns and maintenance of registers by small establishments. Establishments where less than 19 persons are employed are exempt from the cumbersome filings of periodic returns and maintenance of registers under various labour legislations. Such establishments are required to maintain a minimal number of registers and make only annual filings for the purpose of all labour legislations. There is a proposal to increase the threshold from 19 persons to 40 persons to cover a larger number of establishments. The Indian Government has also proposed changes to provide more flexibility in the hiring and firing of labour in order to increase productivity, efficiency and allow a more flexible adjustment process in the changing demand market.

During the past year, employment litigation in the private sector has been in the areas of dismissal, termination, retrenchment compensation claims, social security claims, claims on right to notice of retrenchment by daily wagers and right of workmen on transfer pursuant to sale of undertaking.

Given the changing economic environment and the constant need to restructure business segments to keep up with the same, sale of business undertakings is a recurring phenomenon. Under Indian labour regulations, employees are divided into two categories, i.e. workmen and non-workmen. Hence in the cases of transfer of workmen pursuant to transfer of business, the workmen category of employees are protected under the statute governing industrial disputes which provides for the payment of retrenchment compensation in case of redundancy arising out of transfer of a business undertaking. The non-workmen category however is governed by employment contracts and company policies, and unless such policies provide for severance compensation, the non-workmen are not entitled to any severance on redundancy, due to transfer of business. In this context, the most significant case has been in relation to the transfer of workmen on sale of a factory undertaking. The courts have held that it is a settled position of law that a workman cannot be transferred to another employer without his consent whether express or implied. The courts further held that termination of employment as a consequence of refusal to transfer requires payment of retrenchment compensation to workmen employees. The requirement of obtaining consent for the transfer of employment applies to both workmen and non-workmen.

Litigations in the area of social security during the last year have been in the nature of insurance claims in cases of accident and death, provident fund claims and gratuity claims. The courts have not granted the right to claim insurance where the accident/death did not occur in the course of employment. The director of a company has been held to be a defaulter and punished with imprisonment where there has been a default in remittance of provident fund contribution. Provident fund payments have been held to take precedence over all other payments in insolvency proceedings of a company under Indian law by the apex court. Withholding of gratuity payments have been held to be *ultra vires* and illegal. Part time workers have been held to be entitled to notice of retrenchment and retrenchment compensation. Casual labour have been granted maternity benefits on a par with regular workers. In the cases on dismissal, the courts have upheld the principles of natural justice.

The labour laws in India are predominantly in favour of workmen and it has been customary for the courts to rule in the favour of the workmen in most cases. While this trend continues, the courts do not rule out the tendency of frivolous claims by workmen against *bona fide* employers.

Key case law affecting employers' decision making over dismissal, redundancies dismissals etc.

On a review of the recent judicial decisions pronounced by the higher courts in India in the field of labour litigation, it is observed that a majority of cases pertain to dismissal/termination of employees on the grounds of misconduct, misrepresentation and abandonment of services/unauthorised leave of absence. Such litigation is mostly in relation to employment in the government/public sector as opposed to the private sector.

General trends in employment litigation suggest that before an employee is dismissed from service, a fair, impartial and proper enquiry is required to be conducted and the employee must be given a reasonable opportunity to be heard and prove his case. The Supreme Court of India has in the case of *Amar Chakravarty and Ors.* v. *Maruti Suzuki India Limited* ((2011) 2SCC (L&S) 607) observed that in the event an enquiry has not been conducted, then in such a case the onus falls on the employer to prove that it was not possible to conduct an enquiry and that the dismissal of the employee was justified. Therefore, it was upon the management to prove by adducing evidence that the employee was guilty of the charge and that the action taken by the management was proper. Similarly, in the case of *Diljit Singh Bedi* v. *Shiromani Gurdwara Prabandhak Committee, Sri Amritsar* ((2011) 2 SCC (L&S) 25) the apex court held than an employee can be dismissed from service for bad character only after the charges of misconduct are established in an enquiry conducted by an enquiry committee and such employee can be terminated only when such misconduct is established in an enquiry. Where an employee of a bank had misappropriated money by manipulating and making fictitious entries in a bank's ledgers and remained absent from enquiry for three consecutive dates, the Supreme Court of India held that dismissal of such an employee by its employer was not in violation of the principles of natural justice as the principles of natural justice cannot be stretched to a point where they would render the in-house proceedings unworkable and such in-house proceedings should be allowed to be conducted expeditiously and without any undue loss of time *(S.B.I. v. Hemant Kumar ((2011 (129) FLR 553))*. The High Court of Bombay in the case of *The General Manager (Telecom) v. Zarir* (2011 (4) LLN 556 (Bom.)) observed that the enquiry against the employee was not proper and was not in compliance with the principles of natural justice since no charge-sheet was issued against the employee and no opportunity of cross-examination was granted to him.

The removal of an employee from service for a gross act of indiscipline was justified where an employee had defied orders of transfer, as well as the order to report for duty and did not comply with the orders to appear before the medical board to prove his medical condition after proclaiming that he was medically fit continued to defy the transfer order *(S.P Arya v. Union of India (2012 (132) FLR 134))*.

However, in a case where the services of certain professors of a college were terminated on the ground of insubordination to authority and neglect of duty due to their non-attendance at a seminar organised by the college society and wearing of black ribbons, the court held that their silent or passive participation is not indiscipline or misconduct. The court further held that merely wearing black ribbons may amount to disagreement with the policy or the action of the management and cannot be construed as misconduct much less warranting such serious punishment as termination of service *(Central Hindu Military Education Society v. Dr. Vivek Vasantrao Raje and Anr. (2012 (132) FLR 44))*.

In the cases relating to dismissal/termination of service on the ground of 'misconduct', the courts in

India have held insubordination, theft, fraud, misappropriation of funds, tampering and manipulating official documents, making fictitious entries, dishonesty, wilful non-compliance with orders, intoxication, peaceful demonstration and failure to report at the place of transfer, within the scope, meaning and ambit of the term 'misconduct'.

Loss of confidence has been upheld as a valid ground for termination of employment by the Supreme Court of India in the case of *Divisional Controller, KSRTC* v. *M.G. Vittal Rao* (2012 (132) FLR 348). The apex court observed that once the employer has lost confidence in an employee and the *bona fide* loss of confidence is affirmed, the order of punishment must be considered to be immune from challenge, for the reason that discharging the office of trust and confidence requires absolute integrity and in case of loss of confidence reinstatement cannot be directed.

In another case, where a part-time employee's services were terminated because of his conviction in a criminal case and where such employee had been released on probation, the court held that since the employee was a part-time employee and not a regular employee, he had no legal right to be reinstated *(Puran Lal v. Executive Engineer, Tubewell Division 1ˢᵗ , Bareilly and others (2012 (132) FLR 310))*.

The Indian courts have also considered absence from work without authorised leave or abandoning of work as a valid ground for dismissal of an employee from service by the employer. Where an employee was terminated from service for absenting himself from duty for three days without leave, the Supreme Court held that the order of termination of service of the employee was grossly disproportionate to the charge and the same be substituted with a punishment of censure to be entered in the service record of such employee *(Ashok Kumar v. Union of India and Anr. ((2011) 1 SCC (L&S) 480))*.

In another case, an employee who was charged with overstaying his leave, suppressing information regarding his involvement in a criminal case and for being accused in a criminal case, though acquitted, was dismissed from service after conducting a departmental enquiry. The court held that since the employee was acquitted in the criminal case, he became eligible for reinstatement and the employer denying reinstatement on the ground that his acquittal in the criminal case was on the point of benefit of doubt and did not amount to full exoneration, was not acceptable *(Sarvjeet Singh v. Union of India (2011 (5) LLN 217 (DB) (Del.))*.

Cases where an employee misrepresents himself to gain employment by way of forging documents have been held by Indian courts to be a valid ground for dismissal from service. The Supreme Court, in the case of *Daya Shankar Yadav* v. *Union of India and Ors.* (2011 LAB. I.C. 1072), held that where the employee, knowingly made a false statement regarding his antecedents in the verification form which were relevant for employment in a uniformed service, his dismissal from service by the employer was justified for his not being truthful in giving material information. The Supreme Court in the case of *District Primary School Council, W.B.* v. *Mritunjoy Das and Ors.* (2011 LAB I.C. 3729) held that the dismissal from service of a primary school teacher appointed on the basis of certificate obtained by illegal means was proper. However, in another case, the court held that the dismissal of an employee, a crafts instructor in a school, on the grounds of tampering of marks of a foundation course certificate submitted by him was not proper since the foundation course certificate was neither required for initial appointment, nor for getting selection grade *(M. Palaniswamy v. Chief Educational Officer, Dindigul (2012 LAB.I.C.242))*. In yet another case, where an employee's service was terminated by the employer on account of suppression of material fact of pendency of criminal proceedings against him wherein he was required to give an undertaking disclosing pendency of any criminal proceedings against him at the time of his appointment was considered proper *(Anil Narsingrao Khule v. Assistant Commissioner, Food and Drugs Administration (2011LAB.I.C.2371))*.

Although courts in India favour workmen over the employer, such preference is found more in the law suits relating to social security claims on the ground that social security legislations are employee welfare legislations promulgated for the benefit of employees and hence the balance of convenience vests with the employees unless *mala fide* intent is proved. On termination and dismissal, the courts tend to interfere when the termination is grossly *mala fide* and where the principles of natural justice have not been followed. The courts will grant relief based on the facts and circumstances of each case. Courts have upheld termination and dismissal on valid and cogent grounds where the employer complies with the principles of natural justice.

Recent statutory or legislative changes

There have been significant amendments to the labour laws in India over the last two years. The amendments have been in the areas of social security laws, laws relating to industrial disputes and safety of workers.

The social security legislations were amended to enhance the applicability of the legislations to a wider number of workers by increasing the wage ceiling and in some instances including workers belonging to the disadvantaged group and unorganised sector. The social security legislations enhancing the wage ceiling are the Employees' State Insurance Act, 1948, Employees' Provident Funds and Miscellaneous Provisions Act, 1952, Payment of Bonus Act, 1966, Employee's Compensation Act, 1923, Payment of Wages Act, 1936, and the Minimum Wages Act, 1948. The Indian Government has also recently enhanced the cap in relation to the gratuity under the Payment of Gratuity Act, 1972 to bring the private sector employees on a par with the government employees. The Government has also introduced a new legislation namely the Unorganized Worker's Social Security Act, 2008 for providing social security benefits to the unorganised sector workers. These changes are commensurate with the Government's goal of improving the quality of employment in the country. Henceforth employers will need to make a higher contribution towards the coffer maintained for its employees.

One of the most significant developments in recent times has been in relation to provision of pension benefits to international workers under social security programmes by execution of specific social security agreements by the Indian Government with several countries. To date, social security agreements have been executed with Belgium (September, 2009), Germany (October, 2009), Denmark (May, 2011), Luxembourg (June, 2011), France (July, 2011), Switzerland (July, 2011), Korea (November, 2011), and The Netherlands (December, 2011). The salient features of the aforementioned social security agreements, *inter alia,* are waiver from remittance of social security contribution with respect to employees of home country deputed on short term assignment (usually up to 60 months), export of pension due under the legislation of one country to the other country, aggregation of the contribution periods earned while in service in both the countries. Apart from the above, social security agreements have already been signed with Czech Republic, Hungary and Norway, but not yet made effective. Negotiations are at various stages with Canada, Quebec, Sweden, Finland, Austria, Portugal, Japan, Australia and USA. Government level talks are on with other countries where sizable numbers of Indian workers are employed. The move aims at saving the employers from making double social security contributions for the same set of employees. Given the globalisation of the service industry, where more often than not, employees of foreign origin are deputed to India or *vice-versa,* this move is in the right direction. However in countries with which no such reciprocal agreements are in force, the provident/pension fund contributions with respect to the international workers need to be made by employers of both the countries.

Another aspect relating to employment of foreign national employees in India relates to the visa requirements by such foreign nationals for the purposes of employment in India. Employment visas are only granted to highly skilled and/or qualified professionals expressly excluding unskilled workers. If a foreign national desires to change employment to another company/organisation, he/she will have to leave the country and apply for a fresh employment visa at the Indian mission/post concerned. The Government currently is permitting on a prior approval basis change of employment between a registered holding company and its subsidiary and *vice-versa* or between subsidiaries of a registered holding company.

The Government of India has introduced the National Policy on Safety Health and Environment at Workplace under which a safe and healthy working environment is recognised as a fundamental human right. The concerned ministries/departments have been instructed to work out a detailed action plan *as per* the guidelines mentioned in the aforesaid policy. This approach reflects the increased emphasis on employee welfare and places an onus upon employers to comply with certain minimum norms to prevent hazards at the workplace so as to reduce injury and disease.

Hitherto, the legal framework for settlement of industrial disputes provided that aggrieved workers could raise disputes with respect to dismissal or termination to the relevant State Government. Pursuant to the recent amendment in the law relating to industrial disputes, employees falling under the workmen category can directly approach the labour courts or the industrial tribunals. The amendments also include setting up of grievance settlement machinery by establishments for resolution of disputes arising out of individual grievances.

In order to reduce paperwork and in keeping with the trends in technology, the Indian Government has permitted employers to submit returns and maintain records in electronic forms under the majority of the labour legislations.

The Indian labour laws recognise sales promotion employees in certain specified industries as a separate category for the purpose of wages, leave, social security, procedural formalities etc. and have promulgated the Sales Promotion Employees Act, 1976. The Act has been recently extended to 10 additional industries. This amendment will provide higher job security, pay parity and better working conditions. However, this is likely to raise operational cost for the employers as procedural formalities to be complied with under this legislation will be in addition to the other applicable legislations already applicable to such employers.

Likely or impending reforms to employment legislation and enforcement procedures

The impending reforms to employment laws in India are likely in the matters concerning minimum wages, contract labour, protection of women in workplace and procedural formalities.

There are talks regarding the possible amendment of the law relating to contract labour to bring contract workers on par with regular employees in terms of wages, social security and other benefits as enjoyed by permanent employees.

There is a proposal to amend the law relating to minimum wages and fixing a statutory national floor level minimum wage. Currently the minimum wages for unskilled workers is different in different states and the range varies from minimum of Rs 66.50 to a maximum of Rs 256.

The Protection of Women against Sexual Harassment in the Workplace Bill, 2007 has been introduced in the parliament. The bill provides for prevention and redressal of harassment of women in the workplace. This move is a step towards encouraging greater participation of women in the employment growth trajectory.

***

Acknowledgment

The authors would like to acknowledge the assistance of their colleague, Parika Ganeriwal, in the preparation of this chapter.

Akila Agrawal
Tel: +91 11 2692 0500 / Email: akila.agrawal@amarchand.com
Ms. Akila Agrawal joined Amarchand Mangaldas in April 2002 and is a Partner in the Corporate Transactions Team having the core practice area of Mergers, Acquisitions and Takeovers. Prior to joining the Firm she was a Senior Executive with Wipro Limited, Bangalore.
Ms. Agrawal has wide experience in matters pertaining to acquisitions, disposals, takeover offers, delisting offers, joint ventures, mergers and demergers, employment law matters, commercial contracts and general corporate advisory. She has worked closely with a number of multi-national companies, private equity firms and banks in relation to domestic and international acquisitions, takeovers and joint ventures.

Pooja Ramchandani
Tel: +91 11 2692 0500 / Email: pooja.ramchandani@amarchand.com
Ms. Pooja Ramchandani joined Amarchand Mangaldas in April 2004 and presently works with the Mergers and Acquisition Team. Prior to joining the firm, she has worked with Mulla & Mulla & Craigie Blunt & Caroe, Mumbai.
At the Firm, Ms. Ramchandani has been working very closely on matters pertaining to mergers and acquisitions, joint ventures, private equity, issues under foreign exchange laws and SEBI regulations, employment law related matters, commercial contracts and general corporate advisory.

Devleena Bhattacharya
Tel: +91 11 2692 0500 / Email: devleena.bhattacharya@amarchand.com
Ms. Devleena Bhattacharya joined Amarchand Mangaldas in 2008 and has worked with the Capital Markets and General Corporate teams. Prior to joining the firm, she was pursuing her LL.M. from Columbia University School of Law with focus on U.S. corporate and business laws. She has prior experience in civil litigation, intellectual property matters including trade mark registration and litigation, and general corporate work.

Amarchand & Mangaldas & Suresh A Shroff & Co.

216, Okhla Industrial Estate, Phase III, New Delhi 110020, India
Tel: +91 11 2692 0500 / Fax: +91 11 2692 4900

Ireland

Melanie Crowley
Mason Hayes & Curran

Current and Future Trends in Employment Litigation

Ireland is a small, open, export-dependent economy. In a period of exceptional economic growth, dubbed "The Celtic Tiger", Irish real GDP doubled in less than ten years. Ireland's success during the Tiger era was fuelled by the high proportion of the population being of working age, significantly increased female participation in the labour market, and high levels of educational attainment.

However, in the second half of 2007, the heady pace of Ireland's economic growth ground to a halt. A domestic property and banking crisis ensued and Ireland spiralled into full recession in 2008. The labour force which had been characterised by strong inward migration was deeply affected. Migration trends reversed, with high levels of outward migration by both non-national immigrants and Irish emigrants. Unemployment rose from a level of almost full employment to its current rate of 14.8%.

In contrast, Ireland had one of its most successful years for Foreign Direct Investment in 2011 and is currently ranked second in the world for FDI. Davy Stockbrokers anticipate that Irish exports will grow at a modest, but respectable rate of 2.8% in 2012. There are other "green shoots" as evidenced by the number of high tech companies headquartered in Ireland, including Google, Facebook, Twitter, Linkedin and Intel. Significant expansions by Apple, PayPal and Cisco show a similar confidence in Ireland.

Nonetheless, the current economic climate has impacted upon trends in employment litigation and will doubtlessly have a legacy in future employment litigation developments.

As employees and employers seek to consolidate their respective positions, Irish employment law has had to adapt to the needs of the changing labour environment.

This chapter will explore:
1. Current and future trends in Irish employment litigation.
2. Key Irish case law relating to dismissals and redundancies.
3. Recent legislative changes in Irish employment law.
4. Reforms to Irish employment legislation and enforcement procedures.

Redundancy & Unfair Dismissal

The recession has undoubtedly increased tension in the workplace which in turn has triggered a sharp rise in employment related claims.

The most recent statistics confirm that annual redundancies in 2011 totalled 49,762. This represented a 15.2% decrease compared to the 2010 figure of 58,731. While this is still lower than the 77,001 redundancies in 2009, employment continues to haemorrhage. The rise in redundancies has doubtlessly contributed to the waiting time for hearing dates at the Employment Appeals Tribunal and the Equality Tribunal in Dublin (over one year and up to three years respectively).

The amount of compensation being awarded by Ireland's statutory tribunals has also increased. Given the scarcity of secure alternative employment due to the current economic climate, a redundancy has a greater impact on an employee, and the value of claims has increased accordingly.

Retirement

The economic crisis has also made mandatory retirement ages a live issue in Irish employment law.

As pension values have fallen exponentially, older employees are seeking to consolidate their future positions by remaining in employment longer.

Angela Kerins, Chairperson of the Equality Authority commented in the Authority's Annual Report of 2010 that disability and gender cases, followed by age-related complaints were among the highest received by the Authority. She saw this as *"a consistent and clear indicator that in a shrinking labour market, these grounds can be impacted upon negatively and that the Employment Equality Acts are robust in combating anti-discrimination for minority groups in the Irish workplace"*.

Under Irish equality law it is lawful for an employer to set a mandatory retirement age. However, a number of decisions from the European Court of Justice[1] have thrown doubt on the validity of mandatory retirement ages unless they can be objectively justified. Moreover, the standard State pension age is due to rise from 65 to 66 from 1 January 2014, to 67 from 2021 and ultimately to 68 from 2028.

Against this backdrop, the Employment Equality (Amendment) (2) Bill 2012 was published very recently. In its current format, the Bill proposes to prohibit contractual compulsory retirement provisions subject to the worker meeting the necessary health requirements for the position, unless there is a legitimate aim and no alternative available to the employer. However, the Bill is in a very early stage and it is quite possible that a number of amendments will be made to it before it is passed, if ever.

Fitness & Probity

The new Fitness and Probity regime, which will be discussed in further detail below, raises many complex issues for employers regulated by the Central Bank of Ireland and is likely to place significant administrative and compliance burdens on such employers. It is widely anticipated that implementation of the new fitness and probity regime will generate a significant volume of legal challenges, particularly where a finding is made that an individual does not meet the required Standards. The Head of Financial Regulation of the Central Bank of Ireland, Matthew Elderfield, has stated that he does not *"underestimate the legal challenges that we might have in using our new powers, but we must be prepared to make difficult judgments on fitness and probity..."*.[2]

Defined Benefit Pensions

Within the area of pensions and pensions law, continued considerable pressure has been exerted on all stakeholders in relation to the funding of defined benefit (DB) pension schemes. The range of measures used to address the funding of these schemes (for instance closing Direct Benefit schemes to new entrants, freezing existing benefits and winding up of Direct Benefit schemes) is likely to become a fertile area for potential litigation.

Data Protection in the Employment Context

Data protection is an area which continues to generate considerable issues for employers in Ireland. An employee's right to request access to personal data held by an employer, and the Data Protection Commissioner's efforts to ensure those rights are upheld, has had a significant impact on how employers manage their employees. Employers are well-advised to be constantly on guard about what they write in notes, emails or what they record in circumstances, as they may be required to hand over those notes, emails or recordings to an employee who makes a subject access request.

In his 2011 Annual Report (published on 30 April 2012), the Data Protection Commissioner, Mr. Billy Hawkes, included a Case Study on covert CCTV monitoring in the workplace. He received a complaint from an employee at a gym who stated that he had been remotely monitored by his employer via a CCTV system was which was installed without prior staff notification of the reason for its installation or its purpose. In its response, the gym stated that the CCTV system was installed to monitor the security of the office, but that the CCTV also served a "secondary purpose", as the gym had received numerous complaints from its customers stating that the office was not open or that the office was open and unattended, causing further concern for the security of cash/credit cards.

Ultimately, the Office of the Data Protection Commissioner was satisfied that the gym had used the CCTV system to monitor staff and that such monitoring was in breach of the Data Protection Acts. In his report, the Commissioner stated that *"The improper use of CCTV to monitor employees is a matter of increasing concern to me. Even where employers have sought to legitimise the use of CCTV to monitor staff by referring to it in their company handbook, the position remains that transparency and proportionality are the key points to be considered by any data controller before using CCTV in this manner. We would only expect CCTV footage to be reviewed to examine the actions of individual staff members in exceptional circumstances of a serious nature where the employer could legitimately invoke the provisions of Section 2A (1) (d) of the Data Protection Acts 1998-2003 (the processing is necessary for the purposes of the legitimate interests pursued by the data controller ...except where the processing is unwarranted in any particular case by reason of prejudice to the fundamental rights and freedoms or legitimate interests of the data subject)".*

Key Case Law Relating to Dismissals and Redundancies

Employees in Ireland have common law, constitutional and statutory rights in relation to dismissals. Employees whose employment is terminated may allege that their dismissal is unlawful and claim the dismissal was either wrongful or unfair.

An action for wrongful dismissal is essentially an action for breach of contract and is brought before the civil courts at common law. The onus of proof in a wrongful dismissal action is on the employee.

As part of a wrongful dismissal action, in certain limited circumstances, an employee may make an application to the courts for an interlocutory injunction restraining his/her dismissal. The High Court has shown a willingness to grant this relief where it can be shown that damages would be an inadequate remedy, despite the traditional jurisprudence against the specific performance of employment contracts. In order to secure an injunction, the traditional three-tiered test applied by the courts involves answering the following questions: (i) is there a "serious" question to the tried; (ii) are damages an adequate remedy; and (iii) does the balance of convenience favour the granting of an injunction. Of late, the courts have gone a step further and held that in the context of a mandatory employment injunction, an employee must establish that he/she has a strong arguable case before a court will grant interlocutory relief.

A claim for unfair dismissal (as opposed to a claim for wrongful dismissal) is brought under the Unfair Dismissals Acts 1977–2007, and with the exception of constructive dismissal claims, the onus is placed on the employer to prove, on the balance of probability, that there were substantial grounds and justified reasons for the dismissal and that the dismissal was procedurally fair. Circumstances where a dismissal may be deemed to be fair include a dismissal based on the capability, competence or qualifications of the employee and the conduct of the employee.

Redundancy Case Law

Decisions of the Employment Appeals Tribunal have, over the past number of years, emphasised the need for employers to consult with employees in relation to seeking alternatives to redundancies, such as part-time working or pay cuts, and for generally seeing redundancy as a last resort before making a decision about making positions redundant.

The requirement for employers to show that a redundancy was transparent and reasonable was highlighted in *JVC Europe v. Panisi.*[3] In that case, Mr. Panisi worked as general manager of JVC in Ireland until he was dismissed by reason of redundancy in 2008. A short time later, JVC advertised for a new sales manager in Ireland.

In his judgment, Mr. Justice Charleton notes that the job description for the sales manager role *"very closely mirrors the job then being done by Jerome Panisi".* He went on to hold that *"the dismissal of Jerome Panisi from his job as general manager of JVC in Ireland was not a genuine redundancy",* but was rather *"a plan, implemented through an apparent redundancy, for the new post of sales manager Ireland to be filled by the existing national account manager".*

The court awarded Mr. Panisi €197,000 in damages as supplement to an *ex gratia* payment which Mr. Panisi had already received. The case emphasised that for an employer to defend a claim for unfair dismissal, adherence to stated principles and policies in effecting a redundancy is essential.

Refusal to Transfer Case Law

The vexed question of what happens when an employee refuses to transfer when the European Communities (Protection of Employees' Rights on Transfer of Undertakings) Regulations 2003 ("the TUPE Regulations") applies, was addressed in a seminal decision of the High Court in 2010.[4]

Until this decision was issued, there had been two schools of thought in Ireland. Some practitioners believed that in a situation where an employee refused to transfer, his/her employer was obliged to find alternative employment, failing which his/her position was redundant and an entitlement to redundancy pay ensued. Other practitioners were of the view that an employee who refuses to transfer in a situation where his/her terms and conditions of employment are guaranteed, was effectively resigning.

The case involved the outsourcing by Symantec Limited of its maintenance function to a third party provider. Messrs. Lyons and Leddy refused to transfer to the new provider and sought redundancy payments.

At first instance, the Employment Appeals Tribunal ("EAT") held that *"in a transfer of undertaking, the employee is not obliged to accept the new employer"*. The EAT reasoned that should an employee refuse to transfer, they would remain employed by the transferor. Where no alternative position could be offered by the transferor to the employee, the position becomes redundant and the employee would be entitled to any redundancy payment payable.

However, the decision of the EAT was overturned by the High Court which held that a refusal to transfer is, in fact, a resignation and as such, no entitlement to redundancy or other severance payment arises.

While the decision of the High Court has been appealed to the Supreme Court, the decision reflects the current position in Irish law.

Legal Representation Case Law

The issue of whether an employee is entitled to legal representation at disciplinary meetings can be something of a thorny issue. The Irish Code of Practice on Grievance and Disciplinary Procedures states that an employee may be represented by a trade union representative or a colleague at grievance or disciplinary meetings, but does not provide for legal representation.

The High Court, in its case law on wrongful dismissal, tended towards the view that legal representation could be required, in some cases at least. The court took the view that while there was no general entitlement to legal representation, there may be such an entitlement where the disciplinary process involves issues which may be best handled by a lawyer including issues of law, cases involving cross-examination of witnesses, or cases involving the admissibility of evidence, for example. However, in a relatively recent Supreme Court case[5], the Supreme Court found that the issue of whether legal representation is required essentially boils down to a consideration of whether legal representation is desirable in the interest of a fair hearing.

The court held that the following factors must be analysed in ascertaining whether or not legal representation is necessitated for a fair hearing to be held:
(a) the seriousness of the charge and of the potential penalty;
(b) whether any points of law are likely to arise;
(c) the capacity of a particular prisoner to present his own case;
(d) procedural difficulty;
(e) the need for reasonable speed in making the adjudication; and
(f) the need for fairness between the prisoner and prison officers.

Thus, while it remains the position that an employee has no general legal right to legal representation at an internal disciplinary meeting, the Supreme Court has, at least, now set out in some detail, the factors which it considers relevant in determining whether legal representation might be appropriate.

Recent Legislative Changes

Central Bank Introduces a new Fitness & Probity Regime

As part of its response to the financial and banking crisis, the Central Bank of Ireland ("the Central Bank"), in September 2011, published new Standards of Fitness and Probity ("the Standards") for persons who carry out certain functions (Pre-Approval Control Functions (PCF) and Control Functions (CF)) in all regulated financial service providers ("RFSPs"), except for Credit Unions. This includes banks, insurance undertakings, investment firms, fund administrators and custodians, amongst others.

The Central Bank has openly stated that it made a conscious decision to impose more demanding

Standards than those in place in other jurisdictions because Ireland has suffered more than most countries in the financial crisis. To comply with the Standards, a person performing a PCF or CF role is required to be: (i) competent and capable; (ii) honest, ethical, and must act with integrity; and (iii) financially sound.

Each RFSP is required to satisfy itself, on reasonable grounds, that each and every employee and director occupying a CF (including a PCF) complies with the Standards both on entry into the RFSP and on an on-going basis thereafter. In so doing, employers are required to carry out due diligence to ensure the Standards are met and to record how it reached its decisions in this regard. This will be a significant task and the importance of documenting the process cannot be overstated.

Protection of Employees (Temporary Agency Work) Bill 2011

This Bill, which will transpose the EU Directive on Temporary Agency Work (Directive 2008/104/EC), ensures equal treatment in relation to basic working and employment conditions between temporary agency workers and workers employed directly by the organisation where the agency worker is placed. The Bill also contains whistleblowing provisions.

When the Bill is enacted it will have retrospective effect to the transposition date of 5 December 2011.

Disclosure in the Public Interest Bill 2012

On 27 February 2012, the Minister for Public Expenditure and Reform, Brendan Howlin TD, published the General Scheme of the Protected Disclosures in the Public Interest Bill 2012 ("the Bill").

The proposed legislation seeks to protect public and private workers where they disclose information or "whistle-blow" relating to wrongdoing in their workplace. The Bill provides three avenues for the employee to make a protected disclosure: an internal disclosure outlet; a regulatory disclosure outlet; and an external disclosure.

The proposed legislation also envisages granting immunity against civil liability and criminal liability to the disclosing employee in certain circumstances.

The full Bill is expected to be published in the second quarter of this year.

Industrial Relations (Amendment) Bill 2011

Under Ireland's current industrial relations landscape, there is a mechanism whereby Joint Labour Committees ("JLC") can be established by the Labour Court to oversee the pay rates and working conditions of workers in the sector the particular JLC represents. The JLCs set minimum rates of pay and conditions for employees working in certain sectors over and above the minimum pay and conditions required under employment legislation. JLCs are empowered to petition the Labour Court for an Employment Regulation Order (ERO) establishing rates of pay and working conditions. Therefore, not only does this system allow for mandatory rates of pay above the national minimum wage, it also has the potential to require employers to pay employees mandatory overtime, sick pay, Sunday *premia* and to provide holidays over and above the statutory minimum. This means that two employers located beside each other could have very different staff overheads depending on whether or not they are covered by the JLC system.

In early 2011, the Quick Service Food Alliance ("the Alliance") successfully challenged the catering JLC. In *John Grace Fried Chicken Ltd v The Catering Joint Labour Committee*[6] Mr. Justice Feeney held that some provisions of the Industrial Relations Acts 1946 and 1990 (which empower the making of EROs) are unconstitutional. Furthermore, it was held that the JLC system unlawfully interfered with the constitutionally protected property rights of the plaintiffs. The court also concurred with the Alliance's proposition that only the Irish legislature could establish binding provisions in relation to employees' terms, conditions and payment. The net effect of this decision is that the issuing and enforcement of EROs is now unconstitutional.

The Industrial Relations (Amendment) Bill 2011 aims to reform the JLC/ERO system in light of the High Court decision. The Bill proposes to reduce the number of JLCs and to construct a JLC system that is cognisant of the challenging commercial climate faced by traders. In particular the Bill states that in making proposals to the Labour Court, the JLC must have regard to (a) the legitimate interests of the workers, (b) the legitimate interests of the employers, (c) the prevailing economic circumstances, (d) the prevailing employment circumstances of the workers, (e) the prevailing commercial circumstances of the employers, and (f) the terms of any National Agreement relating to pay and conditions.

Employment Equality (Amendment) Bill 2012

The 2012 Bill proposes to amend Section 37(1) of the Employment Equality Acts 1998 to 2004. The Bill proposes prohibitions on both positive and negative discrimination against employees on the basis of their civil status or sexual orientation.

Protection of Employees (Amendment) Bill 2012

This Bill proposes an extension to the notice periods required in the context of collective redundancies. It also proposes broadening the definition of insolvency under section 4 of the Protection of Employees (Employers' Insolvency) Act 1984 to confer additional protection on employees whose former employer has ceased trading, but has not been formally designated as being in liquidation.

Public Service Agreement 2012-2014 ("the Croke Park Agreement")

In 2010 the Public Service Agreement 2012-2014 ("the Croke Park Agreement") was introduced. The Agreement is a commitment by public servants and their managers to increase efficiencies across the public service. The Government made the following commitments to public servants on the delivery of such efficiencies:

- save for the pay reductions made in 2009 and 2010, pay rates will not be reduced any further;
- there will be no compulsory redundancies in return for cooperation from public servants in relation to redeployment;
- in relation to the pay reductions heralded in January 2010, for an extended period these reductions will now be disregarded for the purposes of calculating pensions; and
- an annual review of the Agreement will be carried out to re-evaluate the Government position on public service.

The first annual review by the Implementation Body, which was tasked to oversee the Agreement, was published on 15 June 2011, reviewing the Agreement's implementation for the twelve months to the end of March 2011. The Body reported that:

> "..estimated sustainable pay bill savings of approximately €289m had been achieved during the review period. This saving was driven primarily by a 5,349 reduction in staff numbers but also other factors such as reductions in overtime costs (down 5.2%) and pay bill savings accruing from changed work practices...".[7]

In addition, the Body reported that:

> "public service bodies are succeeding in generating significant non-pay cost savings through better use of resources".[8]

The Body concluded that:

> "the level of sustainable savings delivered during the first year of the Agreement has exceeded the targeted savings for the public service pay bill in 2011...".[9]

Redundancy Rebate

Budget 2012 heralded a significant change to the employer rebate on statutory redundancy payments. As of 1 January 2012, the rebate rate was reduced from 60% to 15%. The new rate applies to rebates on payments to employees made redundant on or after 1 January 2012.

Reforms to Employment Legislation and Enforcement Procedures

Reform of the Employment Law Fora

Irish employment law is governed by over 30 pieces of legislation and five redress or enforcement bodies: the Labour Relations Commission; the Employment Appeals Tribunal; the Equality Tribunal; the Labour Court; and NERA, the National Employment Rights Authority. The absence of a unified claim form for launching proceedings and the multitude of appeal venues has made the infrastructure of Irish employment law fora complicated and cumbersome.

The current economic crisis has highlighted the need for economies of scale within the public sector and the duplicity currently experienced in Irish employment law fora was targeted by the Minister for Jobs, Enterprise and Innovation, Mr. Richard Bruton in July 2011.

In his address to the High Level Conference on the Resolution of Individual Employment Rights Disputes at the School of Law, University College Dublin, Minister Bruton stated his intention to streamline the current system. His vision of reform centres on the amalgamation of the five aforementioned redress bodies to create an institutional structure with a single entry point for claims and a single accessible advice and information service.

In January 2012, the Minister realised these objectives. All first instance individual complaints and referrals to the Rights Commissioner Service, the Employment Appeals Tribunal, the National Employment Rights Authority, the Equality Tribunal and the Labour Court are now initiated though a single complaint form. Further, a single point of contact called the Workplace Relations Customer Services of the Department of Jobs, Enterprise & Innovation was established, which has responsibility for providing information in relation to employment and industrial relations matters, as well as having responsibility for the registration of all first instance complaints. The new body will also deal with enquiries regarding the progress of any complaints made.

Further reform targets were set out by the Minister in March 2012. Minister Bruton announced that he will publish and enact the Workplace Relations (Law Reform) Bill in the third quarter of 2012. The legislation will create a compact, two-tier Employment Rights and Industrial Relations structure made up of two statutorily independent bodies, i.e. a single body of first instance and a separate appeals body. The first instance body, to be named the Workplace Relations Commission, will amalgamate the Equality Tribunal, the National Employment Rights Authority, the Labour Relations Commission and the first instance functions of the Employment Appeals Tribunal. The appeals body will integrate the appellate functions of the Employment Appeals Tribunal into the Labour Court. When enacted, the Law Reform Bill looks set to revolutionise the landscape of institutional employment rights and industrial relations in Ireland.

* * *

Useful References

For information on the Rights Commissioner Service and the Labour Relations Commission: www.lrc.ie.
For information on the Employment Appeals Tribunal: www.eatribunal.ie.
For information on the Labour Court: www.labourcourt.ie.
For information on the Equality Tribunal: www.equalitytribunal.ie.
For information on the Health and Safety Authority: www.hsa.ie.
For information on the civil courts: www.courts.ie.
The Employment Status Group has issued a useful code of practice on the topic of employment status of workers: www.revenue.ie/leaflets/code-of-practice-on-employment-status.pdf.

Endnotes

1. For example, *Palacios de la Villa v Cortefiel Servicios SA* (C-411/05).
2. Address to the MacGill Summer School, 25 July 2011.
3. 2011 IEHC 279.
4. [2010] 1 I.L.R.M. 112 In the Matter of the Redundancy Payments Acts 1967-2007 and in the Matter of an Appeal Pursuant to s.39(14) of the Redundancy Payments Act 1967, Symantec Limited v Declan Leddy and Symantec Limited v Diarmuid Lyons.
5. *Burns & anor v The Governor of Castlerea Prison* [2009] IESC 33.
6. High Court Number 10663P.
7. Implementation Body, Public Service Agreement 2012-2014, First Progress Report, at ii.
8. Implementation Body, Public Service Agreement 2012-2014, First Progress Report, at ii.
9. Implementation Body, Public Service Agreement 2012-2014, First Progress Report, at ii.

Melanie Crowley
Tel: +353 1 614 5230 / Email: mcrowley@mhc.ie
Melanie Crowley is a Partner with Mason Hayes & Curran. Her practice areas are Employment Law and Industrial Relations Law. Melanie has been with the firm for 15 years. She is involved in all aspects of contentious and non-contentious employment law on both the employer and employee side. Melanie assists clients in drafting employment contracts, agreements and HR policies and procedures. She provides on-going support to HR managers in relation to internal reorganisations and rationalisations, terminations, and audits employment related documentation. In contentious areas, Melanie is regularly involved in employment related civil actions including injunctions, actions for breach of contract, employer liability claims and personal injury actions for stress and bullying. She regularly appears before the High and Circuit Courts and the Employment Appeals Tribunal.

Mason Hayes & Curran

South Bank House, Barrow Street, Dublin 4, Ireland
Tel: +353 1614 5000 / Fax: +353 1614 5001 / URL: http://www.mhc.ie

Italy

Mattia Persiani & Aldo Calza
hELP – the Employment Law Plant – Studio Legale Persiani

Recent statutory or legislative changes

<u>Introduction</u>

The last two years have seen a variety of reforms which have substantially altered the face of employment law in Italy and although less revolutionary than initially anticipated, they have had a marked effect on the rules governing employment litigation, as well as the rights and protections enjoyed by employees. And this is not all; there are more changes on the way, amongst which the much-debated and highly-publicised reform of Article 18 of the Workers' Statute, which is giving rise to increased tension amongst the trade unions ("Unions"). Briefly, this norm provides that workers of a business with more than 15 employees, who are found to have been unfairly dismissed, are entitled to the dual remedies of: i) reinstatement; and ii) damages equal to the amount of the remuneration they would have received between the date of dismissal and the date of reinstatement.

This additional round of reforms, which are under discussion by the legislature at the time of writing, will be examined in more detail later on in the chapter, but as a precursor, we first need to take a closer look at the most significant reforms in the labour market in the past couple of years.

<u>Abolition of obligatory attempt at mediation</u>

Without doubt the most important recent reforms can be found in Law no. 183 of 4 November 2010, the so-called "*Collegato Lavoro*" that came into force on 24 November 2010 and introduced important changes in the field of employment law. One of the most notable of these was with regard to employment claims and the abolition of the obligatory attempt to settle disputes by way of mediation as a necessary prerequisite to commencing court proceedings (which rule had originally been introduced in 1998 in the hope of reducing the number of court cases).

It is worthwhile at this juncture stopping to take a brief look at what the situation had been up until then. Basically the civil procedural code required that anyone seeking to raise court action under an employment contract, a contract of commercial agency or a consultancy contract, had first of all to make an attempt at settling the dispute by filing a request with the appropriate local government offices. The effect of this was to interrupt prescription and stop any deadline running until twenty days after such a request had run its course. This attempt at settlement had to be concluded within 60 days from the date of submitting the request, which in practice, rarely happened. The deadline having expired, even if the parties had not been granted a hearing before the mediation committee of the local employment office, meant that the process was deemed to been completed, allowing the interested party to go ahead with litigation.

The upshot of the 2010 reforms was that the attempt at settlement is no longer a mandatory pre-requisite to court proceedings and has become optional, except for disputes regarding "certified" contracts, for which it remained obligatory. Where the optional attempt at mediation is made, the request has to be sent not only to the local employment office or other relevant body, but also to the counterparty (by registered post with return receipt) and needs to contain a statement of the facts, and the grounds for the claim. In doing this, the legislature has transformed the request for an attempt at settlement into a kind of "preview" of the claim form, probably with a view to focusing the parties' attention on the risks they run in going to court, which it has to be said, they are often oblivious to until they find themselves before a judge. The reformed procedure provides that the "defendant" in the mediation process has to file defences with the mediation committee within 20 days of receiving the request, including exceptions in fact and law, as well as any counter claims. If the counterparty does not file anything, the attempt to settle the dispute is deemed to have run its course and both parties are free to revert to litigation. If, on the other hand, defences are filed, the committee is bound within 10 days to fix a date (no more than 30 days hence) in which the parties will appear together at the appropriate office in an attempt at settlement. If mediation is successful, even in part, a settlement agreement is signed by the parties and the committee, which agreement can be subsequently declared enforceable by a court. If the parties fail to reach an agreement, the committee is obliged to formulate a settlement proposal and put it to the parties. If the proposal is rejected, this is minuted together with a note of the terms of the proposal and the evaluation of same by the parties. Any future court decision regarding the dispute takes into account the proposal by the committee and the unjustified rejection of same by the parties. The documents and minutes from the mediation must be attached to the claim form.

<u>Deadlines for challenging dismissals</u>

In modifying the existing framework, the legislator was seen to intervene decisively as regards time limits. The 2010 reforms introduced a double time limit concerning the right to challenge a dismissal. The first challenge needs to be made within 60 days of receipt of the dismissal letter while the second deadline is much longer, i.e. 270 days from the date of the said challenge, in which to file a claim or submit a request to go to mediation or arbitration, on pain of rendering the challenge ineffective.

If mediation or arbitration fails, then a third time limit of 60 days is provided for, in which the claim has to be filed. The new regime effectively introduces an additional deadline of 270 days, in which to raise proceedings, in addition to the already existing 60-day period in which to challenge the dismissal. The backdrop to this is that article 18 of the Workers' Statute provides that if the employee is successful in his claim for unfair dismissal, then damages are calculated from the date of the dismissal to the date of reinstatement. Therefore, the purpose of the double time limit is to protect the interests of the employers: i) in knowing within a reasonable time whether or not the employee intends to bring court action for unfair dismissal; and ii) to avoid the employee taking advantage of the fact that after having challenged the dismissal within the 60-day period, he/she can then file proceedings at their leisure.

This new and more complex framework applies not only to all cases of unfair and unlawful dismissal, but also to cases where the far longer time limit of prescription previously applied, for example, dismissals where the category of the employment relationship itself was questioned as not being "subordinate" (e.g. project based contracts, contracts for services and casual labour, i.e. types of work that are considered "precarious"). Applying the new regime for open-ended employment contracts, to these types of contracts, has come in for a lot of criticism, given that it further penalises those workers who do not enjoy the rights and protections that "subordinate" employees have, forcing them to choose between challenging the dismissal within 60 days and thus running the risk of never working again for the employer in question, or not exercising their rights in the hope that the contract will be renewed.

The above provisions do not apply to illegal work, which in most cases does not require any written notice of termination.

The new framework also applies to fixed-term contracts, unless such a contract has already been renewed beyond the duration of 36 months allowed by law. The new rules apply both to fixed-term contracts currently running at the date the new provisions came into force, as well as contracts that have already expired - with the effective date deferred to the date of the law coming into force. This last provision has attracted much criticism as impacting on employment relationships that have actually expired and making them potentially annullable. This is not the only change in fixed-term contracts that has caused an uproar, as we shall see below.

The new regime of time limits also applies to: i) the termination of employment contracts in the ambit of a transfer of undertaking transaction, in which case the time limit starts to run from the date of transfer; ii) illegal employment agency contracts; and iii) all other cases in which the employee is accountable to an employer who is different from the employer named in the contract. With regard to iii), there is no mention of when the time limit starts to run. The most consistent interpretation would be from the date of termination of the employment with the fictitious employer.

Fixed-term contracts: employee protections

Article 32(5) of the *Collegato Lavoro* has also introduced more changes in the realm of fixed-term contracts, by substantially altering the system for damages where the fixed-term nature of the contract is found to be unlawful. It establishes that the court in converting the contract to an open-ended one, can award the worker damages ranging between a minimum of two and a half months and a maximum of 12 months of the last total salary. This new regime attracted much criticism as it applies to all court cases pending at the date of the law coming into force. It was even said by some to be unconstitutional, and in fact, in one case the Supreme Court judges awarded damages to a worker following conversion of the contract, based on the amount he would have been entitled to under the pre-reform rules. In fact, such damages were previously quantified on the basis of the total salary at the end of the fixed-term contract up until reinstatement, with the possibility of reducing the level of damages by the amount that the employee could have been reasonably expected to have earned in the intervening period had he made all reasonable efforts to find alternative employment.

The new regime has been upheld as lawful by the Constitutional Court in judgment no. 303 of 11 November 2011, in which it rejected the issues raised by the referring judges of the Supreme Court and the Employment Court of Trani respectively. The judge pointed out that the conversion of the employment contract into an open-ended one and the protections this entails was paramount, while the award of damages was secondary. The level of damages must take into account the fact that the employer, in any event, has to pay all the remuneration from the date of the judgment to the date of reinstatement, which sum cannot be reduced even if the worker has found alternative employment in the meantime, between the date of dismissal and the outcome of the court case.

Industrial relations reform

The Fiat case

This now historical case occurred between the end of 2010 and the beginning of 2011. It involved the Fiat factories in Naples (*Pomigliano d'Arco*) and Turin (*Mirafiori*) and reignited the debate on certain unresolved issues pertaining to Italian industrial relations law: on the one hand Union representation within companies; and on the other hand the effectiveness of collective bargaining agreements (CBA) and the relationship between them at different levels.

Fiat, the biggest manufacturing group in Italy, entered into "separate" agreements with the Unions at Pomigliano and Mirafiori, thus highlighting the urgent need to plug a gap in the rules that had come about by the non-implementation of article 39 of the Constitution. This had resulted in CBAs at national level (signed by the company and the Unions) not being applicable *erga omnes,* i.e. to everyone, but only to the parties – employers and employees – who are members of the Unions who had signed the agreements, or rather as case law is given to interpreting, the parties who have expressly made reference to the CBA in their employment contracts and who actually apply it *de facto*.

To briefly summarise what happened: in 2010 Fiat, under the management of Sergio Marchionne, announced a new project, *Fabbrica Italia,* which would bring an investment of around €20 million to the company and double car production, in return for the company guaranteeing continuity of production and maximum utilisation of machinery. There followed very difficult negotiations with the Unions, particularly with regard to production in Pomigliano, which ended with the Unions signing an agreement on 15 June 2010 ("Agreement"), regarding the organisation of work at the factory and the setting up of a new company: *Fabbrica Italia Pomigliano*. The said Agreement made provision for some amendments to the national CBA for metal workers as regards: increased flexibility in shifts; overtime; breaks; and above all absenteeism (in a factory which had a poor track record of absenteeism well above the national average). In addressing this last mentioned issue, the agreement made provisions for the company to alter the framework as set out in the national CBA, in the event that the level of absenteeism did not drop to the national average within a year of setting up the new company. In that case, there would be no cover for the first three days of sick leave (which according to the CBA, would normally have been borne by the company) in the cases of absence due to collective industrial action or absence from work to take part in demonstrations. While the terms of the agreement modify what is written in the CBA, they do not breach the Law, i.e. article 2110 of the Italian Civil Code which governs injury, sickness and maternity leave.

The Agreement was signed by some of the metalworkers' Unions at both national and local level, but not by FIOM-CGIL (the Union with the biggest number of members amongst the Fiat workers), who opposed any changes to the working conditions, as laid down in the CBA. The Agreement was subsequently put to a referendum of the factory workers on 22 June 2010 and approved by the majority (63%). The question then arose as to whether the new conditions contained in the agreement were applicable to the workers who were members of the Union that was not a party to the Agreement. Subsequently, on 7 September 2010, Fiat gave notice of withdrawal from the national CBA for metalworkers, which was due to expire on 31 December 2011, and therefore, as from 1 January 2012, the Fiat Group would no longer be bound by its terms.

A similar scenario was playing out in relation to the project to re-launch the factory at Mirafiori in Turin, with the setting up of a new Fiat Chrysler company, which company was not registered with the employers confederation (*Confindustria*) – that was a party to the CBA for metalworkers – and thus not bound by its terms. An agreement was signed between Fiat and the metalworker Unions ("Mirafiori Agreement") in Turin on 23 December 2010, again with the exception of FIOM-CGIL, and was approved by a majority of the workers at referendum. This meant that FIOM-CGIL could not appoint their own Union representatives within the new company and thus were not able to exercise their Union rights within the biggest manufacturing company in Italy.

On 29 December 2010, in the wake of the Mirafiori Agreement, a new contract was signed between Fiat and all the metalworkers Unions (except FIOM-CGIL) for the workers of *Fabbrica Italia Pomigliano* hired for the production of the new Panda. Just as happened with the Mirafiori Agreement, FIOM-CGIL's refusal to sign effectively excluded them from having a Union presence in the Pomigliano factory.

Trade Unions Agreement of 28 June 2011

The discussions between the Employers Confederation (*Confindustria*) and the Unions regarding the rules on Union representation and the possibility of applying CBAs at company level *erga omnes,* as an exception to the national CBAs, reached an initial consensus with the signing of a multi industry agreement on 28 June 2011 by the Employers Confederation and the three major Unions: CGIL; CISL; and UIL. This was the first time in Italian history that rules were introduced on Union democracy in industrial relations that possibly herald the end of Union conflict.

First of all, the agreement regulated the relationship between CBAs at different levels, on the one hand reaffirming the predominance of national CBAs, but at the same time reserving the right of the CBAs at company level to adapt the provisions of the former to bring them into line with reality. Secondly, the agreement established criteria in which to measure Union representation in any given category, i.e. a minimum threshold of representation of at least 5% of the total workers in the industry to which the national CBA applies.

But the most important aspect of the multi-industry agreement was the understanding reached between the parties as to the effectiveness of company level CBAs towards all workers in the company and all the Unions who signed the multi-industry agreement, even where they were not a party to the company CBA, on the condition that the agreement had been approved by the majority of the Unions represented in the company and was passed by a referendum of the workers. The agreement contains a so-called "Union ceasefire", i.e. an undertaking by the Unions not to call strikes for a fixed period following the signing of the CBA.

The "Collective Bargaining Agreements of Proximity"

Following closely on the heels of the multi-industry agreement of 28 June 2011, Parliament passed article 8 of Legislative Decree no. 138 of 13 August 2011 (modified and converted into article 1 of Law no. 148 of 14 September 2011), which revolutionised not only industrial relations in Italy but also the job market, by introducing a new type of CBA, namely the "contract of proximity", which is defined as a CBA at company or regional level signed by a majority of the most highly represented Unions at national or regional level, pursuant to the rules and multi-industry agreements in place, including that of 28 June 2011. In this way, the law allows certain agreements, which conform to certain conditions, to have the effect *erga omnes* as an exception to both the national CBAs and the Law. The purpose of article 8 was to create higher employment, improve the quality of employment contracts, adopt measures to allow employee participation in profit schemes, expose illegal work, increase competitiveness and salaries, help companies in financial difficulty and encourage new company start-ups. Article 8 (2) lists the matters that can be covered, under the umbrella of organisation of the workforce and production, which are:

- installation of audio visual systems and the introduction of new technology;
- workers' duties, job positions and qualifications;
- fixed-term contracts, contracts for reduced, modular or flexible working hours;
- the framework of joint liability in the tender process;
- use of employment agency workers;
- rules on working hours; and
- types of hiring and rules governing employment contracts, including project-based contracts, contracts for services (VAT registered), the transformation and change of employment contracts and the consequences of withdrawal from the employment contract, with the exception of discriminatory dismissals, dismissal of a worker on the occasion of her marriage, dismissal of a female worker from the period running from the beginning of her pregnancy up until the child is one year old, dismissal due to the worker requesting or using up parental leave, or taking leave due to illness of the child, taken either by the mother or father, and dismissal in the event of adoption or fostering.

As regards the abovementioned areas, the contracts of proximity can operate as exceptions to the rules of Law and the provisions of the national CBAs, even if the application of such rules is to the employees' detriment, as long as they comply with the employee protections contained in the Constitution as well as those found in EU regulations and international conventions. In short, the specific agreements pursuant to article 8 of Legislative Decree no. 138/2011 can waive employee protections which had, up until then, been untouchable. Companies, even those not registered with any confederation, can, with the agreement of the most representative Union(s) at national or regional level, introduce changes with a view to increasing employment, managing the reduction in business, stimulating new investment and setting up new companies.

Pension reform

Overview

The economic crisis that hit Italy in the summer of 2011 saw the fall of the Berlusconi government and the appointment of a new government of so-called "technocrats" made up predominantly of academics and backed by a broad cross section of the parliamentary majority. This government was specifically formed to bring about fundamental long-awaited reforms in a variety of areas, including pensions. On taking office, the government quickly carried out a radical reform of the pensions system with the ambitious goal of stabilising the balance sheet of the state pension fund; given the increased life expectancy of the population, the sustainability of long term pension costs and the impact on the gross national product.

The pension reform can be found in:
- Law no. 14 of 24 February 2012.
- Legislative Decree no. 216 of 29 December 2011.
- Law no. 214 of 22 December 2011.
- Legislative Decree no. 201 of 6 December 2011.

Article 24 of Legislative Decree no. 201/2011 introduced new pension rules, effective as from 1 January 2012, based on the following principles and criteria:
a) Equitable and uniform treatment of people of the same generation and people of different generations.
b) Flexibility in accessing pension schemes.
c) Incentives to extend people's working life span.

d)   Adapting the requirements for entry to the changes in life expectancy.

e)   Simplification, harmonisation and expenditure.

Before launching into the details, it is worth noting that the most important change brought about by the reform lies in the fact that, as from 1 January 2012, the contribution period accrued after 31 December 2011 will be calculated for all workers by reference to contributions actually paid, and not as happened in some cases, on the average of the remuneration received in the final years of a person's working life.

This change is particularly important for those workers who would otherwise have continued to benefit from a pension scheme which calculated their pension rights with reference to contribution periods and pensionable earnings. Now, however, they will draw a pension calculated *pro rata* using both systems, (i.e. the part attributable to seniority after 1 January 2012, will be calculated on the basis of contributions paid).

The reform also amends the prerequisites for entry to the state pension system and the benefits given in return. However to better understand these changes we need to take a look at the old system and compare it with the new one.

A) The Old System

The system pre-reform comprised three different types of pensions.

A1) **Retirement pension**. Entitlement to this pension was based on 40 years' paid up contributions. However, the legislator had also provided for a system that suspended payment, based on the so-called "sliding window" principle and deferred payments, which, as of 1 January 2011, was 12 months for employees and 18 months for self employed workers.

A2) **Old age pension**. The requirements in this case were a bit more complex. For workers already part of the system as at 31 December 1995, the requirement was 60 years of age for women and 65 years of age for men, together with 20 years' paid up contributions, whereas for those entering the system after 31 December 1995, the age requirement was the same but with paid up contributions of five years.

A3) **Early old age pension**. 1 July 2009 saw the introduction of the so-called "quota system" whereby the right to a pension matured on reaching a quota, which quota was calculated by combining the actual age of the worker plus at least 35 years' contributions, which for employees was: a) 59 years of age and having reached a quota of 95, in the period between 1 July 2009 and 31 December 2010; b) 60 years of age and having reached a quota of 96, in the period from 1 January 2011 to 31 December 2012; and c) 61 years of age and having reached a quota of 97, starting from 1 January 2013.

The quota system for self employed workers was different, namely: a) 60 years of age and having reached a quota of 96, in the period between 1 July 2009 and 31 December 2010; b) 61 and having reached a quota of 97, in the period from 1 January 2011 to 31 December 2012; and c) 62 years of age and having reached a quota of 98, starting from 1 January 2013.

B) The new System

The new system provides that, as from 1 January 2012, and with reference exclusively to the workers who have the necessary prerequisites to retire as at that date, the three types of pension referred to in paragraphs A1, A2 and A3 above shall be replaced by two types of pension, namely the old age pension and the early retirement pension.

B1) **Old age pension.** This is based on the following minimum requirements:

i)   62 years of age for female employees, which will increase to 63 years and six months as from 1 January 2014; to 65 years of age as from 1 January 2016; and reaching 66 years of age as from 1 January 2018;

ii)   63 years and six months for self employed females, which will increase to 64 years and six months as from 1 January 2014; to 65 years of age and six months as from 1 January 2016; and reaching 66 years of age as from 1 January 2018; and/or

iii) 66 years of age for male workers – both employees and self employed.

Thus the equal treatment of men and women, as required by the European Union, is reached by 2018.

It should be noted that the requirements are "moveable" in that they are subject to adjustment from time-to-time to take into account increased life expectancy.

The underlying principle in all these cases is the right to an old age pension only on reaching a minimum of 20 years' contributions.

B2) **Early retirement pension.** This replaces the retirement pension, which up until now was based on 40 years' contributions (see A1 above) and is based exclusively on the following prerequisites, both for employees and self employed workers:

i)   42 years and one month of contributions for men; and

ii)   41 years and one month for women.

These prerequisites are gradually increased by another month for 2013 and yet another for 2014, as well as being subject to adjustment from time-to-time to take into account increased life expectancy.

In all cases, choosing to retire early triggers a penalising mechanism which provides for a reduction in the part of the pension attributable to the contribution period prior to 1 January 2012, of 1% for each year of early retirement before 62 years of age. This reduction is increased to 2% for each year of early retirement prior to 60 years of age. This reduction does not apply, however, to those who meet the requirements of the contribution period by 31 December 2017, if during the said period the person actually worked (this includes periods of maternity leave, military service, injury, sickness and redundancy).

The reform has abolished the mechanism of quotas and the "sliding window" of deferred payments. Now, both old age pensions and early retirement pensions are effective as of the first day of the month immediately following maturity, on the condition that the person stops working for third parties as from the effective date of the pension. However, this condition does not apply to self employed people.

The reforms introduce greater flexibility in deciding when to retire. Apart from the public sector, which has specific limits, workers in the private sector can decide themselves when to retire, between 62 and 70 years of age, with the resulting application of the relative coefficients to convert the capital accumulated, using the method of calculating contributions up until 70 years of age.

The pension reforms above described do not apply to workers who are entitled to retire under the old rules by 31 December 2011. There is also an important exception with regard to female employees with 35 years or more contributions and aged 57 or above (58 or above for self employed female workers). By way of experiment, up until 31 December 2015, they can retire on an amount calculated under the less favourable rules as long as they do so by 31 December 2015.

Another exception is available to male workers in the private sector. If by 31 December 2012 they have accrued 35 years of contributions and meet the previous criteria for quotas as regards the early old age pension, they can retire on turning 64. The same applies to female workers who, as at 31 December 2012, have matured at least 20 years of contributions and are at least 60 years of age; they can retire early on turning 64.

The reform has attracted bitter criticism in trade union quarters as well as in a large section of public opinion, given that the change over to the new framework was not a gradual one and badly affected the expectations of those workers who were close to retirement under the old rules. Basically, this section of the population found themselves in the unpleasant position of being just about to cross over the finishing line to find that it had been moved forward.

This issue was only partially resolved by the setting aside of funds to cover the needs of a broad range of workers who had accepted redundancy on the basis of an agreement with the Unions whereby they were guaranteed an income up until they qualified for a pension.

While it is true that any radical pension reform, as is the case in Italy, has to be pushed through to ensure the sustainability of the whole social security system, undoubtedly there is one generation in particular that is sacrificed for the greater good.

There is no doubt that Italian society has paid a high price for these reforms, but some consolation can be taken from the fact that the newly reformed Italian state pension system is considered by the international institutions and the European Community as one of the best in the world.

Impending reforms to employment legislation

There is a draft Bill called "*Disposizioni in materia di riforma del mercato del lavoro in una prospettiva di crescita*" passing through the Italian Parliament at the moment aimed at: i) encouraging more flexibility and mobility in the workforce; ii) reducing the rate of unemployment; and iii) making businesses more agile and competitive in the marketplace. The Bill was endorsed by the Cabinet on 23 March 2012 and handed over to the Chamber of Deputies in order to complete the legislative process, which is still ongoing. The most pertinent reforms under consideration can be divided into 3 categories.

1) Simplification of employment contracts

The Bill affects first and foremost the so-called "project-based contract" or rather the type of long-term consultancy contract that has become widespread in Italy over the last 20 years, but which in practice often conceals an ordinary employment relationship and is simply a way of avoiding the high costs associated with standard employees.

The Bill specifies that should the project consist merely of taking instructions and carrying out repetitive tasks, then it is highly likely that the relationship would be relabelled as a standard employee/employer one. Likewise, the use of project workers to carry out tasks normally performed by the employees of the company is expressly prohibited.

The Bill introduces an assumption (unless proved otherwise) that a person, who is VAT registered and performs services, is in fact self-employed. However, in the circumstances where at least 2 out of 3 conditions occur, namely: a) the provision of services lasts more than 6 months; b) the remuneration paid represents more than 75% of the worker's total annual earnings; and/or c) the worker has a workspace in the company's offices, then such a relationship can be relabelled as an ordinary employment one due to the lack of any project.

The mere enrolment of the worker in a professional society, institute or association (e.g. lawyers, architects, etc.) is not sufficient to avoid application of the rules regarding project-based contracts and could result in the judge converting the status of such workers into that of ordinary employees.

The pending reforms will also have an impact on fixed-term contracts, with a view to reducing the so-called "precarious" workers and to do away with one of the prime sources of litigation, i.e. the duty to give reasons when entering into a fixed-term contract. Thanks to a long-awaited reform, companies will be allowed to enter into an initial fixed-term contract, maximum duration 6 months, without specifying the reasons for doing so. In addition, the Bill would levy on businesses that hire on a fixed-term basis, an increase of 1.4% on unemployment insurance premiums, partly recoverable only where the contract is converted into an open-ended one.

The Bill stresses, however, that the apprenticeship contract remains the most favoured channel of entry into the workplace, as regulated by Legislative Decree no. 167/2011, which in the current market is the type of contract which offers the most financial and regulatory incentives.

2) Dismissals and Section 18 of the Workers Statute

The reform of the employment market also affects the regime of individual dismissals, with a view to guaranteeing businesses certainty and predictability as regards the cost of dismissal and in order to encourage international investment.

It is worth noting that the reform only applies to companies with more than 15 employees locally or more than 60 nationwide. It does not affect businesses with 15 or fewer employees, for whom unlawful dismissal is punished by payment of damages in an amount of between two and a half and six months' salary (in exceptional circumstances increased to 10 and 14 months respectively).

As far as discriminatory or retaliatory dismissals are concerned, nothing changes and there remains in place the strictest of protections, pursuant to article 18 of Law no 300/1970, i.e. the right to be reinstated as well as a payment of damages which comprises the salary from the date of dismissal to the date of reinstatement.

On the other hand, it is all change where the court finds that there is no just cause or subjective reasons for dismissal. If the facts and circumstances on which the dismissal was based, are discovered to be untrue or not pertaining to the employee, or rather do not constitute a lawful reason for dismissal either in terms of the collective bargaining agreements or disciplinary codes, then the judge will order reinstatement and payment of a maximum amount in damages equal to one year's salary.

In all other cases where the grounds for dismissal are other than just cause or subjective reasons, there is no remedy of reinstatement and the judge can only order the company to pay damages in the amount of between 12 and 24 months' salary.

The reform also has a bearing on redundancies made for economic or objective reasons in that it introduces a duty to carry out a particular mediation procedure, initiated by the employer by sending a letter to the regional employment office and a copy to the employee. The letter generates a joint consultation process in the hope of reaching an agreement, which, if reached, allows the employees made redundant to be covered by the state unemployment insurance fund (ASPI) and assisted by an outplacement agency. On the other hand, in the absence of an agreement, the employer can go ahead with the redundancies. Where a dismissal in such cases is held by the court as null and void due to breach of the procedure or lack of the required reasons, the dismissed employee cannot expect to be reinstated but only to receive compensation of between 6 and 12 months' salary.

3) New social measures to lessen the impact of the global economic down turn

Finally, it is worth mentioning in passing that the Bill envisages a substantial overhaul of the system of unemployment benefits. However, given that the more important aspects of this suggested reform would not come into force until 2016, it is decidedly premature to enter into any in-depth analysis at the moment. Suffice to say that a lot of the current subsidies will be gradually replaced by a single scheme called ASPI, providing higher payments to a broader range of employees on a more egalitarian basis.

All in all it has to be said that what started off as a proposal to simplify the rules surrounding dismissals, with a view to encouraging foreign investment, looks likely to be stifled by a law, which is yet again far too complex.

Note

The information contained in this chapter is up-to-date as of May 28, 2012.

Acknowledgment

The authors would like to acknowledge the assistance of their colleague Sharon Reilly, Partner, in the preparation of this chapter. Tel: +39 02 3673 6350 / email: sharonreilly@help-pers.com.

Mattia Persiani
Tel: +39 06 8069 1974 / Email: mattiapersiani@help-pers.com
Professor Mattia Persiani is the Chairman of the firm. As a highly-esteemed and time-honoured professor, he is a renowned authority in the field of Employment, Labour Relations and Social Security Law. As a lawyer, clients recognise his uncommon ability and expertise in the field.

Emeritus Professor of Labour Law at the University of Rome "La Sapienza", he has taught at the University of Pescara, Sassari and Venice; he is Chairman of the Scientific Committee of AGI (Italian Employment Lawyers Association). Mattia Persiani was also Director of the graduate school of Labour law and Social Security at the University of Rome "La Sapienza".

Founder and editor of the magazine "Argomenti di diritto del lavoro", Mattia Persiani has published an impressive number of books and articles.

Professor Persiani is ranked as a Senior Statesman in Chambers Europe 2012.

Aldo Calza
Tel: +39 02 3673 6350 / Email: aldocalza@help-pers.com
Aldo Calza is the Managing Partner of the firm. Aldo has always practised exclusively employment, industrial relations, pensions and social security law and has acquired an impressive breadth and depth of expertise over the years working for national and international clients in a variety of industry sectors. He is an experienced and passionate litigator and is particularly adept at handling the labour relations aspects of large restructuring projects. Clients appreciate his expertise and precision. Aldo is ranked Band 2 in Chambers Europe 2012.

He speaks Italian, English and French.

hELP – the Employment Law Plant – Studio Legale Persiani

Via Pietrasanta, 12, 20141, Milan, Italy
Tel: +39 02 3673 6350 / Fax: +39 02 3673 6379 / URL: http://www.help-pers.com

Japan

Masao Torikai & Koichi Nakatani
Momo-o, Matsuo & Namba

Japan continues to recover from the effects of the Great East Japan Earthquake. Last year many companies faced government-imposed electricity shortages and adjusted headcount as a result. Although this year many companies have not faced government-imposed electricity shortages so far, many still need to adjust headcount due to many reasons such as appreciation of the yen. Therefore, how to adjust the workforce (i.e., termination, non-renewal of fixed-term contracts, etc.), remains one of the most pressing employment law issues here.

Theory regarding termination

General theory

One of the most important features of Japanese Labour Law is that the discharge of regular employees is very difficult.

In most companies, employment contracts between regular employees and the employer do not have a fixed term. Although basically an employer has the right to terminate an employment contract, according to Article 16 of the Labour Contract Act ("LCA"), the discharge of an employee shall be an abuse of right, and therefore null and void, if such discharge lacks objectively reasonable grounds and is not deemed proper in general societal terms. The application of an employer's right to discharge its employees is severely restricted by the LCA.

There is extensive case law regarding the restriction of an employer's right to discharge its employees. Generally speaking, unless a discharge satisfies the conditions for one of the following three types of discharge (i.e., Usual Discharge, Discharge as a Disciplinary Measure and Discharge Based on Bad Financial Condition), it is likely that the courts will find that such discharge is an abuse of employer's right of discharge and consequently shall be null and void. If a discharge is null and void, an employer shall reinstate an employee who is the subject of discharge to his or her original position, and shall pay his or her salary from the time of discharge to return plus interest.

Usual Discharge (Tsujo Kaiko)

Usual Discharge is one option an employer has in the case of an employee's inability to work due to injury or disease unrelated to work, or inefficient performance.

Since many companies have adopted performance-based wage systems, how to deal with an employee's inefficient performance has become an important issue in Japan. Please note that there is no clear theory with regard to discharge based on a target employee's inefficient performance. In other words, the court decides whether the discharge is null and void on a case-by-case basis.

Generally speaking, Japanese courts are pro-employee and tend to request clear and persuasive evidence of the target employee's inefficient performance. Some judges have requested evidence showing that there is no possibility that the employee's performance will improve. Also, in many cases, courts have held that the discharge is null and void if the employer could have taken other measures to avoid discharge such as demotion, transfer or salary cut. Please note that even if the target employee's salary is rather high and the target employee's performance did not meet the employer's expectations, the court does not always hold that the discharge is valid. In other words, the court might find that the fact that the employee did not meet the employer's expectations does not mean that the employee's performance was inefficient.

Therefore, generally speaking, in order to prove that employer took possible measures to avoid discharge, it is necessary for an employer to collect objective evidence to prove inefficient performance such as warning letters to the employee or the subject employee's insufficient sales results.

There is one exception to the above. If an employee is hired for a specific position (such as sales department head) and the employer can prove that such employee is incompetent for the position, sometimes the court holds that the discharge is valid even if the employer did not take measures to avoid discharge.

Discharge as Disciplinary Measure *(Chokai Kaiko)*

The conduct of the subject employee should fall into one of the causes for disciplinary measures prescribed in the company's Work Rules *(Shugyo-kisoku)* and discharge should be prescribed as one of the disciplinary measures in said Work Rules. However, disciplinary discharge will be rendered invalid unless the conduct of the subject employee in question is serious enough to justify such an extreme measure as discharge.

Discharge Based on Bad Financial Condition *(Seiri Kaiko)*

Even where conditions (i) or (ii) above are not satisfied, an employer can discharge its employees if it becomes necessary to do so as a result of the employer's bad financial condition. According to case law, discharge of employees based upon an employer's bad financial condition may be allowed only when all of the following four (4) conditions are satisfied: (a) existence of necessity to cut the number of employees (for example, the employer is facing severe financial problems); (b) existence of necessity to choose discharge; (c) reasonable criteria for selecting employees to be discharged; and (d) reasonable procedures for discharge. In the above four factors, the most important factor is (b). Generally speaking, in order for the employer to satisfy (b) above, it shall implement various measures such as a voluntary resignation programme, salary cuts, transfer and no new hiring. However, to what extent an employer takes various measures to satisfy (b) above would vary depending on the financial difficulty the employee is facing ((a) above). In other words, if the employer's overall financial situation has not deteriorated greatly, the court is likely to request that the employer take almost all possible measures to avoid discharge. On the other hand, if the employer is facing a very severe financial crisis, it is possible that the court might not request that the employer take all measures to satisfy (b) above.

Recent important case

In the *JAL* case, the Tokyo District Court issued its opinion on March 29, 2012 and on March 30, 2012 regarding whether the termination of the employment contracts of 148 employees of Japan Airlines Co., Ltd. ("JAL") was valid. JAL applied for corporate reorganisation procedure (the Japanese version of Chapter 11 of the U.S. Code) on January 19, 2010. After that, JAL took various measures to cut costs such as salary cuts, solicitation of voluntary resignation, and the cessation of the hiring of fixed-term employees, etc. JAL made a reorganisation plan which was approved by the creditors' meeting on November 19, 2010. JAL terminated 148 employees based on the reorganisation plan on December 31, 2010. The court held that the termination was valid, stating that it was necessary to terminate employees based on the reorganisation plan. This is the leading case where the validity of the termination of employees during a corporate reorganisation procedure was contested and the theory of this case could serve as a useful reference for similar cases moving forward.

As stated above, it is not easy to terminate regular employees in Japan. Therefore, many companies use fixed-term employees or dispatched employees in order to easily adjust headcount.

Fixed-term employees

General

In Japan, no legal restrictions exist on concluding or renewing a fixed-term contract. The only legal restrictions on fixed-term contracts are that the term may not exceed three (or five) years in order to avoid unduly long periods of obligatory servitude of an employee to an employer, and that it is extremely difficult for an employer to terminate a fixed-term contract during the term. Since there is no restriction on the renewal of fixed-term contracts, it is legally possible to renew a short-term contract, such as a three-month contract, as many times as desired. Theoretically, a fixed-term employment contract terminates automatically upon expiration of the time period specified therein. Since the termination upon expiration of the term is not a discharge, Article 16 (Discharge) of the LCA does not apply directly. Accordingly, when reduction of workforce is required, many Japanese employers have refused to renew fixed-term contracts due to the fact that the discharge of regular employees is severely restricted.

Fixed-term contracts have functioned as shock absorbers to protect regular employees against fluctuating economic circumstances. However, the case law restricts non-renewal of fixed-term contracts in order to protect fixed-term employees. In the *Toshiba-Yanagi-cho* case, the Supreme Court held on July 22, 1974 that fixed-term contracts were *de facto* indistinguishable from non-fixed-term contracts, the refusal to renew is tantamount to a discharge and that, accordingly, the legal theory concerning discharge applies by analogy. In the case, employees with two-month employment contracts were denied renewal after having such contracts renewed, depending on the case, from five to 23 times. The renewal of the contracts had been informal and some of them were not renewed precisely at the expiration of the term. There was also a desire for continued employment on the part of the employees and the employer.

After the *Toshiba-Yanagi-cho* case, in order to avoid the characterisation that the renewal of fixed-term contracts is "indistinguishable from non-fixed-term contracts", Japanese employers executed more precise contracts and more strictly administered fixed-term contract renewals. In the *Hitachi-Medico* case, the Supreme Court held on December 4, 1986 that even where there is a fixed-term contract, the theory concerning discharge shall apply by analogy when there was an expectation of continued employment and the contract was renewed five times.

After the *Hitachi-Medico* case, a lower court held further that even if a fixed-term contract was not renewed repeatedly, a justifiable reason is necessary for not renewing it if there was a reasonable expectation of continued employment. Nevertheless, the protection of fixed-term employees is still inferior to that of regular employees with no-fixed-term contracts. The Supreme Court has held that when it is necessary to adjust workforce, it is reasonable to terminate fixed-term employees prior to regular employees and management need not solicit voluntary retirement from regular employees before terminating the employment of fixed-term employees. Therefore, based on the case law, there is a big difference between fixed-term employees and non-fixed-term employees in the extent of protection of employment security.

The Bill for Amendment of the LCA

This year, the Ministry of Health, Labour and Welfare ("MHLW") proposed to amend the LCA. The important contents of the bill are as follows:

(i)   In principle, if a fixed-term contract is renewed and the total of the contract period exceeds five years (without a cooling-off period of less than six months), such fixed-term contract will be transformed into a non-fixed term contract if the employee requests to do so.

(ii) If there are differences between conditions of fixed-term contracts and non-fixed term contracts, the differences should not be unreasonable.

The most significant amendment for companies is (i) above. If a fixed-term contract will be transformed into a non-fixed term contract, it will become difficult for the employer to easily adjust head counts, since it is difficult to terminate non-fixed term contracts under Japanese law. If such a bill would be passed by the Congress, many companies would terminate fixed-term employees before the total length of the term exceeds five (5) years.

Dispatch of Workers

General

Recently many companies have been utilising dispatch (or temporary) workers. In the case of dispatched workers, an employment agreement exists only between the worker's dispatching agency and the dispatched worker. There is no employment agreement between a client company (recipient of the dispatched worker) and the dispatched worker even though the client company instructs and supervises the worker. A client company enters into an agreement regarding the dispatch of workers with a dispatching agency. In addition, a client company is liable regarding the relationship of employment, including working hours, rest periods, and work concerning dangerous and harmful materials. Typically, if a client company suffers financial problems, a client company terminates the agreement with a dispatching agency, stops acceptance of dispatched workers and adjusts its workforce. According to the MHLW's guideline, if a client company wishes to stop acceptance of dispatched workers, it owes certain obligations to the dispatching agency such as to help it find a new client company, to inform it 30 days in advance, and to compensate it for damages. However, this guideline is not enforceable. Currently the employment security of dispatched workers is a very important issue in Japan due to the fact that these types of workers constitute a significant portion of the workforce.

Amendment of the Workers Dispatching Law ("WDL")

The WDL was amended in March this year. Several important points are included in the amendment. For example, if a client company accepts dispatched workers knowing that such dispatch of workers violates the WDL, such client company is deemed to have offered employment to dispatched workers. Details of the amendment would be decided by the MHLW's ministerial order which would be enacted by this fall. Apparently, the amendment will take effect by April 2013.

Illegal Disguised Contract Labour (Giso Ukeoi)

Illegal Disguised Contract Labour *(Giso Ukeoi)* means an illegal contract relationship to avoid undertaking obligations under the WDL. Let us assume that company A entered into a service contract with company B (as service provider) and company B uses its contract worker X to perform its obligation for company A. In principle, since the relationship between company A and company B is based on a service contract, contract worker X is not a dispatch worker and company A is not liable for various obligations related to contract worker X. However, according to the public notice by the MHLW, if a company instructs and supervises workers of another company, such company needs to have a dispatching agreement, not a service contract agreement, and such company shall be liable for several obligations under the WDL. Therefore, if company A instructs and supervises contract worker X, company A should have entered into a dispatching agreement with company B.

In the case of Illegal Disguised Contract Labour, penalties will be imposed on both companies (i.e., employer of contract workers, "company B" in the above case; and a company which accepts contract workers, "company A" in the above case) pursuant to the Industrial Safety and Health Law. In addition, contract worker X may claim that a tacit employment agreement has been established between contract worker X and company A due to Illegal Disguised Contract Labour.

In the *Matsushita Plasma Display* case, the Osaka High Court on April 25, 2008 acknowledged the existence of a tacit employment agreement between contract workers and a company which accepts contract workers ("company A" in the above case) in case of Illegal Disguised Contract Labour. The Osaka High Court stated that the employment agreement between contract worker X and company B, and service contract agreement between company A and company B, were null and void since the relationship among contract worker X, company A and company B constituted Illegal Disguised Contract Labour and was in contravention of the WDL. The Osaka High Court expressed a new opinion that the relationship which violates the WDL was null and void and created an employment relationship with a company actually used the contract worker.

However, the Supreme Court on December 18, 2009 reversed the judgment of the Osaka High Court and denied the existence of a tacit employment agreement between contract worker X and company A. The Supreme Court stated that the employment agreement between contract worker X and company B was not null and void without exceptional circumstances even if the relationship among contract worker X, company A and company B violated the WDL and was Illegal Disguised Contract Labour. In addition, the Supreme Court denied the establishment of a tacit employment agreement since company A did not get involved in company B's hiring process of contract worker X, company A did not actually decide the amount of contract X's salary, and company B had the authority to decide contract worker X's working conditions to some extent. Based on the Supreme Court's decision, the risk of the establishment of a tacit employment agreement is small if companies A and B satisfy the following conditions: company A's non-involvement in the hiring process and decision of the salary of contract worker X and company B's authority regarding contract worker X's working conditions to some extent such as authority to deploy worker X.

Elderly Workers

General

Many companies in Japan used to have a rule of mandatory retirement at the age of 60. However, the typical Japanese worker has been rapidly "graying" and pension payments have accordingly/also/ thus increased drastically. Therefore, in 1985, the Japanese government raised the minimum pension-qualified age from 60 to 65 and revised the Law concerning Stabilization of Employment of Older Persons (the "LSEOP"). According to the revised LSEOP, a company which had decided a retirement age of 60, shall need to implement the following measures: (i) raise the mandatory retirement age to 65*; (ii) introduce a continued employment programme (a programme whereby a company will continue to employ older workers currently in the company's employment beyond the mandatory retirement age if such workers wish to continue in employment) until 65*; or (iii) abolish the system of mandatory retirement age. (*In order to avoid rapid change, as a transitional measure, the new retirement age has been decided to be gradually changed. The current new retirement age is 64 and from April 1, 2013, the retirement age will be 65.)

Continued Employment Programme

Most companies choose (ii) above (i.e., continued employment programme). If a company chooses a continued employment programme, such company could set a standard to select eligible employees by a labour-management agreement. Such labour-management agreement could be made between employer and a representative of employees. According to the instruction by the MHLW, if a company wishes to set a standard for selection of employees for its continued employment programme, the standards need to be reasonable and clear enough in order for employees to be able to know whether they satisfy the standards.

There have been several recent cases involving continued employment programmes. One of the important issues in these cases is whether an employee is able to claim an employment relationship with his employer if the employer's continued employment programme does not satisfy requirements decided by the MHLW, or the employer mistakenly refused to apply a continued employment programme to the employee despite the employee satisfying the standards for selection of employees. The conclusion of the courts has been divided. In some cases, courts have held that the employee is not able to claim an employment relationship with his employer, although the employee is entitled to damages. However, in other cases, the courts have held that the employee is able to claim an employment relationship with his employer. According to the latter position, the courts could potentially decide the various working conditions of the employment relationship such as term and salary. Therefore, we are of the opinion that the former position is the most persuasive.

The Bill for Amendment of the Law concerning Employment of Older Persons

The MHLW has submitted a proposal to amend the LEOP. This bill has not yet passed the Diet. It basically states that a company which introduces a continued employment programme cannot set a standard to select eligible employees by a labour-management agreement. In other words, all employees would be eligible for a continued employment programme. It is not certain when the bill will be passed by the Diet and the Congress.

Non-competition clause

General explanation

Companies sometimes want to include non-competition clauses (along with a confidentiality clause) in employment contracts, or to alternatively execute non-competition clauses during an employee's employment. These are to prevent an employee from engaging in activities which would compete with their original employer for a certain period of time after leaving their position of employment and to protect that employer's confidential information. It is extremely hard for any employer to prove the breach of confidentiality clauses, since many activities violating the confidentiality clauses are conducted secretly.

Usually it is stipulated that in case of violation of a non-competition clause, the employee will lose entitlement to the retirement allowance.

Such clauses are likely to be inconsistent with the Constitutional right to choose a job. However, simultaneously, employers also have the right to do business, and in some circumstances employers could require some means of protection from a competitor company that employs former high-level employees who have significant confidential information of the former company. In an effort to balance these contradictory needs, Japanese courts interpret such non-competition provisions on a case-by-case basis, but mostly the courts tend to treat such provisions to the advantage of the employee. The courts would take the following factors into consideration: (a) a company's legitimate interest to be protected by imposing such provision on ex-employees; (b) the position of the ex-employee in the company; (c) the adequacy of the monetary compensation in consideration of compliance with the non-competition; and (d) the length of period for non-competition and the area of non-competition. Usually regarding (a) above, the courts have deemed that (i) protecting trade secrets or know-how, and/or (ii) maintaining existing relationships with customers established through substantial time, efforts and investments would constitute a company's legitimate interest.

Recent case

In *American Life Insurance Company* case, the Tokyo District Court on January 13, 2012, held that the non-competition clauses could not be enforced against an ex-employee of the company. The duration of the obligation was two (2) years and no monetary compensation was paid to the ex-employee with regard to the non-competition clauses. Although there was the fact that the ex-employee's position was rather high-level and he received a large annual salary, the court held that the non-competition clauses were invalid and that the ex-employee was entitled to a retirement allowance which was about 30 million (30,000,000) Japanese Yen. In this case, it is important that the court held that the protection of the company's know-how and customer information was not a legitimate reason to impose a non-compete obligation which is not similar to other judgments.

This judgment was rather surprising since it seems not to take into account the necessity by companies in utilising such non-competition clauses. We need to wait and see whether this will become a prevailing opinion by the courts.

Persuasion to retire

General

As stated Section 1 hereof, it is not easy to validly terminate employment contracts. Therefore, employers usually avoid unilaterally terminating employment contracts in order to circumvent the possibility of losing the case as well as some time-consuming, onerous and costly procedures.

Employers rather tend to attempt to persuade employees to retire voluntarily. Typically, the offers include payment of special severance allowances in addition to the normal retirement allowances.

In some cases, employees request compensation for mental damages claiming that the employer tried to force them to retire illegally (i.e., persuasion by employer to resign was in fact extortion to retire).

Regarding the issue of under what circumstances the persuasion to retire could be deemed as a torturous act, the Supreme Court held as follows: employees are able to freely decide whether or not they accept persuasion to retire. Although an employer is trying to make encourage employees to voluntarily retire by persuasion to retire, if the actual persuasion to retire was not conducted in a socially appropriate way and as the result of this, employees did not have freedom to decide by their own, such persuasion could be regarded as a torturous act.

Recent case

Regarding the issue of whether or not an employer can continue the persuasion to retire even if the employees refused to accept such persuasion, the Tokyo District Court in the *Japan IBM* case held on December 28, 2011 as follows:

The court acknowledged that the employer has a culture that all employees should improve their performance, the employer selected subject employees based on employees' performance evaluation and that the employer offered generous severance packages. The court held that the employer shall not be obliged to immediately stop persuasion to retire even if the employees show negative intentions regarding such persuasion to retire. As long as persuasion to retire is conducted in a socially appropriate manner, the employer is able to explain in detail the outcomes if the employees continue to work for the employer (such as expected bad performance evaluations) and how generous the offered severance packages are, and to confirm whether the employees seriously reviewed the offered conditions of the severance packages, and request them to review again the offered conditions.

We believe that this case is helpful to understand how to validly conduct the process of persuasion to retire.

Exempt employees

General

According to the Labour Standards Act ("LSA"), if an employee works more than 8 hours per day or 40 hours per week, their employer shall pay an overtime premium to such employee. In addition, if an employee works nighttime work (i.e., from 10 p.m. to 5 a.m.) or holidays, such employee is entitled to a nighttime work premium and a holiday work premium.

In order to avoid the increase of amounts of overtime premiums, companies can introduce a discretionary work system that includes special or management work. If employees satisfy requirements for the discretionary work system, such employees are deemed to work for a certain number of hours (a number which is decided by agreement between management and employees) regardless of actual work hours. However, since requirements for a discretionary work system are rather severe, generally speaking, it is very difficult for companies to apply a discretionary work system to many of their employees. Accordingly, many companies designate many employees as "employees who have administrative or supervising positions" ('Exempt Employees'). According to Article 41, Item 2 of the LSA, employers do not need to pay overtime premiums and holiday work premiums to Exempt Employees even if they work more than 8 hours per day or 40 hours per week or work on a holiday. However, if they work from 10pm to 5am, employers shall pay a nighttime work premium to them.

Since the wording of Article 41, Item 2 of the LSA (i.e., "employees who have administrative or supervising positions") is unclear, the range of Exempt Employees is an important issue in Japanese Labour Law.

The MHLW has issued several notices regarding the interpretation of "employees who have administrative or supervising positions." Such interpretations do not make it completely clear, but in any case, the range of Exempt Employees is very narrow according to the interpretations.

The courts tend to follow the MHLW's position and limit the range of Exempt Employees very narrowly.

Recent Case

In the famous *McDonald's* case, the Tokyo District Court held on January 28, 2008 that the head of a McDonald's restaurant could not be treated as an Exempt Employee. In many companies, the range of Exempt Employees is broader than the MHLW's opinion. In other words, it is possible that many companies need to pay a large amount of unpaid overtime premiums to their employees if their employees file a lawsuit against them claiming unpaid overtime premiums. However, employees tend not to file a lawsuit regarding unpaid premiums against their employers as long as the employment relationship exists. Therefore, even if employers did not change the range of the Exempt Employees based on the MHLW's opinion, they have not been forced to pay premiums to their employees. Since the McDonald's judgment has become very famous, many companies have changed the range of Exempt Employees. Such companies must carefully implement the amendment of the range of Exempt Employees, since such change might let their employees understand that certain Exempt

Employees are entitled to unpaid premiums. The statute of limitations for unpaid premiums is two (2) years.

Injuries/death caused by work (Workers' Accident Insurance and damages claim against employer)

Workers' Accident Insurance

In Japan, if employees get injured, suffer disease, or die due to work, such injury, disease or death could be deemed as a work-related injury, disease or death under the Workers' Accident Compensation Insurance Law. The Workers' Accident Compensation Insurance System provides insurance benefits to employees (or to their survivors) who suffer injury, disease, disability or death arising from employment. Upon due application, insurance benefits are paid to the employees, or their survivors. The decision to pay, or not to pay, is made by the Chief of the Labour Standards Inspection Office (*Rohkisho-cho*, the "CLSIO"). Only after this payment decision is made does the afflicted employee, or his or her survivors, acquire a concrete right to claim insurance benefits from the Japanese government. Basic benefits under the Workers' Accident Compensation Insurance System are as follows: medical compensation, compensation for disabilities, survivor's compensation, payment of compensation in installments and funeral expenses.

Damages claim against employer

Relationship between damages claim against employer and Workers' Accident Insurance

In addition to Workers' Accident Compensation Insurance, an employee involved in a work-related accident (or the worker's survivors) may assert a claim for compensation against the employer. The legal theory of such claim is as follows: an employer owes a duty to care for the safety of its employees. Therefore, if an employer neglected to exercise such duty, such employer is responsible for damages due to such negligence. With regard to a claim for lost profit, legally speaking, an employer is responsible for that portion of the claim that exceeds the amount of Workers' Accident Compensation Insurance benefits. Regarding a claim for mental damages, an employer is responsible for the amount of such claim in full.

Please note that the two issues in one case can be different (i.e., a] whether an employee's injury or death will be treated as a work-related injury or death, and b] whether compensation against the employer shall be admitted). However, generally speaking, the compensation claim against the employer is more likely to be admitted. Therefore, there are many cases where the court admits the claim against the employer, although the injury or death of an employee is not admitted as a work-related injury or death. On the other hand, it is rare that the court does not admit the claim against employer when the employee's injury is admitted by the CLSIO as work-related injury or death. In other words, the CLSIO's decision that a certain accident is a work-related injury or death is exceedingly important evidence in a civil procedure against the employer.

As stated above, it is very important whether an employee's injury is classified as a work-related injury or death. However, if the CLSIO decides that a certain employee's injury or death is not a work-related injury or death, such employee or his or her survivors may appeal. However, if the CLSIO decides that a certain employee's injury is a work-related injury or death, the employer is not able to appeal. Therefore, it is important that an employer take measures to prevent the CLSIO's decision that an employee's injury or death is work-related.

Recent Case

The *Daisyo* case is the case where a new employee has died after four (4) months of work due to excessive work. The parents of the employee made damage claims against the employer and four (4) directors of the employer. At the employer, long and excessive work was taken for granted and there were various schemes for long and excessive overtime work. For example, employees' monthly salary would be reduced if their overtime work was less than eighty (80) hours per month. In this case, the Kyoto District Court held on May 25, 2010 that in addition to the employer, four (4) directors of the employer, who knew the schemes for long and excessive work but did not know the employee personally, shall pay damages. This judgment was affirmed by the Osaka High Court on May 25, 2011.

Mental Health

Damage claims against employer

After the collapse of Lehman Brothers, many Japanese companies have reduced their headcount and remaining employees have been faced with even more work. Currently, in many companies, there are employees who have asserted claims that they suffer from mental disease such as depression due to overwork. If such employees' mental disease is deemed a work-related disease, as stated above, the employee is entitled to certain benefits and is able to claim damages against the employer. Please note that basically the diagnosis of mental disease will be made based on a patient's statement of his own symptoms. In other words, an employee can obtain a medical certificate that he has suffered mental disease if he is able to state symptoms which are those of a mental disease (even if he does not actually suffer such symptoms).

On the other hand, some doctors have made out medical certificates simply based on the request of the patients without investigating the health of the patient further. Therefore, because of this, the number of cases where an employer doubts whether a certain employee really suffers from mental disease has been increasing.

Leave due to mental disease

Even if an employee suffers mental disease which is not caused by work and he is not able to work, an employer is not able to immediately terminate such employee. Generally speaking, such employee could take sickness or injury leave (leave of absence), the term of which is stipulated by the applicable Work Rules. If the subject employee could not return to work at the end of sickness/injury leave, such employee usually would be deemed to have resigned at the end of sickness/injury leave. In other words, sickness/injury leave would work as moratorium on the termination by employer.

The important issue with sickness/injury leave issue is how to decide whether the subject employee could return to work or not. Usually it is not so difficult for the employee who wishes to return to work to obtain and submit a doctor's medical certificate which states that they can return to work. Some medical doctors tend to accept their patients' request and to write a medical certificate that the employee can return to work, even if they do not believe that they can really return to work. Therefore, in some cases, an employer would have a suspicion that the employee has not recovered to return to work.

In such case, how to rebut the employee's doctor's medical certificate which states that the employee could return to work, is a very important issue from view of the defence.

Recent Case

In the *Nihon Tuun* case, although the doctor designated by the employer was not able to see the subject employee by himself, the doctor provided advice that the employee did not recover to return to work, based on information obtained from the employee's doctor who wrote a medical certificate which stated that the employee could return to work. The Tokyo District Court held on February 25, 2011 that it is permissible that the employer can follow the judgment of the doctor designated by the *employer* and determined that the subject employee resigned at the end of sickness leave based on the facts of the case.

Sexual Harassment and Power Harassment

Sexual Harassment

Article 11 of the Act on Securing etc. of Equal Opportunity and Treatment between Men and Women in Employment states as follows: employers shall establish necessary in terms of employment management to give advice to workers and cope with problems of workers, and take other necessary measures so that workers they employ do not suffer any disadvantage in their working conditions by reason of said workers' responses to sexual harassment in the workplace, or in their working environments do not suffer any harm due to said sexual harassment.

If a female employee suffers sexual harassment, she may claim damages against both the person who conducted the sexual harassment and the employer. In some cases, due to sexual harassment, victims suffer mental disorders such as depression. The CLSIO usually decides whether a certain disease is a work-related disease or not based on the standards prepared by the MHLW ("Standards"). Although it is very rare that the CLSIO decides that a mental disorder suffered by victims of sexual harassment is a work-related disease, the MHLW plans to amend the Standards in order that it will become easier for the CLSIO to decide that mental disorders suffered by victims of sexual harassment are work-related diseases.

Power Harassment

General

Power Harassment is a phrase that was created based on the Japanese corporate environment. It means harassment deriving from the environment of the workplace. It includes a range of behaviour from mild irritation and annoyances to serious abuses which can even involve forced activity beyond the boundaries of a job description. These days there are many lawsuits involving power harassment in Japan. Usually plaintiffs claim mental damages caused by power harassment. Generally speaking, the court decides whether certain activities by the plaintiff's superiors constitute power harassment on a case-by-case basis. Therefore, sometimes the court is very strict against the plaintiff's superiors. In the *"A" Insurance Company* case, Tokyo District Court dated April 20, 2005, the head of a centre sent his subordinate, an assistant-section chief who did not improve his performance, and other section members an email stating, "I think you should quit the company if you are not ambitious or motivated to work. Do you know how many personnel we can hire for your salary?" In this case, on December 1, 2004, the Tokyo District Court rejected the claim by the assistant-section-chief. However, on April 20, 2005, the Tokyo High Court reversed the judgment and admitted the claim of the assistant-section-chief. The court awarded 50,000 Japanese yen as mental damages.

Recent Cases

In the *Sanyo Denki Consumer Electronics* case, an HR section head had a meeting with an employee who conducted inappropriate actions such as the spreading of baseless rumours about an employee and requested the employee to amend her activities. However, since she looked away sullenly and defiantly during the meeting, the section head became emotional and scolded her loudly. She secretly recorded the conversation during the meeting. After the meeting she was seconded to another company. She filed a lawsuit claiming mental damages caused by his statement. On March 31, 2008, The Tottori District Court awarded her three million (3,000,000) Japanese yen as mental damages (which included mental damages for secondment). Although the Hiroshima High Court on May 22, 2009 held that the section head's statement during the meeting was inappropriate, it decreased the amount to five hundred thousand (500,000) Japanese yen taking into consideration the background of the case.

In the *Fukoku Life Insurance Company* case, a superior scolded a female manager of an insurance company who controlled the sales personnel team by stating: "Do you think you are up to being a manager with such bad sales results?" And, "You can resign from being a manager at any time." The manager quit the company and filed a lawsuit against the company and the superior claiming that she quit because of depression due to power harassment. The Yonago Branch of the Tottori District Court held on October 21, 2009 that the company and the superior shall pay damages to the manager in the amount of three million and three hundred thousand (3,300,000) Japanese yen.

As stated above, the courts decide the boundaries of instructions by superiors on a case-by-case basis. Some cases are difficult to understand based on the facts in the judgment. Currently, many employees easily claim power harassment against instructions or guidance by their superiors if they do not like the instructions or guidance. Since it is still not clear what kinds of activities/statements shall be deemed power harassment, many superiors now hesitate to impose tough guidance or instructions on their subordinates.

Masao Torikai
Tel: +81 3 3288 2080 / Email: torikai@mmn-law.gr.jp

Masao Torikai is a Senior Partner of Momo-o, Matsuo & Namba. He has over 16 years of international legal experience in general corporate law and specialises in labour and employment matters. He received a LL.B from the University of Tokyo in 1987 and a LL.M. from Northwestern University in 1998. Mr. Torikai routinely represents the management of publicly-held multinational corporations in labour and employment dispute resolution and litigation including collective bargaining and issues involving Labour Standards Inspection Offices. He has advised clients on a wide range of employment issues including the preparation and amendment of rules of employment; dismissal and voluntary resignation; employment and secondment contracts; disciplinary actions; occupational and mental health (including death or suicide due to overwork); sexual and power harassment claims; whistleblowing; employment of the aged, disabled and transgendered; and protection of employee data. Mr. Torikai's practice also includes the areas of labour and social insurance (including workers' compensation) and pension plans.

Koichi Nakatani
Tel: +81 3 3288 2080 / Email: nakatani@mmn-law.gr.jp

Koichi Nakatani is a Partner of Momo-o, Matsuo & Namba. He has over 14 years of international legal experience in general corporate law and specialises in labour and employment matters and IP law. He obtained a LL.B. from Keio University in 1992 and a LL.M. from the University of Washington in 2007. Having served as in-house counsel for IBM Japan, Ltd. for seven years, Mr. Nakatani possesses extensive experience with the HR management practices of publicly-held multinational corporations. His experience spans matters such as early retirement programmes and the shutdown of offices and transfer of employment in the course of M&A. He also frequently represents the management of multinationals in labour and employment dispute resolution and litigation, including disciplinary dismissal cases. His practice includes advising clients on a wide range of other employment issues including protection of employee data.

Momo-o, Matsuo & Namba

Kojimachi Diamond Bld. 6F, 4-1 Kojimachi, Chiyoda-ku, Tokyo 102-0083, Japan
Tel: +81 3 3288 2080 / Fax: +81 3 3288 2081 / URL: http://www.mmn-law.gr.jp

Luxembourg

Guy Castegnaro & Ariane Claverie
CASTEGNARO

General labour market trends and latest/likely trends in employment litigation

The Luxembourg labour market is notably characterised by an international and multicultural working environment, an exceptional rate of foreign labour and an unemployment rate below the European average.

Indeed, with an unemployment rate at 6.0% in March 2012, the Luxembourg unemployment rate is largely below the European unemployment rate which was at 10.9% in March 2012.

Generally, the growth of employment in Luxembourg has moderated since mid-2008 until the end of the year 2009, which was a year of stagnation. Employment growth then started to go down slightly at the end of 2011, due notably to the crisis in the European economy.

The decline of employment in Luxembourg is also due to the increase in the number of companies declared bankrupt. Indeed, while approximately 30,000 companies were registered in Luxembourg in 2011, 961 have been declared bankrupt compared to 918 in 2010.

Nevertheless, it must be noted that even if the number of bankruptcies has gone up and the employment growth has slightly decreased since 2008, Luxembourg employment growth remains positive (the employment growth rate was of 3.1% in the last 12 months).

In this context of economic crisis and of lower growth in employment, Luxembourg courts do not seem to be adopting stricter measures against employers. On the contrary, Luxembourg courts seem to declare most employee dismissals – and notably economic dismissals – as fair when the reasons for the dismissal are precise, real and serious.

As a reminder, according to Luxembourg labour law, the motivation letter must precisely indicate the reasons for the dismissal and the facts which have led the employer to take the decision of the dismissal. In case of redundancy, the employer must indicate the reasons arising from the operating needs of the business, establishment or department.

For example, the Luxembourg employment tribunal decided in February 2012 that an employer who only indicated in the motivation letter that the economic dismissal was due to the "financial crisis", without indicating comparable figures, had breached the law, as it did not indicate precisely the reasons for the economic dismissal *(Employment tribunal, 6 February 2012, n°592/2012)*. Indeed, the employer should have indicated comparable figures and the reasons justifying the need to reorganise the company, as well as the reasons which have led it to choose this employee over another.

It must be noted that even if compensations allocated by the courts in case of unfair economic dismissal are slightly higher than those allocated in case of dismissal based on personal reasons, these compensations remain very low (between 3 to 6 months' gross salary for an employee who has a length of service of less than 10 years; between 6 to 8 months' gross salary for an employee who has a length of service of between 10 to 20 years).

This was not the case for dismissals pronounced in 2008, as the courts seemed to award a higher amount of damages to employees who were unfairly dismissed in that year.

Key case law affecting employers' decision making over dismissal, redundancies dismissals etc.

- The Court of Cassation ruled in October 2011 that an employer going into dissolution or judicial dissolution has to establish a social plan when the conditions of collective dismissals are fulfilled. *(Court of Cassation, 27 October 2011, n°58/11, 2752 of register, Court of Cassation, 27 October 2011, n°62/11, 2753 of register*, and *Court of Cassation, 3 March 2011, n°15/11, 2822 of register and n°16/11, 2823 of register.)*

- In case of redundancies, the employer does not have to look for a redeployment of the dismissed employee in the area of his/her company nor in the area of another company of the group before terminating the employment contract. *(Court of Appeal, 28 October 2011, n°35913.)*

- In case of redundancy, the company's financial difficulties have to be appreciated at the group level when the Luxembourg company has no administrative and financial autonomy with regard to the group. In such cases, the motivation letter has to indicate precisely the financial situation of the group. *(Court of Appeal, 1 March 2012, n°37078.)* Nonetheless, an appraisal of the economic difficulties in cases of economic dismissal has to be assessed at the Luxembourg company level when the group of companies to which the Luxembourg company belongs is composed of separate legal entities. *(Court of Appeal, 22 March 2012, n°36037.)*

- The Court has also ruled that once a frontier worker has moved to Luxembourg (after his/her dismissal) she/he is entitled to unemployment benefits in Luxembourg even though she/he was living abroad at the moment of the dismissal. This decision challenges article L.521-3 of the Labour Code. *(Court of Cassation, 3 March 2011, n°15/11, 2822 of register and n°16/11, 2823 of register.)*

- As regards the situation of the employee who has been dismissed during her pregnancy, the Court has ruled that the employee is allowed to either:

  - ask the President of the Labour Court to state the nullity of her dismissal within 15 days of the termination of her employment contract; or

  - ask the Labour Court for damages for her unfair dismissal. However, if the pregnant employee has already requested the nullity of her dismissal to the President of the Labour Court, she will not be allowed to also claim damages to the Labour Court. *(Court of Appeal, 1 December 2012, n°36402.)*

- The notification of a dismissal letter neither signed nor dated by its author is valid and does not constitute a formal irregularity. Only the following are considered as formal irregularities by Labour Courts:
  - when notification of the dismissal letter is sent only by ordinary postal letter and not by registered letter; and
  - failure by the employer to invite the employee to attend a preliminary meeting when the employer employs 150 or more persons. *(Court of Appeal, 30 June 2011, n°35362.)*

- Dismissal for gross misconduct is allowed when an employee has exercised, during his/her sickness leave, a parallel remunerated activity, even if this activity is a non-competitive activity. *(Court of Appeal, 12 January 2012, n°36488.)*

Recent statutory or legislative changes

- <u>Law of 18 January 2012</u> which creates a new labour administration: the "Agency for the development of employment". This law modifies Art.L.621-1 to L.623-2 of the Labour Code. It has also modified the name of the Labour Administration: the *"Administration de l'Emploi"* is now the *"Agence pour le développement de l'emploi"*. This law has extended the right to benefit of unemployment benefits to nationals (and their family members) of European Union countries, of the European Economic Area or of the Swiss Confederation and to third-country nationals holding long-term resident status, as well as third-country nationals having a valid residence permit. This law also allows an employer, who has declared a vacant position to the Labour Administration, to request 3 weeks after this declaration a document certifying the employer's entitlement to employ the person of his/her choice, and notably nationals of European Union countries and third-country nationals.

- Law of 31 January 2012 which modifies some modalities of the sliding salary scale. This law mainly provides that there will be only one index increase per year in 2012, 2013 and 2014. According to this law, there must be at least a 12-month interval between each indexation.

- Law of 8 December 2011 which modifies the law of 29 August 2008 on immigration to introduce the EU Blue Card for highly qualified workers in the Luxembourg legislation. This law implements the European Directive 2009/50/CE of 25 May 2009 on the conditions of entry and residence of third-country nationals for the purposes of highly qualified employment. It also introduces the European Blue Card in the Luxembourg legislation. This law eases the employment in the European Union of highly qualified workers and their movements in the European Union area. This law also ensures equal treatment of highly qualified workers with nationals after the first 2 years of Blue Card validity.

- Grand-Ducal regulation of 25 January 2012 which modifies the Grand-Ducal regulations of 26 September 2008 and 5 September 2008, defining the level of the remuneration needed for a third-country national in order to request a EU Blue Card for highly qualified workers. This Grand-Ducal regulation determines the minimum level of remuneration for highly qualified workers. Thus, the gross annual salary of a highly qualified worker shall not be lower than one-and-a-half times the gross annual salary determined by Grand-Ducal regulation. The Ministerial regulation of 15 February 2012 determines this gross annual salary for the year 2012.

- Law of 19 April 2012 which modifies articles L.126-1 and L.541-1 of the Labour Code. This law allows the employee whose employer has been declared bankrupt, to request to the Labour Administration an advance of his/her "super privileged" debts (arrears of salary) as soon as his/her debt is declared without waiting for the later verification by the Bankruptcy Trustee.

- Law of 28 March 2012 which modifies the law of 19 December 2008 on the vocational training reform. According to this law, the participation of the government notably rose from 14.5% to 20%.

- Grand-Ducal regulation of 25 April 2012 which modifies the Grand-Ducal regulation of 6 December 1989 on the political leave of mayors and communal councillors. This law provides additional hours (9 hours) for elected representatives who have been elected as "delegates in the associations of municipalities" of which the municipality is member, in order to exercise their mandate.

- Grand-Ducal regulation of 29 May 2012 which modifies the Grand-Ducal regulation of 5 September 2008 to establish the conditions and procedures for obtaining a residence permit as an employee.

Likely or impending reforms to employment legislation and enforcement procedures

- Bill n°6101 modifying articles L.243-1 and L.243-5 of the Labour Code on positive actions (equal treatment between men and women) is under process.
- Bill n°6387 reforming the pensions insurance and modifying 1) the social security code, 2) the modified law of 3 August 1998 creating the special pension regime applicable to civil servants, and 3) the Labour Code, is under process. This bill focuses on:
  - the mechanism of fixed and proportional increases;
  - supplementary qualifying courses for pension rights;
  - the coverage period;
  - the adjustment mechanism; and
  - the transition to retirement.
- Bill n°6401 modifying article L.521-3 of the Labour Code and repealing the current legal provision prohibiting the combination of unemployment benefits with a retirement pension or with a disability pension.
- Draft bill n°6404 notably modifying the Labour Code, the Penal Code, and the modified law of 29

August 2008 on immigration, and implementing Directive 2009/52/EC which provides minimum financial, administrative and criminal sanctions in case of employment of illegal migrants.

- Bill n°6373 on the European Works Council, implementing Directive 2009/38/EC of the European Parliament and of the Council of 6 May 2009 on the establishment of a European Works Council or a procedure for Community-scale undertakings and Community-scale groups of undertakings for the purposes of informing and consulting employees.
- Bill n°6234 on 'time savings accounts' is currently under process. It will allow employees to save days of paid leave on their account, for private reasons or vocational training. Time savings accounts already exist in Luxembourg, especially in the banking sector. However, the new law will give a legal frame to this tool.
- Bill n°6442 modifying the Labour Code extends, until December 2013, the measures provided by the Luxembourg government to maintain the employment in Luxembourg. This bill also proposes to modify the provisions of the Labour Code as regards partially unemployed workers by extending the duration of short-time working for a 10-month period.

Guy Castegnaro
Tel: +352 268 6821 / Email: guy.castegnaro@castegnaro.lu
Guy Castegnaro is an *Avocat à la Cour* admitted to practice before the High Court of Justice. He is the founder of CASTEGNARO, the only niche employment law firm in Luxembourg. Mr Castegnaro is also a founding member and member of the Board of Ius Laboris, an alliance of leading human resources law practitioners. His qualifications include Master of Laws (University of Paris I, Panthéon-Sorbonne, France, 1991), Master of Laws (LLM) in German Law (University of Kiel, Germany, 1993) and Advanced Course of Law (University of Luxembourg). Mr Castegnaro participated in the establishment of the Luxembourg Labour Code. He is also a speaker at numerous conferences on employment law topics and teaches social security law at the University of Luxembourg.

Ariane Claverie
Tel: +352 268 6821 / Email: ariane.claverie@castegnaro.lu
Mrs Ariane Claverie is an *Avocat à la Cour* admitted to practise before the High Court of Justice. Her qualifications include Master of Laws (University of Bordeaux, France, 1992) with a specialisation in public, international and European law (1992-1993), a DEA in European Law (University of Nancy, France, 1994) and Advanced Course of Law (University of Luxembourg). Now partner at CASTEGNARO, Mrs Claverie first became in-house counsel before joining the Luxembourg Bar in 1997. She quickly specialised in labour law and joined Guy Castegnaro in 2001. Mrs Claverie is notably specialised in employment law in all its aspects and especially in the protection of personal data, duration of work, employee's sickness, and employer and employee's liability. She participated in the establishment of the Luxembourg Labour Code. She is also a speaker at conferences and the author of articles on employment law matters.

CASTEGNARO

33 Allée Scheffer, L-2520 Luxembourg
Tel: +352 268 6821 / Fax: +352 2686 8282 / URL: http://www.castegnaro.lu

Malaysia

Teh Eng Lay
Cheah Teh & Su

Malaysia's Employment & Labour laws are shaped by statutes and case law. For the last three years, this area of the law has seen greater activism from Parliament with amendments made to the Employment Act 1955[1] and the Industrial Relations Act 1967[2] as well as the enactment of the National Wages Consultative Council Act 2011[3]. These measures were followed by the passing of the Minimum Retirement Age Bill 2012 on 28 June 2012. When in force, this piece of legislation will fix the retirement age of private sector employees at 60 years of age when hitherto there was no prescribed retirement age with it being left to contract.

These developments are to do with the private sector employees and not government employees, the latter being under the purview of the Public Service Commission established by Article 139 of the Constitution of Malaysia. For government employees, amendments have been made to the Pensions Act 1980, the Pensions Adjustment Act 1980 and the Statutory and Local Authorities Pensions Act 1980 to improve their civil service pension scheme.

In respect of case law, the word "life" in Article 5(1)[4] of the Federal Constitution has been liberally interpreted to include "right to livelihood". Thus, one cannot be deprived of his employment save in accordance with the law.

Statutory Framework and Adjudication System

The principal Acts of Parliament[5] regulating employment relations for the private sector are the Employment Act 1955 (applicable to Peninsular Malaysia and Federal Territory of Labuan[6]) and Industrial Relations Act 1967.

The Labour Court

The Employment Act 1955 is generally applicable to employees whose wages do not exceed RM2,000 a month and those falling within the First Schedule of the Act. The First Schedule defines an employee as:

1. *Any person, irrespective of his occupation, who has entered into a contract of service with an employer under which such person's wages do not exceed RM2,000 a month.*

2. *Any person who, irrespective of the amount of wages he earns in a month, has entered into a contract of service with an employer in pursuance of which –*

    (1) he is engaged in manual labour including such labour as an artisan or apprentice:

    Provided that where a person is employed by one employer partly in manual labour and partly in some other capacity such person shall not be deemed to be performing manual labour unless the time during which he is required to perform manual labour in any one wage period exceeds one-half of the total time during which he is required to work in such wage period;

    (2) he is engaged in the operation or maintenance of any mechanically propelled vehicle operated for the transport of passengers or goods or for reward or for commercial purposes;

    (3) he supervises or oversees other employees engaged in manual labour employed by the same employer in and throughout the performance of their work;

(4) he is engaged in any capacity in any vessel registered in Malaysia and who –

    (a) is not an officer...;

    (b) is not the holder of a local certificate as defined in Part VII of the Merchant Shipping Ordinance 1952...; or

    (c) has not entered into an agreement under Part III of the Merchant Shipping Ordinance 1952; or

(5) he is engaged as a domestic servant.

3. For the purpose of this Schedule, "wages" means wages as defined in Section 2, but shall not include any payment by way of commission, subsistence allowance and overtime payment.

However, certain provisions, for example the new provisions on sexual harassment, are applicable to all irrespective of their wages.

This Act prescribes the basic terms of a contract of service, e.g. payment of wages, hours of work and rest days, maternity protection, employment of women, children and young persons, termination, lay-off and retirement benefits; and any term which is less favourable than those prescribed under Act is void. However, any term which is more favourable is to prevail.

Pursuant to Section 69 of this Act, the Director General of Labour is empowered to inquire into and decide disputes in respect of wages and any other payments in cash due to an employee (those within the categories in the First Schedule of the Act). The access to this adjudication system is also extended to employees whose wages exceed RM2,000 a month but does not exceed RM5,000 a month[7].

When carrying out this function, the Director General of Labour acts as the "Labour Court". Arising therefrom, an appeal to the High Court may be undertaken by any person affected financially by the decision of the Labour Court. Nevertheless, if a dispute falls within the Industrial Relations Act 1967 or is pending before the Industrial Court, the Labour Court would cease to have jurisdiction over the dispute[8].

The Industrial Court

The Industrial Court is empowered to deal with cases for recognition of collective agreements, and if referred to the court by the Minister of Human Resources – unjust dismissal cases, trade union complaints and trade disputes. For these latter three types of cases, employees do not have direct access to the Industrial Court. The complaint will have to be lodged with the Director General of Industrial Relations who will conduct a conciliation process and report to the Minister of Human Resources. If the conciliation process fails, the Minister will decide on whether to refer the dispute to the Industrial Court[9]. The Industrial Court will only be seized with jurisdiction upon a reference by the Minister.

No. of Cases Referred to the Industrial Court (2005 – 2011)

	Year						
	2005	2006	2007	2008	2009	2010	2011
Total cases carried forward	4143	3723	4566	4612	3342	2627	2552
Total cases referred	1859	2990	2346	665	647	1437	1346
Total awards handed down	2403	2332	2599	2170	1485	1640	1838
Total cases pending	3723	4566	4612	3342	2627	2552	2251
Total cases disposed	2209	2233	2367	1980	1390	1528	1670

Statistics from the Industrial Court of Malaysia at http://www.mp.gov.my

In this regard, the Minister exercises a referral discretion and his decision (be it a reference or a non-reference) is susceptible to judicial review by the High Court. From the High Court, a litigant may then pursue an appeal to the Court of Appeal. Thereafter, subject to obtaining the leave of the Federal

Court (the apex court), an appeal to the Federal Court. Often, this process results in significant delay in the resolution of the dispute.

In respect of unjust dismissal cases (referred by the Minister to the Industrial Court), the Industrial Relations Act 1967 provides for the relief of reinstatement. This is the statutory exception to the common law rule that a contract of service will not be specifically enforced by compelling its performance. In this regard, it must be noted that the use of a contractual termination clause (with notice or otherwise) to terminate the service of an employee would not exculpate an employer as the Industrial Court acts *"according to equity, good conscience and the substantial merits of the case without regard to technicalities and legal form"*[10] and will enquire into any termination case as a dismissal case.

In respect of relief, if a dismissal is found to be without just cause and excuse, the Industrial Court may make an award for reinstatement of the employee or compensation *in lieu* of reinstatement to be paid to the employee, both with award of backwages to the employee.

However, the relief of reinstatement is often illusory because of the significant amount of time taken for the Minister's decision to refer the dispute to the Industrial Court, the possible judicial review of the Minister's decision and finally the hearing at the Industrial Court. Meanwhile, the law has not come to recognise interim reinstatement or interim injunction issued to preserve the employment and to allow the employee concerned to continue working while the dispute undergoes the adjudication process.[11]

Arising from an Industrial Court's award (whether for the employee or the employer), there is no appeal process. But the Industrial Court's award is subject to judicial review by the High Court. Thereafter, an appeal to the Court of Appeal and subject to obtaining leave from the Federal Court, an appeal to the Federal Court. If the entire appellate procees is undertaken there would be a significant delay in the final resolution of the matter.

Employee (Workman) vs Independent Contractor

The question of whether one is an employee or an independent contractor persists in the adjudication system, as protection and reliefs are statutorily provided only to employees (workmen), and not independent contractors. Furthermore, the Industrial Court in adjudicating a dispute has the power to create new rights and obligations[12] in the employer-employee relationship. Thus, the question of employee-or-independent-contractor becomes the primary (if not preliminary) issue in many cases[13].

The Statutory Definitions

As remarked by the Federal Court[14], the statutory definitions of "workman", "employee", "contract of employment" and "contract of service" are circuitous and far from clarity.

Under the Industrial Relations Act 1967, a "contract of employment" means an agreement to employ one as a workman, and a "workman" means any person who is employed under a contract of employment. Similarly, the Employment Act 1967 provides that a "contract of service" means an agreement to employ one as an employee and "employee" means any person who is employed under a contract of service. Hence, in many cases, the Labour Court and the Industrial Court have to deal with this pertinent mixed question of fact and law[15] – whether one is an employee or an independent contractor. The law continues to be premised upon the common law divert of employee and independent contractor, and has not recognised any hybrid category as in other jurisdictions.

The Legal Test

"There is not a single satisfactory test that is available for the determination of the issue"[16], and the control test is said to be *"based on the simpler socio-economic conditions of the by-gone days"* and it *"must be modified if it is to be valid"*[17].

Towards this end, the courts in Malaysia look at both the traditional control test and the integration test to determine this issue[18]. Under the latter test, where a man is employed as part of the business and his work is done as an integral part of the business, there is an employment and the work is done under a contract of service. Where his work, although done for the business, is not integrated into the business but is only accessory to it, there is no employment and the work is done under a contract for services.

Analysis of Industrial Court Awards of Dismissal Cases (2005 – 2011)

Types of dismissal	Year						
	2005	2006	2007	2008	2009	2010	2011
Constructive	22	42	97	126	140	135	91
Misconduct	2144	2051	1200	878	613	608	639
Retrenchment	16	32	422	155	114	67	90
Others	0	0	402	573	328	479	640
TOTAL	2182	2125	2121	1732	1195	1289	1460

Statistics from the Industrial Court of Malaysia at http://www.mp.gov.my

Analysis of Industrial Court Awards of Non-Dismissal Cases (2005 – 2011)

Subject	Year						
	2005	2006	2007	2008	2009	2010	2011
Non-compliance of Award	60	136	109	124	113	131	107
Non-compliance of Collective Agreement	60	66	30	40	34	27	27
Interpretation of Award/ Collective Agreement	16	10	6	4	5	8	4
Variation of Award/ Collective Agreement	7	1	7	2	3	3	5
Amendment to Collective Agreement (by Court Order)	1	1	0	0	0	0	0
Collective Agreement (Terms and Conditions)	46	37	61	39	37	47	36
Victimisation	0	0	1	0	0	20	4
Trade Disputes	0	0	38	15	13	21	27
TOTAL	202	259	228	232	195	239	210

Statistics from the Industrial Court of Malaysia at http://www.mp.gov.my

The courts, however, are not concerned with nomenclature[19]. The focus is on the person's duties and functions and the conduct of the parties in order to ascertain what is the true nature of the relationship of the parties, and labels do not change the nature. In this connection, the fact that statutory contributions have not been made to the Employees' Provident Fund[20] and the Social Security Organisation[21] (commonly known as Socso) is not decisive in the resolution of the question of whether there was an employer-employee relationship[22]. Similarly, the fact that schedular tax deductions[23] have not been remitted to the Inland Revenue Board is not decisive. In this connection, the Industrial Court acts *"according to equity, good conscience and the substantial merits of the case without regard to technicalities and legal form"*[24].

Fixed Term Contract

A related matter is the popular use of fixed term contracts, particularly in the employment of expatriates and also in the construction industry where employees are commonly engaged on a project basis.

The main issue that presents itself is whether there is a genuine fixed term contract or there is an employment on a permanent basis dressed up as several fixed term contracts. A permanent employment would entail security of tenure in that the person is employed until he retires. More often than not, in such cases, statutory contributions to the Employees' Provident Fund and Socso as well as schedular tax deduction would have been made. That, however, as mentioned above is not decisive.

There is no clear legal test on this issue, and nor has legislation addressed this issue. The question the courts will enquire into is whether there was an "ulterior motive" behind the fixed term contract. This makes each case fact-sensitive and the courts are to deal with each case on its own facts[25].

Non-Citizen Employees

In respect of employment of non-citizens, there are several restrictions. Section 5 of the Employment (Restriction) Act 1968 stipulates the requirement of a valid employment permit. A fine not exceeding RM5,000, or a prison term not exceeding 1 year, or both, may be imposed on the employer and the employee respectively for a breach of this section.

Further, on the part of the employer, it is an offence under Section 55B of the Immigration Act 1959/1963 to employ *"1 or more persons, other than a citizen or a holder of an entry permit, who is not in possession of a valid pass"*. A heavier penalty of a fine of not less than RM10,000, up to a maximum of RM50,000, or a prison term not exceeding 1 year, or both, is imposed under this section. Also, Section 60M of the Employment Act 1955 prohibits the termination of a local employee for the purpose of employing a foreign employee.

In respect of an application for an employment permit, the procedure varies depending on whether the person concerned is a professional or unskilled, and the industry/sector as well as the state/area (Peninsular Malaysia or Sabah or Sarawak) in which the person concerned will be engaged. The Malaysian Industry Development Authority has laid down the following guidelines on the employment of expatriates as as follows:

(1) Manufacturing companies with foreign paid-up capital of US$2 million and above:
   (a) Automatic approval is given for up to 10 expatriate posts, including five key posts.
   (b) Expatriates can be employed for up to a maximum of 10 years for executive posts, and five years for non-executive posts.

(2) Manufacturing companies with foreign paid-up capital of more than US$200,000 but less than US$2 million:
   (a) Automatic approval is given for up to five expatriate posts, including at least one key post.
   (b) Expatriates can be employed for a maximum 10 years for executive posts, and five years for non-executive posts.

(3) Manufacturing companies with foreign paid-up capital of less than US$200,000 will be considered for both key posts and time posts based on current guidelines which are:
   (a) Key posts can be considered where the foreign paid-up capital is at least RM500,000. This amount, however, is only a guideline and the number of key posts to be allowed depends on the merits of each case.
   (b) Time posts can be considered for up to 10 years for executive posts that require professional qualifications and practical experience, and five years for non-executive posts that require technical skills and experience. For these posts, Malaysians must be trained to eventually take over the posts.
   (c) The number of key posts and time posts to be allowed depends on the merits of each case.

(4) For Malaysian-owned manufacturing companies, approval for the employment of expatriates for technical posts, including R&D posts, will be given as requested.

Apart from the Malaysian Industry Development Authority, there are also several approving authorities for the employment of expatriates in the relevant industry/sector. These are:

1. Multimedia Development Corporation	Expatriate Post and skilled foreign workers in Information Technology-based companies which have been granted "Multimedia Super Corridor" (MSC) status.
2. Public Service Department	Doctors and nurses working in government hospitals or clinics. Lecturers and tutors employed in Government Institutes of Higher Education. Contract Posts in Public Services. Recruitment process jobs offered by the Public Service Commission or government-related agencies.
3. Central Bank of Malaysia	Expatriate posts in the following sectors: • Banking • Finance • Insurance
4. Securities Commission	Expatriate posts in Securities and Share market.
5. Expatriate Committee	Expatriate posts in private and public sectors other than those under the jurisdiction of the above agencies/authorities.

There is also the Residence Pass-Talent introduced in April 2011 by the government to attract and retain talent in the country[26]. This Residence Pass-Talent is valid for 10 years as opposed to the two or three years in the usual Employment Pass. The spouse of the Residence Pass-Talent holder is also eligible to work in Malaysia.

Application for this pass is made to Talent Corporation Malaysia Berhad established under the Prime Minister's Department. Its primary function is to formulate and facilitate initiatives to attract, retain and nurture talents in support of the country's economic programme.

Recent Developments

Award of Backwages in the Industrial Court

Prior to 28 February 2008, the Industrial Relations Act 1967 does not stipulate the maximum amount in backwages the Industrial Court may award.

The basic approach had been that the employee is awarded a sum of backwages arrived at by multiplying his monthly remuneration with the number of months between the date of his dismissal and the date of the award. Although the Industrial Court Practice Note No 1 of 1987 ('Practice Note') stipulates a maximum of 24 months' backwages, the Industrial Court had always retained discretion to award more than the said 24 months' backwages.

The Industrial Relations Act 1967, since the amendments which came into effect on 28 February 2008, now contains a Second Schedule: Factors for Consideration in making an Award in relation to a Reference under subsection 20(3). In essence, this limits the award of backwages to a maximum of 24 months. In the case of a probationer who has been dismissed, the maximum is 12 months' backwages.

Further, a percentage of any post-dismissal earnings (i.e. income from elsewhere after the dismissal) shall be deducted from the backwages, and the Industrial Court is to decide on the percentage. Compensation for loss of future earnings is also excluded, while contributory misconduct of the employee will be considered.

Maternity Leave

Prior to the amendments in 2012, the maternity provisions under the Employment Act 1955 were applicable only to female employees earning RM1,500 per month and below and those falling within the First Schedule of the Act. By virtue of Section 44A (added *vide* the amendments), this protection is now extended to all female employees irrespective of the amount of wages.

The maternity provisions in essence stipulate the maternity leave of 60 days and the entitlement to payment of maternity allowance. It also provides that an employer who terminates the service of a female employee during the period in which she is entitled to maternity leave commits an offence.

Sexual Harrassment

In 1999, the Minister of Human Resources acknowledged that "the problem does exist at least in certain workplaces especially those with very large female workforce", and that "the situation already warrants due attention and remedial action so that it does not get worse"[27].

There was, however, no specific employment legislation on sexual harassment in the workplace. In respect of civil service, this area was regulated by the Public Services Department's circular dated 10 September 2005 known as Guidelines for Handling Sexual Harassment in the Workplace Among the Civil Servant No. 22 of 2005. As for private sector employees, the Code of Practice on the Prevention and Eradication of Sexual Harassment in the Workplace 1999 served as guidelines.

By virtue of the new Part XVA of the Employment Act 1955 (inserted *vide* the amendments in 2012), employers now have a duty to act. An employer is liable to a fine not exceeding RM10,000 if he fails to conduct an inquiry into a complaint of sexual harassment, or inform the complainant why he refuses to conduct an inquiry, or conduct any inquiry when directed to do so by the Director General of Labour, or submit a report of inquiry to the Director General.

Briefly, a complaint of sexual harassment includes that made by an employee against another employee, an employee against any employer, and an employer against an employee[28]. Sexual harassment has been defined as "any unwanted conduct of a sexual nature, whether verbal, non-verbal, visual, gestural or physical, directed at a person which is offensive or humiliating or is a threat to his well-being, arising out of and in the course of his employment"[29]. By virtue of Section 81G, the provisions on sexual harassment extend to every employee irrespective of their wages.

On receiving a complaint, an employer has to conduct an inquiry unless the complaint has previously been inquired into and no sexual harassment has been proven, or the employer is of the opinion that the complaint of sexual harassment is frivolous, vexatious or is not made in good faith[30]. If the employer refuses to hold an inquiry, he must inform the complainant of the refusal and the reasons for the refusal within 30 days of the complaint[31]. The complainant may then refer the matter to the Director General who may direct the employer to conduct an inquiry if he thinks the matter should be inquired into, or inform the complainant no further action will be taken if he agrees with the employer's decision not to hold an inquiry[32].

In respect of the action which may be taken by an employer, the amendments provide that where the employer has conducted an inquiry and is satisfied that sexual harassment is proven, the employer shall:

(a)   in the case where the person against whom the complaint is made is an employee, take disciplinary action which may include dismissing the employee without notice, downgrading the employee, or imposing any other lesser punishment as he deems just and fit, and where the punishment of suspension without wages is imposed, it shall not exceed a period of two weeks; and

(b)   in the case where the person against whom the complaint is made is a person other than an employee, recommend that the person be brought before an appropriate disciplinary authority to which the person is subject.

Quite apart from the above, a complainant may lodge a complaint directly with the Director General[33]. The Director General will then assess the complaint and may direct an employer to inquire into such complaint and submit a report to the Director General within 30 days[34].

If the complaint is made against the employer who is a sole proprietor, the Director General would conduct the inquiry[35], unless the complaint of sexual harassment has previously been inquired into by the Director General and no sexual harassment has been proven, or the Director General is of the opinion that the complaint of sexual harassment is frivolous, vexatious or is not made in good faith[36]. The Director General has to inform the complainant within 30 days[37] if he refuses to conduct an inquiry.

If the Director General decides that sexual harassment is proven against the employer who is a sole proprietor, the complainant may terminate his contract of service without notice and be entitled to termination benefits and wages as if the complainant has given the notice of the termination of contract of service.

These provisions however do not create a cause of action for sexual harassment, nor provide any monetary relief to the complainant for having suffered the sexual harassment. The Director General is also not empowered to award any relief to the complainant. Therefore, the complainant would have to resort to civil suit for damages.

Children and Young Persons (Employment) (Amendment) Act 2010

The Children and Young Persons (Employment) Act 1966 regulates the employment of children and young persons by restricting the type of work in which they may be engaged as well as limiting their hours of work and number of days of work.

Prior to the Children and Young Persons (Employment) (Amendment) Act 2010, "child" was defined as any person who has not completed his 14th year of age and "young person" as any person who, not being a child, has not completed his 16th year of age. Now, "child" is defined as any person who has not completed his 15th year of age, and "young person" as any person who, not being a child, has not completed his 18th year of age. The specific protection of child and young persons has thus been been extended.

National Wages Consultative Council Act 2011 and Minimum Wages

This Act repealed the Wages Council Act 1947 and dissolved all wages councils previously formed. The National Wages Consultative Council established under this Act is charged with the responsibility of studying minimum wages and making recommendations to the government on matters of minimum wages.

Pursuant to Section 23, where the government agrees with the recommendations of the council, the Minister of Human Resources will issue a minimum wages order stipulating the minimum wages rates, the coverage of the rates according to sectors, types of employment and regional areas, the non-application to any sectors, types of employment and regional areas or to any person or class of persons, and the commencement of the minimum wages order. Pursuant to Section 24, the rates stipulated in a minimum wages order will replace any lower rates of wages agreed in a contract of service between an employer and an employee.

Nevertheless, under Section 25, the council has the duty to review the minimum wages order at least once in every two years, and may on its own accord or upon the direction of the government, review the minimum wages order.

On 16 July 2012, the Minister of Human Resources issued the Minimum Wages Order 2012 fixing the minimum wages rates payable to an employee (except a domestic servant) as follows:

Regional Areas	Minimum wage rates	
	Hourly	Hourly
Peninsular Malaysia	RM900	RM4.33
Sabah, Sarawak and the Federal Territory of Labuan	RM800	RM3.85

In respect of probationary employees, the Order provides that the minimum wages rates may be reduced not more than 30% of the minimum wages rate and that the reduction is allowed only for the first 6 months of the probationary contract.

The Order will come into operation on 1 January 2013 in relation to an employer who employs more than five employees and an employer who carries out a professional activity[38] classified under the Malaysia Standard Classification of Occupations (MASCO) regardless of the number of employees employed. As for all other employers with five employees or less, the operational date is on 1 July 2013.

In this connection, an employer who fails to pay the basic wages *as per* the minimum wages order is liable to a fine of not more than RM10,000 for each employee[39]. The Court may further order the employer to pay the difference between the minimum wages rate and the basic wages paid by the employer to the employee[40].

Private Retirement Scheme

In Malaysia, it is a mandatory requirement that both employer and employee contribute to the Employees' Provident Fund[41], a government operated scheme of savings for employees' retirement.

Following the amendments to the Capital Markets and Services Act 2007, which came into operation on 3 October 2011, private retirement schemes are now permissible. It is part of the government's effort to develop the private pension industry. In contrast to the Employees' Provident Fund, this scheme is a voluntary retirement savings scheme structured and managed by private sector fund providers. Licensing and approval from the Securities Commission, however, is required.

Towards this end, the Securities Commission has issued the Capital Markets and Services (Private Retirement Scheme Industry) Regulations 2012 and the Guidelines on Private Retirement Schemes. On 6 April 2012, the Securities Commission announced the approval for eight Private Retirement Scheme Providers. And on 18 July 2012, the Private Retirement Administrator was established[42].

Private Sector Retirement Age

In the private sector, the retirement age has always been a matter of contract. That has changed with the Minimum Retirement Age Bill 2012 which was passed in Parliament on 28 June 2012. When in force[43], this piece of legislation will fix the retirement age of private sector employees at 60 years of age and an employer who *"prematurely retires an employee before the employee attains the minimum retirement age"*[44] is liable to a fine not exceeding RM10,000.

The minimum retirement age is not applicable to probationary employees, apprentices, non-citizen employees, domestic servants, part-time employees, students employed on a temporary term, employees on a 24-month fixed term contract of service and *"a person who, before the date of coming into operation of this Act, has retired at the age of 55 years or above and subsequently is re-employed after he has retired"*.[45]

Conclusion

The government's Economic Transformation Programme is expected to create more than three million jobs by 2020. Coupled with the coming liberalisation of services sectors, Malaysia will see more statutory reforms to Employment & Labour laws.

* * *

Endnotes

1. Employment (Amendment) 2012 came into operation on 1 April 2012.
2. Industrial Relations (Amendment) Act 2007 came into operation on 28 February 2008.
3. National Wages Consultative Council Act 2011 came into operation on 15 September 2011 and repealed the Wages Council Act 1947.
4. "No person shall be deprived of his life or personal liberty save in accordance with law"; and the Federal Court's decision in Sivarasa Rasiah v Badan Peguam Malaysia & anor [2010] 2 MLJ 333; also the Court of Appeal's decisions in Tan Tek Seng v Suruhanjaya Perkhidmatan Pendidikan & anor [1996] 1 MLJ 261 and Hong Leong Equipment Sdn Bhd v Liew Fook Chuan and another appeal [1996] 1 MLJ 481, and the Federal Court's decision in R Rama Chandran v The Industrial Court Of Malaysia & anor [1997] 1 MLJ 145.
5. Other Acts of Parliament which relate to employment are *inter alia* Employees Provident Fund Act 1991, Employees Social Security Act 1969, Workmen's Compensation Act 1952, Factories and Machinery Act 1967, Occupational Safety and Health Act 1994, Employment (Restriction) Act 1968, and Children and Young Persons (Employment) Act 1966.
6. Employment Act 1955 is applicable to West Malaysia and Federal Territory of Labuan. In East Malaysia, Labour Ordinance 1950 is applicable to the state of Sabah and Labour Ordinance 1952 to the state of Sarawak.
7. Section 69B of the Employment Act 1955.
8. Section 69A of the Employment Act 1955.
9. Section 20 of the Industrial Relations Act 1967.

10. Section 30(5) of the Industrial Relations Act 1967.
11. Dr David Vanniasingham Ramanathan v Subang Jaya Medical Centre Sdn Bhd [2007] 1 MLJ 713, Court of Appeal.
12. Viking Askim Sdn Bhd v National Union of Employees in Companies Manufacturing Rubber Products [1991] 2 MLJ 115 and Section 30 of the Industrial Relations Act 1967.
13. Subang Jaya Medical Centre Sdn Bhd v Dr David Vanniasingham Ramanathan [2012] Unreported.
14. Hoh Kiang Ngan v Mahkamah Perusahaan Malaysia [1995] 3 MLJ 369.
15. Hoh Kiang Ngan v Mahkamah Perusahaan Malaysia [1995] 3 MLJ 369, Assunta Hospital v Dr A Dutt [1981] MLJ 115, Dr A Dutt v Assunta Hospital [1981] MLJ 304 and Menteri Sumber Manusia v John Hancock Life Insurance (M) Bhd [2007] 1 CLJ 366.
16. Hoh Kiang Ngan v Mahkamah Perusahaan Malaysia [1995] 3 MLJ 369.
17. EPF Board v MS Ally & Co Ltd [1975] 2 MLJ 89, Federal Court.
18. Mary Colete John v South East Asia Insurance Bhd [2010] 2 MLJ 222, Court of Appeal affirmed in Mary Colete John v South East Asia Insurance Berhad [2010] 6 MLJ 773, Federal Court. This is a personal injury insurance case where the issue of employee or independent contractor arose.
19. Hoh Kiang Ngan v Mahkamah Perusahaan Malaysia [1995] 3 MLJ 369 and Mary Colete John v South East Asia Insurance Bhd [2010] 6 MLJ 733.
20. The fund established under the Employees' Provident Fund Act 1991.
21. The Social Security Organisation, commonly known as SOCSO, is the body established to enforce the Employees Social Security Act 1969. It operates the Employment Injury Insurance Scheme and Invalidity Pension Scheme.
22. Kuala Lumpur Mutual Fund Berhad v J Bastian Leo & Anor [1988] 2 MLJ 526 and Great Eastern Mills Bhd v Ng Yuen Ching & Ors [1998] 6 MLJ 214.
23. Income Tax (Deduction from Remuneration) Rules 1994 made under the Income Tax Act 1967 applicable to employment income.
24. Section 30(5) of the Industrial Relations Act 1967.
25. M. Vasagam Muthusamy v Kesatuan Pekerja-Pekerja Resorts World, Pahang & Anor [2005] 4 CLJ 93.
26. http://www.talentcorp.com.my; see also http://www.expats.com.my.
27. The preface to code of practice on the Prevention and eradication of Sexual harassment in the Workplace, Ministry of Human Resources.
28. Section 81A of the Employment Act 1955.
29. Section 2.
30. Section 81B(3).
31. Section 81B(1) and (2).
32. Section 81B(4) and (5).
33. Section 81D(1).
34. Section 81D(2).
35. Section 81D(3).
36. Section 81D(4) and (5).
37. Section 81D(6).
38. Science And Engineering Professionals, Health Professionals, Teaching Professionals, Business And Administration Professionals, Information And Communications Technology Professionals, Legal, Social And Cultural Professionals, Hospitality, and Retail And Services Professionals (see http://www.mohr.gov.my/MAJOR_GROUP_2.pdf).
39. Section 43 of the National Wages Consultative Council Act 2011.
40. Section 44.
41. The fund established under the Employees' Provident Fund Act 1991.
42. News articles of 18 July 2012 and 19 July 2012 at thestar.com.my.
43. This legislation will come into force on a date appointed by the Minister of Human Resources.
44. Clause 5 of the Minimum Retirement Age Bill 2012.
45. Schedule to the Minimum Retirement Age Bill 2012.

Teh Eng Lay
Tel: +603 6203 6918 / Email: Englay@ctslawyers.com.my
Mr Teh Eng Lay was admitted as an Advocate & Solicitor of the High Court of Malaya in 2001. He regularly appears before the Industrial Court and the High Court of Malaya and also as junior counsel in the Court of Appeal and the Federal Court of Malaysia. He handles a variety of litigation cases involving matters on employment and industrial relations, administrative and public law, land transactions and contractual disputes.

Cheah Teh & Su

L-3-1, No. 2 Jalan Solaris, Solaris Mont' Kiara, 50480 Kuala Lumpur, Malaysia
Tel: +603 6203 6918 / Fax: +603 6203 6928 / URL: http://www.ctslawyers.com.my

Morocco

Amin Hajji
Hajji & Associés

General labour market trends and latest/likely trends in employment litigation

The recent Moroccan labour law of 11th September 2003, organised as a code together with its implementing decrees, has definitively modernised and simplified the rules governing the relationship between employers and their employees. This law has already maintained a very favourable social protection to employees and Moroccan case law has confirmed at length that the applicable law provides good protection to employees.

Along with Moroccan labour law, social security regulation is part of the applicable law governing the relationship between employers and employees. The Social Security Law of 31st December 1959 aims at guaranteeing employees' pensions and cover against disability, medical expenses and/or any harm incurred by the employee during his duty and/or any career illnesses.

Generally, employment contracts must be in writing but they can be entered orally, except when the contract is for a fixed term, or part-time. Indeed, oral fixed-term contracts and oral part-time contracts are categorically deemed to be indefinite-term contracts. Definite-term contracts can occur only if they are required for substitution of an employee by another in case of suspension of contract of employment, or if there is a temporary increase of the company's activity, or if the proposed work of the candidate has a seasonal character. Part-time employees can be hired for a maximum of 6 months, non-renewably. Nevertheless, the part-time employment contract, which must necessarily be in a written form, should specify respectively the reason justifying part-time hiring, the term of the employment task, the amount of the salary, and the salary payment mode, together with the probationary period if any.

Moreover, the new Moroccan constitution of July 2011 and the applicable labour law strictly prohibits discrimination on the basis of country of origin, name, political opinions, trade union activities, ethnic group, race, religion, health, sex or family situation of the persons and of the employees. Discrimination is a criminal offence subject to judicial sanctions.

The employment contract may provide for various covenants such as non-compete and confidentiality clauses. Specifically, the non-compete clause should take into consideration the particularities of the job position of the employee concerned, but it should be limited both geographically and in time. Moroccan case law considers that two years is the maximum limit of a non-compete clause, and no financial compensation is necessary to enter into such a covenant. The employer is free to consider confidentiality clauses.

Among other responsibilities, employers must inform employees about any changes to terms and conditions relating to the collective labour rules, the measures concerning health and security, mandatory membership of the national health and pensions organisation, and the name of the insurance company covering employees against work injury and occupational diseases.

It should be noted that a recent personal data protection law of 18 February 2009 has been published and come into force, and is applicable to employers, who must comply with said employees' data protection law.

In addition, should an employee be in trouble with his employer or if his employment is terminated, he may at no judicial cost file a claim against his employer before his residency judicial court near his residence. Thus, Moroccan courts are overloaded with often tendentious social cases necessarily ruled by the courts until final judgement. Hopefully, recent labour law has put an end to the previous court's discretionary power in awarding at-discretion damages to dismissed employees. The maximum amount of damages cannot exceed 1.5 months' net salary per year of service capped to 36 months, regardless of the number of years of the employee's service with their employer.

Besides, the labour law regulates for the first time the temporary employment agencies whose employees are very often hired on a long-term basis, mainly with corporations, but in full breach of related applicable law.

Generally, the new labour law as practised for nearly ten years as of today, has clarified a number of unpredictable and risky situations to employers. Specifically, it states in one document a code for precise figures as to an employee's probationary period, notice period, compensation for supplementary worked hours, annual leave, severance and damages if any. Indeed, an investor starting its business and hiring employees may calculate in advance the legal risk and related financial exposure it faces for any possible future reorganisation of its business, or when deciding its closure.

Key case law affecting employers' decision making over dismissal, redundancies dismissals etc.

Moroccan courts are very formalistic toward the enforcement or even interpretation of the applicable labour law. For example, when an employer decides to terminate an employee for a serious fault such as theft, fraud, drunkenness, insulting behaviour, etc. it cannot take such a decision without summoning the disorderly employee to a meeting in order to give him a chance to argue with or challenge such a serious charge, in the presence of the employee's representative. Should such a meeting not be held, the court would consider the termination as abusive and the dismissed employee would be entitled to full compensation including severance and a separation amount.

It should be noted that the role of the labour authority has become much more constructive, specifically when an employment relationship is close to being terminated but with some dispute between employer and employee about the compensation to be paid. Here, the law authorises the competent labour authority to undertake a conciliation between employer and employee and, if successful, to settle under minutes duly executed by both parties as a final and binding decision, for the termination amount to be paid to the employee. Such a conciliation will close for good the employment relationship, removing all possible claims the employee may file before the courts.

Furthermore, redundancies are generally characterised by employees, labour authority and courts as termination with no cause, and they generally proceed to full compensation of the terminated employees. There are indeed very few situations where local authorities approve when informed about such a large economic pay off. Here again, economic issues are subordinated to the social side of the situation.

With respect to employers who notify newly hired employees about their required compliance with the company's code of conduct, such a document being in digital or in hard copy, it must be executed and duly accepted without any reservation by the employees, with periodic renewal of the same procedure when the code is amended. Unfortunately, Moroccan courts do not consider breach of the said code of conduct provisions as a serious fault, and they rather generally focus on article 39 of the labour law. This states a list of serious faults which may lead to the termination of an employee without any compensation, and on the same law's article 36 which provides for the non-valid grounds for dismissal.

In conclusion, the internal dismissal process is very precise and formal and the employer should comply with all of its details – for example, the termination of a general manager of a company being simultaneously an employee and a legal representative with the employing company, cannot be decided with a simple revocation of the manager's social mandate. Such a partial decision will give full rights to the former general manager but, while he remains an employee of the company, full rights to compensation based on an abusive termination of his employment contract.

Recent statutory or legislative changes

No statutory or legislative changes are foreseen at the date of this chapter. The main general project relates to the implementation of a national programme giving minimum revenues to unemployed persons having lost their jobs, and free medical care named "RAMED" to persons with financial difficulties.

Likely or impending reforms to employment legislation and enforcement procedures

After nearly ten years of existence and practice of the law, it is very likely that the Moroccan government shall undertake the lifting of the Moroccan Labour Law which is often considered by investors as a considerable risk to their business and sometimes unfair to their interests. The new trend, embodied by the development of temporary employment agencies, is to give much flexibility to employers to adapt their human resources to the evolution of their business. The right to employment for life has evaporated and the evolution of the modern workplace requires rapid adaptation by young workers. Therefore, such new economical, social and technological trends imply a need to change applicable labour laws in order to comply with the new challenges, giving as much protection as possible to the employees.

Amin Hajji
Tel: +212 522 48 74 74 / Email: a.hajji@ahlo.ma
Education: Juris doctor in Law, Faculty of Law. University Hassan II - Casablanca.
Postgraduate Doctorate in Law, Faculty of Law & Economics of Toulouse - France.
Professional Career: Professor at the Faculty of Law of Casablanca: doctoral studies
in international commercial law and business law.
Associative & Scientific Activities: Founder member of the Moroccan Association of
business lawyers. Acting Chair of the ICC Morocco Commission on Law and Practice.
Working Languages: Arabic, English and French.

Hajji & Associés

28 Bld Moulay Youssef, Casablanca, Morocco
Tel: +212 522 48 74 74 / Fax: +212 522 48 74 75 / URL: http://www.ahlo.ma

Portugal

Rita Garcia Pereira
Garcia Pereira SP

Portugal Labour Law System

Portugal has been notable, for several years, for its alleged lack of flexibility in the employment law system, notably because of the legal situation on dismissals. This apparent rigidity has been accompanied by a very deficient efficacy of the rules, especially within companies, as the majority of the lawsuits exemplify. The most flagrant examples are individual or mass dismissals, the economic fundamentals of which usually are not judicially controlled, while short-term contracts, although exceptional according to law, are an ordinary practice all over the country and faced by employees like a trial period.

Therefore, the practice in Portugal is very different from the theory, depending on the rules in force. The recent reforms have increased flexibility in areas like schedules, dismissal procedures and supplementary working time, for example. The main idea is to increase employment by reducing costs.

Nevertheless, there are several sources governing employment relations in Portugal.

Besides the international and European laws (like the Treaty of Rome and the European Social Charter), as a Member of the European Union, Portugal has a labour law system which is similar to those of its Community partners, particularly those in Southern Europe, in terms of both its structure and solutions. Note that Portugal's membership of the EU led to the incorporation of European Rulings and Directives with regard to labour relations, which apply generally throughout the EU. As Portugal belongs to the ILO (International Labour Organization) its conventions are indirectly applicable, as they provide guidelines regarding employment relations. On another side, Portugal has also concluded numerous bilateral treaties regarding social security, not only with the European Union Members but also with other countries all over the world.

At a national level, the highest source is the Portuguese Constitution, stating a certain number of basic principles and dedicating an entire chapter to the rights and guarantees of workers. The Portuguese Constitution establishes, for example, the right to labour and security in employment, so that dismissal without fair cause is forbidden all over the country, and that is the basic principle in labour relations.

Although the primary legal source of Labour Law in Portugal is the Labour Code, which was progressively amended in 2009 (by Law no. 7/2009, of 12th February), in 2011 (by Law no. 54/2011, of 14th October) and in 2012 (by Law no. 3/2012, of 10th January and by Law no. 23/2012, of 25th June, which was rectified by the Declaration, of 23rd July), modifying most essential aspects of the law then in force (Law no. 99/2003). Before 2003, the legal rules were dispersed in several documents, some of them from 1969.

In addition to the law referred to above, there are also regulations, which govern labour activities. Amongst these, the most important are collective instruments (collective bargaining agreements, adhesion agreements and arbitration awards in voluntary arbitration proceedings). The most common of these are collective agreements, which are contracts made between trade unions and employers' associations, the purpose of which is to regulate employment within the sectors in question. The law also provides for company agreements, which are agreements made between a trade union and the employer with regard to a single enterprise or establishment. These are very detailed and deal with almost all foreseeable situations, and prevail over the parties' intentions. Sometimes, this kind of regulation is extended to all companies by a Government act, stipulating, for example, the minimum wage for that activity or sector or alterations to the maximum duration of working time. The individual contract and its uses in companies are also recognised sources, since they don't contradict the highest source, such as the imperative legal rules. The Portuguese Labour Code establishes many imperative rules, like the amount of the dismissal compensation, the personality rights and the situations that allow term contracts.

Some of the values and rights present in, and still actively defended by, the Portuguese labour laws, are: the protection of employees, such as in the event of illness, work accident, bullying or 'mobbing', and from discrimination on the grounds of age, gender or race; equal opportunities; maternity rights and the right to vocational training; and the participation of employee representatives in the life of the company, or in the definition of the general rules governing economic activity in Portugal.

The principal institutions concerning Labour Law are:
1. Labour Inspection Services (ACT), which is the entity responsible for promoting the improvement of labour conditions, the professional risks prevention and also to monitor compliance with the legal rights of employees; every private employee has the possibility to access information and to denounce any irregularity committed by a company.
2. Commission for Equality at Work and on Employment (CITE), which is responsible for promoting equality and non-discrimination and protection of maternity and paternity rights. This institution has a very important role in the dismissal of pregnant employees because it has to expressly agree with the measure.
3. Economy, Innovation and Development Ministry, which is the government department responsible for the definition, orientation and practice of the labour and employment politics and social security. It also has an important role in collective dismissals, since it is mandatory to participate in the information and negotiation phase.
4. Labour courts, where employment rights and obligations are enforced. The social section of the Court of Appeal is the second degree and, depending on the type of lawsuit and the amount in discussion, there may be a third degree by the Supreme Court of Justice.

All these solutions will only be potentially applicable if the person in the case is considered a subordinated worker, and not if he is self-employed. Nevertheless, the designation that both parties gave to the contract is immaterial, because Portuguese Law determines that, if the requirements are fulfilled, the relationship will be qualified as a labour one, even if both parties agree it is not.

So, Portuguese law assumes that the professional has an employment contract if:
1. The activity is performed on premises pertaining to the beneficiary or determined by him.
2. The working tools used pertain to the beneficiary.
3. The professional respects a schedule determined by the beneficiary.
4. The amount paid is fixed and regular.

Depending on the nature of the relationship, there are different obligations and rights for both parties, especially for the purposes of social security (the hiring party doesn't have to pay contributions for independent contractors) and when it comes to ending the relationship. In fact, the terminating of an independent contract is very simple. By contrast, Portugal has very strict rules for terminating employment relationships. However, that distinction is, most of the time, only theoretical since many so-called independent contractors, after the termination, sue the companies, alleging they had an employment relationship, with the aim of increasing the amount that the employer has to spend to dismiss an employment contract and the payment of the grants. Recently the courts have enlarged the concept of employee, allowing the qualification to lawyers and others engaged in legal activities.

Regarding types of contracts, the general rule is that employment contracts must be made for an indefinite period (and in this case, a verbal basis is legally accepted) but that rule has diverse exceptions – there is certain information that must be provided in written form, even when the contract is oral. It's common that, although it's not mandatory, contracts are written and include clauses on confidential duties, non-competition and intellectual property rights, besides the legal information.

Accordingly, employment contracts made for a term must be in writing and justified, otherwise the employee is considered permanent.

Short-term employment contracts may only be used in order to meet a temporary need and must terminate as soon as the need in question has been met. The duration of the employment relationship is limited and the contract is subject to a term that can be fixed or uncertain. The relevant circumstances are legally specified and are related to the replacement of an employee, seasonal work, exceptional increases in activity, occasional work, launch of a new activity of uncertain duration, beginning of operations by a company with fewer than 750 employees, and the hiring of workers seeking their first employment, or who are long-term unemployed, or such circumstances as are provided in special employment policy legislation.

In the meantime it is legal to maintain a contract subject to a term that is variable, depending on the basis used, but generally it stays at 3 years and, till 30th June 2013, an extra 18 months. When the maximum duration is exceeded, the consequence is that the employee is considered as permanent – as he will become too if the reason cited in the contract is not real.

On another side, an employment contract remains in force indefinitely until the event or purpose for which it was made, such as the return to work of an absent employee, or the conclusion of the activity for which an employee has been hired. An employment contract for an unspecified term is converted into a contract for an indefinite period whenever the employment of the employee continues for more than 15 days after the end of the term.

Another type of relationship that is possible is intermittent employment contracts (non-continuous work), which presume that the company carries on its business intermittently or with variable intensity, and should also take written form.

Firms that hire according to Portuguese Law may also choose the temporary employment contract, which is an employment contract for a fixed or unspecified term, made between a temporary employment company and a worker, whereby the latter agrees to work, for payment, for third parties, while remaining in the employment of the temporary employment company.

Portuguese Labour Law also admits an e-work employment contract, which involves the employee working away from the enterprise's premises, via recourse to information and communication technologies.

For directors and other leading posts, it is possible to make a service commission agreement, which simply ends with the payment of a compensatory amount, by unilateral decision of the company. If both parties agree on that, they can also celebrate a promise of employment contract, which is often used for foreign people so they can be legalised. That contract obliges the future employer and employee to celebrate a definitive contract but the only consequence for infringement is the payment of compensation.

Apart from the concrete type of contract chosen, the laws and the conventional instruments also provide for a trial period during which the parties may freely rescind the employment contract, without any entitlement or compensation. The length of the trial period varies according to the type of contract. In contracts for an indefinite period, the trial period can vary between 90 and 180 days, depending on the complexity of the task: in the case of management positions and senior staff, it can be as long as 240 days. In the case of fixed term contracts with a term of less than 6 months, or contracts for an unspecified term with a duration that does not exceed 6 months, the trial period is 15 days. This period is 30 days if the term or duration is 6 months or more.

During the contract, if an employee breaches his contractual duties, the employer may take disciplinary action, in what represents a formal procedure. Portuguese law allows the following sanctions: warning; registered warning; payment of a fine; loss of vacation days; suspension from work, with loss of payment and of seniority; and dismissal without compensation.

Regarding the end of the labour relation, employment contracts can terminate by reason of lapse of time, revocation, dismissal or termination on notice.

Employment contracts lapse, on the expiry of the corresponding contractual term, if performance of the contract by the employer, or the employee, is impossible, or when the employee retires; and terminate by agreement between the parties (revocation); or by reason of dismissal (with just cause, on the grounds of mass or individual redundancy, or by reason of the unsuitability of the employee); they also lapse at the instigation of the employee (rescission) and finally, on termination by the employee on notice, in accordance with the provisions of the law.

The law imposes some restrictions on the termination of employment contracts, which include minimum notice periods with regard to dismissal, after the legal procedure.

In the case of fixed term contracts, at least 8 or 15 days' prior notice of termination must be given in writing to the employee, depending on the duration of the contract. Regarding contracts for an uncertain term, the prior notice period varies between 7, 30 and 60 days, depending on whether the duration of the contract is six months, more than six months and less than two years, or more than two years.

The contracts for an indefinite period can only be unilaterally terminated by the employer by the invocation of fair cause, namely by inadmissible behaviour or mass or individual redundancy.

Dismissal with fair cause must be preceded by a special procedure, termed disciplinary proceedings. The final result of the said proceedings can be contested in court by the employee.

No compensation is payable in the event of this dismissal but if the employee wins the litigation, the court will order the employer to pay compensation between 15 and 45 days of wage per year of seniority.

Mass or individual redundancy also obliges a special procedure and the payment of an amount, depending on the seniority and the wage. The mass redundancy procedure counts with the mandatory intervention of the Government Department; as in the individual case, that intervention depends on the employee request. Those redundancies must occur on the grounds of definitive closure of the company, or closure of one or more departments or be based on structural, technological or market reasons. In the collective dismissal, after the initial communication from the employer, a phase of information and negotiation takes place, with the aim of obtaining an agreement as to the scale and effects of the measures to be adopted and also alternative solutions, notably work suspension, professional requalification and early retirement. This phase requires the presence of a member of the Government Department, who will assure that all proceedings have been respected.

According to Portuguese law, certain categories of employee benefit from specific protection concerning dismissal: pregnant employees if they had previously notified the pregnancy, and up to one year after the birth (CITE must be consulted before the dismissal); and employees that belong or had belonged within three years to union associations.

If the employer fails any procedure or the reasons that were indicated are false, the legal consequence is that the dismissal is unfair. When a dismissal is considered unfair, the employer may be obliged to reinstate the employees covered, or the employee may also choose to be compensated for an amount between 15 days and 45 days of basic salary per year of seniority.

Forthcoming legislation

Law no. 23/2012 of June 25, which only came into force on 1st August 2012, introduced several changes to the Portuguese Labour Law and is applicable to old contracts.

This law, like the preceding alterations, is intended to honour the agreement between the IMF, the ECB, the European Commission and the Portuguese Government and implements, in accordance with the agreed schedule, several of the measures foreseen in the MEFP and MoU, including: (i) working time arrangements; (ii) reduction of additional pay for overtime; (iii) reduction of compulsory holidays and elimination of the possibility to have three additional vacation days based on the amount of absence; (iv) revision of the legal framework on reduction/suspension of the employment contract due to the economic crisis, turning it into a more flexible procedure; (v) elimination of the need to follow a specific order of dismissal in case of redundancy of employment position / allow dismissal based on unsuitability even without the introduction of a new technology; and (vi) reduction of the amount due by the employer in case of termination of the employment contract.

In fact, this law reduced the costs for employees as they also made workers' rights more fluid. The most important are:

- When an indefinite-period contract is ended by the employer, the employee is entitled to payment corresponding to 20 days of one month of base salary and seniority payments for each full year (this rule is applicable to older contracts, but the amount to which the employee is entitled due to previous seniority is preserved). This compensation is calculated according to the following criteria:
  (i)   Monthly salary and seniority cannot exceed more than 20 x the minimum wage per year.
  (ii) The total amount of the compensation cannot be higher than 12 times the monthly base salary and seniority or, if the limit above is applicable, 240 times the minimum wage.
  (iii) The daily amount of base salary corresponds to a 30-day monthly salary.
  (iv) If there are fractions of a year, then the compensation has to be calculated on a proportional basis.

- The daily work period must be interrupted for a resting break of at least one hour and cannot exceed two hours. The employee cannot work more than five consecutive hours. If the daily work period is more than 10 hours then the employee cannot work more than six consecutive hours. It is also possible to submit an application to the Portuguese public entity responsible for working issues (ACT) asking for authorisation to reduce or completely exclude the resting break of the worker if he/she consents. The employer needs to prove that it is more favourable to the worker, or that it is justified by the specific activity carried out by him/her. If ACT does not respond within 30 days following the application, the employer can consider it authorised.

- There is no need to send the agreement on working hour exemptions to ACT.

- If the company is in operation during bank holidays and the employee has to work those days, he/she is entitled to an additional resting period corresponding to half of the hours they worked, or to an additional 50% of the daily salary. It is the employer who decides whether to give an additional resting period or pay 50% of the daily pay rate.

- Bonuses for employees based on their attendance of one to three holiday days have ceased, so the normal period of holidays is 22 days. Besides those economic issues, the reasons for dismissal are extended. For example, in the individual dismissal the employer may select the employee not only respecting his seniority but also his productivity and the impediment of not having another job as reason to dismiss an employee has disappeared. This reform was (and still is) very contested because it decreased employees' rights, notably the compensation but also other factors like the schedule and the advantages concerning seniority.

Court Decisions

Every legal action concerning employment must be decided at Labour Courts or at mediation services, although this last avenue is not often used. There are Labour Courts in the most important cities and the Labour Process Code has been reformed in 2009, so that the main processes now are more rapid and simple. If the employee is dismissed in writing, the term to sue the employer is 60 days (previously it was a year). The normal duration of a court action depends on its complexity and which Court is chosen by the employee (he can choose the nearest Court of his residence or the employer domicile).

In this section we quote some of the most recent decisions of Labour Portuguese Courts about general aspects of employment law. Note that as the Labour Code was recently changed, there aren't court decisions about the new legal solutions.

Fixed-term employment contracts: interpretation of the notion of "same labour post" – Supreme Court, P. 539/07.7TTVFR.P1.S1 (10-03-2011)

In addition to the typical full-time or indefinite employment contracts, PLC allows fixed-term contracts to meet enterprises' transitory needs, albeit only for the period of time necessary to comply with those specific needs (Articles 139 to 149 of PLC). Under Portuguese law, the term 'employment contract' is considered an exception to the principle of stability and continuity of the employment relationship. Thus, fixed-term employment contracts may only be entered into under certain grounds expressly provided for by law. These grounds are generally related to situations that are transitory and/or unpredictable (such as the replacement of a sick employee, sudden increase in work, etc.). According to PLC, *"fixed-term employment contracts"* may be entered into for a *"fixed term"* (i.e., for a specific period) or for an *"unfixed term"* (i.e., for the completion of a specific task or the occurrence of a specific event). Given its exceptional nature and to prevent abuse, immediate and successive fixed-term employment contracts are prohibited and only permissible in exceptional cases. According to Article 143 of PLC, the termination of a fixed-term employment contract, as a rule, prevents a new allocation of work to the *"same labour post"* for more than a period equivalent to one third of the duration of the contract, including renewals. In its decision, the Supreme Court clarified the meaning of *"same labour post"* which is not the equivalent of *"the same functions"*. It is, therefore, possible for an employee to perform *functions identical to those previously performed* under a new fixed-term employment contract, provided that they correspond to a new labour post, for example, when the employee initially substitutes another who is on leave and subsequently substitutes another employee who is on vacation, although performing the same activity in both cases.

Undertaking of enterprise – Lisbon Court of Appeal decision of 9 May 2012 – P. 423/10.7TTBRR.L1-4

Acquired Rights Directive (2001/23/EC) (hereinafter "Directive") is transposed into the Portuguese Labour Code in Articles 285 to 287; in a nutshell, Articles 1 and 3(1) of the Directive correspond to Article 285 of PLC (particularly, paragraphs 1, 3 and 5). Accordingly, in the event of an assignment, by any means or form, of ownership of an enterprise or undertaking or part of an enterprise or undertaking, which represents an economic unit, the acquirer assumes the legal position of the employer in the existent employment contracts (paragraph 1); this regime also applies to the assignment, transfer or return of the economic operation of an enterprise, undertaking or economic unit (No. 3). Finally, according to No. 5, for this purpose, an economic unit is a group of organised means with the objective of pursuing a central or ancillary economic activity. In the present case, the Lisbon Court of Appeal held that according to the Directive and ECJ case law, the canteen of a nursery, whose operation was handed over by its owner ("A") to a services provider ("B"), and which the parties qualified as an undertaking, shall be considered an economic unit for the purposes of Article 285 (5) of PLC; accordingly, the ending of the operation of the canteen by the company providing the service, passing it to its respective holder ("A") constitutes a reversion/return with the consequences set forth in the transfer of undertaking of the legal regime (namely, the transfer to "A" of the employment contracts formerly entered into by "B").

Contract of employment vs. services agreement (09-05-2012) – Lisbon Court of Appeal decision of 9 May 2012 – P. 4522/09.0TTLSB.L1-4

Article 11 of PLC (the Portuguese Labour Code) defines an employment contract as an agreement "in which a natural person undertakes, upon remuneration, to provide an activity for another or for others, within an organisation and under its authority". The indirect reference to legal subordination ("under its authority") implies that this is the main criterion distinguishing an employment contract from other similar contracts: if proved, an employment contract is defined without further investigation; Portuguese courts apply the "facts index" system (judge-determined basis). According to this system, each element is only approximate and does not automatically provide an accurate and definitive qualification. Thus, Portuguese courts make an overall assessment of all verified elements: balancing their overall relevance, it is possible to arrive at a conclusion about the contract's legal qualification. In Case 4522/09.0TTLSB. L1-4, the facts considered by the Lisbon Court of Appeal can be summarised as follows: for more than 20 years, architect "A" performed functions on "B"'s premises; (i) "A" never signed "B"'s time sheets, which was mandatory for all employees; (ii) "A" performed a similar activity for other entities; (iii) "A" opened, for a brief period, his own office together with other architects; and (iv) "A" declined "B"'s proposal of including "A" as an employee for social security purposes. Given these elements and in light of the above, the Lisbon Court of Appeal ruled that there were no relevant indications of the existence of an employment contract; in fact, according to PLC, there are certain professions (doctors, lawyers, engineers, architects, designers, etc.) who are traditionally regarded as performing "liberal activities" independently, without legal subordination.

Exemption from a work schedule (*"isenção de horário de trabalho"*) and amount due for overtime – Supreme Court – P. 407/08.5TTMTS.P1.S1 (23-05-2012)

Under Article 218 of PLC, employers may seek an exemption from a work schedule for employees:
* who occupy managerial or supervisory functions; positions of trust; who assist these employees;
* whose jobs entail preparatory or complementary operations, which by their nature can only be performed beyond the normal working hours;
* who regularly perform their functions outside the establishment, not under the direct control of management; and
* who are telework employees (collective regulation instruments may foresee additional situations, where this exemption is included).

PLC foresees three different modalities for exemption from a work schedule (Article 219):
* the employee is not subject to the statutory maximum working hours;
* possibility of an increase of working hours per day or per week; and/or
* the employee is subject to the maximum working hours agreed.

The exemptions (of all kind) must be based on agreements with the employee and entitle him/her to a special allowance, between 1 hour of overtime per day and 2 hours of overtime pay per week (depending upon the kind of exemption agreed – i.e., "A", "B" or "C"), unless collectively agreed otherwise (Article 265 PLC). The entitlement to a special allowance may be relinquished by employees occupying managerial posts.

In all these cases the employee is entitled to the weekly rest period (mandatory or complementary), to public holidays and to daily rest (Article 219, no. 3 of PLC); Article 226, no. 3, a) of the PLC foresees that the work performed by an employee exempt from a timetable in a normal working day shall not be considered as overtime work. An exception is made for the modalities "B" and "C" described above – in these cases, the work performed beyond the agreed hours per day/per week is considered overtime work (Article 226, No. 2 of PLC).

In the judicial decision under review, the employee argued that despite being exempt from a timetable under modality "A" (i.e., not subject to the maximum working hours), the statutory maximum limits for overtime work should also be applicable in this case and that the number of hours worked beyond these limits should have therefore qualified as overtime work and be remunerated accordingly (the maximum limits are referred to in Article 228 of PLC).

In this regard, the employee argued that the Supreme Court had already decided in this sense.

However, a different understanding was applied by the Supreme Court in other judgments, namely in a decision of 16 December 2010 – P. 1806/07.5TTPRT.P1.S1- (available at www.dgsi.pt – Portuguese version).

Given the contradictory decisions, the Supreme Court concluded that the problem had to be addressed and its understanding standardised. In light of the above, it considered that an employee exempt from a timetable under modality "A" is not entitled to extra remuneration for the hours worked beyond the maximum limits foreseen for overtime work. Abusive employer behaviour (when an excessive number of hours is requested from the exempted employee) shall be penalised, but the work performed shall not be considered overtime work.

Source: Supreme Court of Justice' decision of May 23, 2012 – P. 407/08.5TTMTS.P1.S1– published on 25 June in the Official Gazette (http://dre.pt/pdf1sdip/2012/06/12100/0319703211.pdf – Portuguese version).

Conclusion

Currently, Portugal has a modern Labour Law System, considerably simplified since 1st August. Nevertheless, if you want to hire according to Portuguese Law, it's still better to ask for advice from a labour specialist.

Rita Garcia Pereira
Tel: +351 21 358 23 85 / Email: ritagarciapereira@gmail.com
Rita Garcia Pereira has been admitted to a PhD in Labour Law at the Faculty of Law of Lisbon University since 2009 and was a Professor at the Bar Association in 2009. She is a Lecturer in Post-Graduate Courses in Labour Law at the Faculty of Law of Lisbon University and the Faculty of Law of Coimbra University, a Master in Labour Law from the Faculty of Law of the Portuguese Catholic University in 2007 and a Lecturer at Seminars and Academic Conferences. She has been an Associate at Garcia Pereira & Associates since 2002 and Vowel secretary of Lisbon Council of Portugal Bar Association since 2011.

Garcia Pereira SP

Avenida Miguel Bombarda 61,5º-D, 1050-161 LISBOA Lisboa, Portugal
Tel: +351 21 358 23 85 / Fax: +351 21 352 14 02

Slovenia

Barbara Korošec & Martin Šafar
Law firm Šafar & Partners, Ltd

Key case law affecting employers' decision making over dismissal, redundancies dismissals etc.

This chapter reviews the legal deadlines in procedures for employment contract termination by an employer, with a special emphasis on categories of employees under special protection against employment termination (older employees, pregnant employees, parents, breast-feeding employees and disabled employees).

In the Republic of Slovenia, labour relations, including special rights enjoyed by older employees, pregnant employees, parents on parental leave, breast-feeding employees and disabled employees, are regulated by: the Employment Relationships Act (Official Gazette of the RS, nos. 42/2002, 79/2006, 103/2007, 45/2008 and 83/2009, hereinafter: the ERA), which is a general legal act; the Pension and Disability Insurance Act (Official Gazette of the RS, nos. 106/1999, 72/2000, 81/2000-ZPSV-C, 124/2000, 109/2001, 83/2002 Dec. of the CC: U-I-178/02-14, 108/2002, 110/2002-ZISDU-1, 112/2002 Order of the CC: U-I-307/98-38, 26/2003-offic. cons. copy, 40/2003 Dec. of the CC: U-I-273/00-13, 63/2003, 63/2003 Dec. of the CC: U-I-57/00-51, 133/2003 Dec. of the CC: U-I-36/00-52, 135/2003, 2/2004-ZDSS-1 (10/2004 amend.), 20/2004-offic. cons. copy 2, 54/2004-ZDoh-1 (56/2004 amend., 62/2004 amend., 63/2004 amend.), 63/2004-ZZRZI, 136/2004 Dec. of the CC: U-I-273/01-21, 68/2005 Dec. of the CC: U-I-29/04-19, 72/2005, 104/2005-offic. cons. copy 3, 69/2006, 109/2006-offic. cons. copy 4, 112/2006 Dec. of the CC: U-I-358/04-13, 114/2006-ZUTPG, 91/2007 Order of the CC: U-I-325/05-5, 10/2008-ZVarDod, 98/2009-ZIUZGK, 27/2010 Dec. of the CC: U-I-40/09-15, 38/2010-ZUKN, 61/2010-ZSVarPre, 79/2010-ZPKDPIZ, 94/2010-ZIU, 84/2011 Dec. of the CC: U-I-245/10-13, U-I-181/10-6, Up-1002/10-7, 94/2011 Dec. of the CC: U-I-287/10-11, 105/2011, 110/2011-ZDIU12, hereinafter: the ZPIZ-1); and the Occupational Rehabilitation and Employment of Disabled Persons Act (Official Gazette of the RS, nos. 63/2004, 72/2005, 100/2005-offic. cons. copy 1, 114/2006, 16/2007-offic. cons. copy 2, 14/2009 Dec. of the CC: U-I-36/06-18, 84/2011 Dec. of the CC: U-I-245/10-13, U-I-181/10-6, Up-1002/10-7, 87/2011, hereinafter: the ZZRZI). The employment relationships of employees employed at state authorities, local communities and institutions and at other organisations and private undertakings performing a public service are regulated by a special Civil Servants Act (Official Gazette of the RS, nos. 56/2002, 110/2002-ZDT-B, 2/2004-ZDSS-1 (10/2004 amend.), 23/2005, 35/2005-offic. cons. copy 1, 62/2005 Dec. of the CC: U-I-294/04-15, 113/2005, 21/2006 Dec. of the CC: U-I-343/04-11, 23/2006 Order of the CC: U-I-341/05-10, 32/2006-offic. cons. copy 2, 62/2006 Order of the CC: U-I-227/06-17, 131/2006 Dec. of the CC: U-I-227/06-27, 11/2007 Order of the CC: U-I-214/05-14, 33/2007, 63/2007-offic. cons. copy 3, 65/2008, 69/2008-ZTFI-A, 69/2008-ZZavar-E, 74/2009 Dec. of the CC: U-I-136/07-13, hereinafter: the ZJU), which, however, does not include the special provisions discussed by this document.

Slovenian labour legislation has been harmonised with its European counterpart and is subject to all ratified conventions; Council directives have already been integrated into the legislation.

Autonomous sources of law in the Republic of Slovenia are the collective agreements concluded for various industries that apply if an employer is a member of an association of employers' that are signatories of the collective agreement, if the collective agreement contains special provisions on application or if it has expanded application. Collective agreements usually specify employees' rights in broader and more detailed terms than an act.

The purpose of this document is to briefly present the procedures of employment contract termination by an employer, with a special emphasis on legally set deadlines applying to such procedures and the impact of these deadlines on termination of employment contracts of employees that belong to special protected categories of employees: older employees; pregnant employees; parents on parental leave in the form of full absence from work; breast-feeding employees; and disabled employees.

According to the currently applicable provisions of the ERA, an employer may terminate an employment contract for business reasons, due to an employee's occupational disability, for cause and due to disability. Extraordinary termination of an employment contract by an employer is possible in case of a severe breach of contractual and other obligations under the employment relationship and if, by taking into account all circumstances and interests of both contracting parties, it is not possible to continue the employment relationship until the expiration of the notice of termination or until the expiration of the period for which the employment contract was concluded.

An employer may terminate the employment contract only if there is a substantiated reason preventing further work under the terms and conditions of the employment contract. Before terminating the employment contract, the employer must check if it is possible to employ the employee under different conditions, for other work or if the employee could be up-skilled for the work they perform or retrained for a different position. If such a possibility exists, the employee should, along with the termination notice, be presented with a new employment contract for signing.

According to the ERA, special protection against termination is enjoyed by workers' representatives, older employees, parents, the disabled and employees on sick leave. This document focuses on employee categories (older employees, parents and the disabled) that enjoy special protection against termination under the ERA and other regulations in connection with the deadlines that the ERA specifies as preclusive periods within which the employer is obligated to conduct the procedures for termination of an employment contract.

Pursuant to Article 88 of the ERA, an employer must give notice of termination no later than within six months of a substantiated reason arising. In the event of termination for cause, an employer must give notice of termination no later than 60 days from identifying the substantiated reason and no later than six months from the substantiated reason arising. If the cause on the part of the employee has all the characteristics of a criminal offence, an employer may give notice of termination of the employment contract within 60 days of identifying just cause and, regarding the offender, for the entire period in which they may be subject to criminal prosecution.

I. Older employees

The act that was in force before the ERA distinguished between female and male older employees – a male employee was considered older when he reached 55, while for female employees, the age threshold was lower – 50 years. The new ERA will do away with this gender differentiation by gradually increasing the age threshold for female employees; the age threshold will become the same for male and female employees in 2014 (which means that positive discrimination in the Republic of Slovenia is permitted to protect older female employees in comparison with older male employees).

According to the original wording of the ERA, older employees enjoyed special protection against ordinary termination of employment contract for business reasons. Their employment contract could not be terminated (except if they gave special consent in writing) for business reasons until they fulfilled the minimum conditions for old-age pension, unless they were granted the right to monetary compensation deriving from unemployment insurance up until the fulfilment of the minimum conditions for old-age pension. Older employees did not enjoy special protection in case of the employer's winding-up. In all other cases of employment contract termination (for cause, due to occupational disability), older employees did not enjoy special protection against termination. In practice, that meant that if, due to business reasons, an employer could no longer provide work to an older employee (who has not yet acquired the right to old-age pension or was not assured the right to monetary compensation deriving from unemployment insurance) under an employment contract, they could not terminate the employment contract, and the fact that the employer had no work for the employee was legally irrelevant. Since the Act stipulated that an employer cannot terminate the employment contract of an older employee, the employer was not able to offer to an employee other appropriate work in the course of ordinary termination of the employment contract for business reasons, if such work was available. In line with the Pension and Disability Insurance Act, which stipulates conditions for old-age retirement of employees and lays down minimum conditions for retirement of employees, the minimum age of employees (both male and female) is set at 58 years, with male employees obligated to complete a pension qualifying period of 40 years and female employees a period of 38 years (both conditions have to be met cumulatively). As the age increases, the pension qualifying period decreases, but the figures speak for themselves. For a time, employers were unable to terminate employment contracts of older employees even if they had no work for them. If this matter could not be arranged with an employer consensually, the employer was left with only one option: to send the employee home, paying them salary compensation equalling the salary under the employment contract. Once the conditions under the ERA were met and an employer could terminate the employment contract of an older employee for business reasons, the objective period of six months stipulated in Article 88 of the ERA had already passed.

The supplements to the ERA introduced at the end of 2007 brought significant changes in this respect, as it is now possible to terminate an employment contract of an older employee even if the employer offers them appropriate new employment (according to the ERA, appropriate new employment shall be deemed to be employment for which the required type and the level of education are the same as were required for the performance of work for which the employee had the previous employment contract, and for working hours as were agreed under the previous employment contract, and where the location of the work is not at a distance of more than three hours' travel in both directions by public transport or through transport organised by the employer from the employee's place of residence). Without a doubt, this amendment to the ERA relieved employers of a great burden. It is thus more important in the general economic recession that the Republic of Slovenia is in.

II. Parents (protection of pregnant employees, parents on parental leave in the form of full absence from work and protection of breast-feeding employees)

Special protection against employment contract termination is enjoyed by employees during pregnancy and throughout the breast-feeding period and by parents (male and female) in the period when they are on parental leave in the form of full absence from work and for another month after taking such leave (according to the Parental Protection and Family Benefit Act of the Republic of Slovenia, parental leave lasts for 260 days, starting upon the expiry of maternity leave, which lasts for 105 days).

The scope of special protection of the above categories of employees is more extensive than the protection enjoyed by older employees, since during special protection the employment contract of the former cannot expire or be terminated by the employer, and in their case the ERA does not distinguish between employment contract termination for cause and other reasons. It can be concluded from the above that the employment contract and employment relationship of this category of employees can be terminated only if they choose to have it ordinarily terminated or if they agree with the employer on the termination of the employment contract. An employer may legally terminate an employment contract of this category of employees only by extraordinary termination or in the case of winding-up of the employer, subject to previous approval of a labour inspector. If an employment contract of an employee from the above category is unlawfully extraordinarily terminated, a subsequent approval of a labour inspector does not make it lawful.

Since the employer must give notice of termination no later than within six months of a substantiated reason arising and, in the event of termination for cause, no later than within 60 days from identifying just cause and no later than six months from just cause arising, it is obvious that an employer will not be able to lawfully terminate employment contracts of employees from the above category in the period set by the Act. In case of a legal dispute, the court would rule in favour of an employee's claim to repeal the termination of employment contract and find the termination of the employment relationship unlawful. The deadlines set by the Act for the procedure of ordinary or extraordinary termination of an employment contract are preclusive, meaning that even if legitimate grounds exist for the termination of the employment contract, the employer cannot carry out the termination procedure or, if they carry it out past the deadline anyway, the outcome in court would be unfavourable for them, because they failed to carry out the procedure by the prescribed deadline.

In the Republic of Slovenia, the definition of a breast-feeding and pregnant employee is regulated by the Rules on Protection of Health at Work of Pregnant Workers and Workers Who have Recently Given Birth and are Breastfeeding (Official Gazette of the RS, no. 82/2003). According to these Rules, a pregnant worker is a pregnant employee that has informed her employer of her condition by a medical certificate, and protection during pregnancy is deemed to last from the moment when the employer is informed of pregnancy until giving birth. A breast-feeding worker is deemed a breast-feeding employee that has informed her employer of her condition by a medical certificate. If, at the time of termination or during the notice period, the employer is not aware of the pregnancy of the female employee, the Act stipulates that special protection against termination shall apply if the female employee immediately or, in the case of obstacles arising through no fault of her own, immediately after the cessation of such obstacles, but not after the expiry of the notice period, informs the employer of her pregnancy, which shall be proven by submitting a medical certificate.

Since the most common method of employment contract termination is ordinary termination for business reasons, we will focus in this chapter primarily on this method of employment contract termination. Under the ERA, the reasons for ordinary termination of an employment contract for business reasons can be economic, organisational, technological, structural or of a similar nature. Given the situation and the recession present in the Slovenian economy, the most frequent cause of termination for business reasons is a change of work process that renders unnecessary the work for which the employee concluded the employment contract. In practice, the procedure for ordinary termination of employment contract for business reasons starts with changes in organisation and the adoption of a new job classification, with organisational decisions falling with the competence of the employer. Such a position was also adopted by the Supreme Court of the Republic of Slovenia (Judgment op. no. VIII Ips 246/2012 of 17 October 2011). If an employment contract is terminated for business reasons, the employer is obligated to prove justified business reasons, while the court does not review the reasonableness and rationality of a new organisational decision or reorganisation of work process that resulted in the abolishment of a position or type of work or which leads to downsizing of employees at a certain position as these fall in the sole competence of the employer's management. That is understandable, since the employer's management is responsible for operations and performance of the employer. Since the deadline by which the employer is obligated to issue notice of the employment contract termination for business reasons usually expires during the period of employee protection, the procedure that an employer would carry out after such a deadline would be unlawful and the employee's legal claim would be successful. Assuming that the reasons for employment contract termination for business reasons are justified, a question arises as to how to proceed in such a case and whether such legal regulation is appropriate, as it is necessary to point out that the law does not provide for a suspension of the deadline for employment contract termination during the period when an employee's employment contract and employment relationship cannot be terminated under the Act, which would allow the employer to finalise the procedure after the reasons for special protection of an employee have ceased.

Special attention has to be paid to the protection of breast-feeding mothers. During breast-feeding, employees enjoy special protection and their employment relationship cannot be terminated no matter how justified the reason, and the employer may not terminate their employment contract.

The question of duration of breast-feeding was highlighted in judicial disputes before Slovenian labour courts in relation to procedures of ordinary termination of an employment contract before parental leave has been used in full. The expert opinions of specialised paediatricians that submitted their expert opinion in these disputes indicate that the experts, the World Health Organization and Unicef, recommend that children up to 6 months of age be exclusively breastfed and that they continue to be breastfed, together with complementary feeding, until the age of two – or longer if the mother and father so desire, since the upper age is not limited. Breast-feeding after the age of two still represents an important source of nutrition, protecting a child from infections, and there is no evidence suggesting that breast-feeding after the age of two is harmful in psychological or developmental terms. The expert opinions also show that children aged from 2.5 to 7 even expect to be breastfed and that it is normal to abandon breast-feeding by the age of 7. Since the Act does not distinguish between protection in case of exclusive breast-feeding and supplementary breast-feeding after a child has reached 6 months of age, nor is such distinction made by case-law, special legal protection against the termination of an employment contract and an employment relationship by an employer is enjoyed by all breast-feeding employees regardless of the child's age.

If, during the period of special protection, a breast-feeding mother and the employer reach an agreement on other work and the employee voluntarily signs a new employment contract, there are no issues. If, however, for any reason, the employee does not reach an agreement with the employer on other work, the employer has no choice but to send her home and continue paying her salary under the valid employment contract. This problem arises because the protection of breast-feeding mothers lasts for as long as they breast-feed. It may not be a frequent problem, but it is nevertheless significant. It leads to the question of the employer's options in such a case. In case-law, such cases were solved in such a manner that, in spite of unlawful termination of the employment contract, the employer claimed before the court that the employment relationship could no longer continue and substantiated this assertion through evidence, while the court, based on powers vested in it by the ERA, rescinded the employment contract regardless of the fact that it found the employment contract termination unlawful. In case of a court dispute, an employer may refer to and prove the fact that an employment relationship can no longer continue because of circumstances on the part of the employer, meaning that the employer in reality has no need for the employee's work and that the court should decide that the employee's employment relationship with the employer be terminated no later than upon the judgment of the court of first instance. Such an objection may be made only until the end of the main hearing before the court of first instance (Judgment of the Supreme Court of the Republic of Slovenia, op. no. VIII Ips 230/2007), since the court does not at its own initiative or *ex officio* ascertain the circumstances and the interests as regards the inability to continue the employment relationship. In such cases, the court decides on the duration of employment relationship (no longer than until the decision of the court of first instance), acknowledges the years of service of the employee and all rights arising from the employment relationship until termination and awards the employee appropriate monetary compensation equalling no more than 18 monthly salaries of the employee.

The employee is obligated to inform the employer about material circumstances that affect or might affect the implementation of their contractual obligations. However, in practice the employer is the one that periodically calls on the employee to submit medical certificates about breast-feeding. A medical certificate on breast-feeding is issued by a specialised paediatrician.

In a labour dispute where the employer for the second time wanted to terminate, for the same business reasons, the employment contract of a breast-feeding employee who was also the procurator of a third legal person, the Higher Labour and Social Court of Ljubljana ruled in favour of the strict protection of breast-feeding employees through Judgment op. no. Pdp 589/2011. The employer claimed that the employee was abusing the institute of breast-feeding and that, as a procurator, she was performing other profitable activity and thus gaining additional income, however, the Higher Labour and Social Court wrote, as did the Supreme Court of the Republic of Slovenia several times before it, that an employer may terminate an employment contract for a specific business reason only once. It further adopted the position that the wording of Article 88, paragraph 6 of the ERA, which stipulates a six-month period for ordinary termination for business reasons, points to the preclusive nature of this deadline. In case of a preclusive period, the right ceases as the period lapses – in this specific case, the employer's right to submit notice of employment contract termination after the business reason has arisen. No circumstances on the part of the employee (such as breast-feeding) influence the commencement of this period, and the period may not be extended since it is not defined by the ERA.

Nevertheless, in its Judgment op. no. VIII Ips 374/2007, the Supreme Court of the Republic of Slovenia adopted a stance that, for a pregnant employee to enjoy protection, such employee must, according to the Act, take action – i.e., immediately submit a medical certificate about pregnancy (or as soon as obstacles cease). A subsequently submitted certificate may not be considered. Taking action is required also to exercise protection during parental leave, because an employee on parental leave must inform the employer about the intended leave 30 days in advance. The above is not specifically required for breast-feeding employees according to Article 115 of the ERA, since the Act does not impose on the employee an obligation to inform the employer or to submit proof (i.e., a medical certificate) of breast-feeding as soon as possible or, in the case of obstacles arising through no fault of her own, immediately after the cessation of such obstacles. However, in the opinion of the Supreme Court, it is in such case impossible to imagine protection of an employee and the related obligation of the employer to uphold such protection, if the employer has not been informed that the employee is breast-feeding. According to the position of the Supreme Court expressed in the relevant decision, a pregnant employee is required to take action so that she may claim protection, namely she must immediately submit a medical certificate on pregnancy or, in the case of obstacles, immediately after the cessation of such obstacles.

In its Judgment op. no. VIII Ips 217/2009, the Supreme Court of the Republic of Slovenia went even further and explained that under Article 34, paragraph 1 of the ERA, an employee is obligated to keep the employer informed about the relevant circumstances that affect or might affect the fulfilment of their contractual obligations and also of any changes to information that affect the fulfilment of rights deriving from the employment relationship. However, the ERA does not specify relevant circumstances, so these need to be assessed on a case-by-case basis. An employee is obligated to inform the employer mainly about those circumstances that originate from the employee's personal domain and hinder the fulfilment of their contractual obligations (e.g. illness) as well as about the circumstances that allow special protection against termination and which the employer cannot be aware of. Thus, special protection under Article 115 of the ERA does not take effect until the employer has been informed about the pregnancy (by a medical certificate). Taking action is required from an employee also to exercise protection during parental leave, because an employee on parental leave must inform the employer about the intended leave 30 days in advance. In the opinion of the Supreme Court, it is in such cases impossible to imagine protection of an employee and the related obligation of the employer to uphold such protection, if the employer has not been informed that the employee is breast-feeding.

III. Disabled employees

According to the ERA, disabled persons enjoy special protection against the termination of employment contracts due to disability and business reasons. The original ERA specified that the employer may not terminate the employment contract of a disabled employee on the grounds of disability or for business reasons, unless it is impossible to provide them other appropriate work according to the regulations governing pension and disability insurance. The amendments and supplements to the ERA introduced significant changes in this respect. As of 2007, an employment contract of a disabled employee may be terminated due to disability or business reasons in the cases and under the conditions defined in the regulations governing pension and disability insurance or the regulations governing vocational rehabilitation and employment of disabled persons. Naturally, in this case as well, the ERA requires that, before an employment contract is terminated, it should be checked if the disabled person could be employed in another appropriate position.

The procedure of termination for business reasons and for disability is the same, even though the actual situation in the two cases differs. In the first case, the employer may terminate the employment contract of an employee if the need for the disabled person's work under the terms and conditions of the employment contract has ceased due to economic, organisational, technological, structural and similar reasons on the part of the employer, and the employer is, by valid reason, prevented from assuring the disabled employee the right to a transfer to another position. In the second case, a disabled employee is not capable of performing work under the conditions of the employment contract due to disability, and the employer is, by valid reason, prevented from assuring the disabled employee the right to a transfer to another position.

Notice of termination of a disabled employee's employment contract due to disability and business reasons has to be given in a six-month preclusive period that starts on the day of the substantiated reason arising.

The procedure for termination of an employment contract due to disability and business reasons starts in the same manner as the procedure for termination of an employment contract due to business reasons (by written notice of intent of termination). Before giving notice of ordinary termination of the employment contract, the employer must obtain an opinion from a special committee composed of the representatives of the Pension and Disability Insurance Institute of the Republic of Slovenia, the Labour Inspectorate of the Republic of Slovenia, the Employment Service of the Republic of Slovenia and the representatives of employers and trade unions. Owing to the mandatory participation of such a committee, the procedure for termination of employment contracts usually exceeds six months, however, in all cases heard so far (e.g. Judgment op. no. VIII Ips 334/2009 dated 7 June 2011, Judgment op. no. VIII Ips 243/2010 dated 8 November 2011, Judgment op. no. VIII Ips 1/2010 dated 7 March 2011), the Supreme Court of the Republic of Slovenia adopted a stance that the six-month period for terminating the employment contract of a disabled employee due to disability or business reasons does not start until the employer receives the opinion where the above committee legally determines the existence or justification of the reason for termination and above all the (im)possibility of other employment.

The protection of disabled employees in the procedures for termination of employment contracts due to disability and business reasons has been adequately regulated by the Act since 2007 and enables, when inevitable, the termination of an employment contract.

Conclusion

Since the entry into force of the ERA in 2003, the procedures of ordinary or extraordinary termination of employment contracts have been subject to preclusive periods, meaning that if the employer misses the deadline, they lose the right to lawfully terminate an employment contract.

According to the ERA, which entered into force on the 1st of January 2003, an employer was obligated to terminate an employment contract for business reasons, occupational disability or for cause no later than 30 days from identifying the reasons for ordinary termination and no later than six months from the occurrence of the reason. The amendment to the ERA, which entered into force at the end of 2007, did away with the subjective deadline applying to termination due to business reasons and occupational disability, and the employer was obligated to complete the termination procedure in six months from the occurrence of the substantiated reason. This was undoubtedly a positive change, as practical experience has shown that the 30-day deadline – from the time the employer identifies the reasons for termination until giving a termination notice – was too short. Labour courts that are, in the Republic of Slovenia, competent to solve individual labour disputes, collective labour disputes and social disputes sustained the claims of employees that referred to preclusion. Until the ERA was amended, the courts had supported the claims of employees in cases when a termination notice was given past the 30-day deadline, even if the termination procedure was carried out within six months from the occurrence of the reason. After the amendment to the ERA, the courts ruled in favour of employees' claims if the employer failed to give notice of termination in six months from the occurrence of the substantiated reason. In case of termination for cause, the amendment referred to the extended subjective deadline (from 30 days from identifying the reasons for termination to 60 days from identifying just cause), while the objective six-month deadline remained unchanged.

Extraordinary termination of an employment contract is subject to even shorter deadlines, which were, in the original, 15 days from identifying the reasons for extraordinary termination and six months from the reason arising, and then were extended with the 2007 amendment, so that an employer must give extraordinary termination notice within 30 days from identifying the reason for extraordinary termination and no later than in six months from the reason arising.

The set deadlines for terminating an employment contract are now adequate, as practice has shown that ordinary and extraordinary termination procedures are feasible within the projected deadlines. However, the question arises as to whether the procedures of employment contract termination should be subject to preclusive deadlines at all. We believe that preclusive deadlines are suitable in cases of employment contract termination for cause and extraordinary termination by the employer. In these cases, the deadlines are necessary and essential, since an employer with expert departments is thus required to take action, while missed deadlines are always to the benefit of an employee. In practice, the question arose several times as to when a substantiated reason for termination of employment occurred and in each individual case the courts determined the occurrence of reason by adopting the position that the reason cannot arise until it is familiar to the employees that have the power to take action. In cases of employment contract termination for business reasons, the courts determined when one of the reasons for termination actually arose, which means that a change in organisation or job classification was not always crucial for setting the deadline.

In our opinion, the situation is different as regards preclusive periods that apply to procedures of employment contract termination for business reasons, occupational disability and disability. In these cases, the employer's failure to take action leads to an extension of employment relationship that is favourable for the employee. We therefore believe that the most adequate solution would be to not legally set the preclusive period.

Legal preclusive periods in procedures of terminating employment contracts of special protected categories of employees in reality mean that an employer who misses the deadline cannot carry out a lawful procedure of employment contract termination. Namely, the Act does not provide for a suspension of the deadline for the period during which an employee enjoys protection that would allow the employer to continue with the procedure after the reasons for protection have ceased.

An employer cannot terminate the employment contract of an older employee for business reasons if such an employee's protection prevents the contract from being terminated in six months, however, the employment contract could be terminated for the same reason after six months have passed from the day of the substantiated reason arising.

The same applies to parents, pregnant and breast-feeding employees, the only difference being that their employment contracts cannot be terminated in any case (neither ordinarily for any reason nor extraordinarily). Once special protection of this employee category ceases, the deadlines for taking legal action have usually passed.

The situation is different with disabled persons whose employment contract is terminated for business reasons or due to disability: the day of the substantiated reason arising is not considered to be the day when the employer established that they do not need the employee or the day when the disability certificate becomes final and enforceable but rather the day when the employer receives the opinion of a special committee. The court adopted this position because it cannot be determined if other appropriate employment can or cannot be offered to an employee until the employer receives the opinion of the committee.

We fully support the position that protection against the termination of employment contracts of certain employee categories is essential and necessary and, after all, prescribed by regulations that the labour law in the Republic of Slovenia has to be harmonised with. However, in our opinion there is no reason that, after the cessation of special protection, an employer could not lawfully carry out the procedure to terminate an employment contract of an employee from any of these categories, provided of course that such is provided for by law. A possible solution is to introduce a suspension of the employer's right to carry out the employment contract termination in a set period or simply abolish the six-month preclusive period.

The work material for proposed amendments to the ERA from January 2011 projects also the changes discussed herein, namely the abolishment of the six-month legal preclusive period for giving termination notice that commences on the day the substantiated business reason arises. It also envisages that the prohibition to give notice of termination to a breast-feeding employee should apply only until the child reaches the age of one year. If these amendments to the Act are adopted, they will undoubtedly contribute to greater flexibility of employment and to reducing the uncertainty of employers regarding the lawfulness of termination of employment contracts of employees that enjoy special protection.

Barbara Korošec
Tel: +386 1 432 2084 / Email: barbara.korosec@op-safar.si
Barbara Korošec studied law at the University of Ljubljana, where she, in 2003, graduated *cum laude* and is continuing her studies at an M.Sc. level. She is a Founding Partner in the Law firm Šafar & Partners Ltd. She counsels clients on a wide range of labour and civil law matters. She regularly represents clients in courts and other state authorities in all kinds of labour law and civil law matters. She is a member of the Bar Association of Slovenia, and can represent her clients at every level of the court system, all the way up to the Supreme Court. She speaks English, Croatian and Serbian.

Martin Šafar
Tel: +386 1 432 2084 / Email: martin.safar@op-safar.si
Martin Šafar is a Founding and Managing Partner in the Law firm Šafar & Partners Ltd. He counsels clients on a wide range of employment and labour law, as well as other, matters. He also practises in the areas of company disputes, commercial litigation and contracts. Martin also specialises in insolvency cases.
Together with his partners, he counsels some of the most important companies in Slovenia. His clients hold him in high regard for his litigation skills. He regularly represents companies in courts in all kinds of civil law matters. He is a member of the Bar Association of Slovenia, and can represent his clients at every level of the court system, all the way up to the Supreme Court.
Martin Šafar studied law at the University of Ljubljana where he graduated *cum laude* and is continuing his studies at a doctoral level. He is fluent in English, Croatian and Serbian, he also understands and speaks German and French.

Law firm Šafar & Partners, Ltd

Resljeva cesta 25, 1000 Ljubljana, Slovenia
Tel: +386 1 432 2084 / Fax: +386 1 234 2770 / URL: http://www.op-safar.si

South Africa

Claire Gaul & Nicholas Robb
Webber Wentzel

Employment in South Africa

Introduction

Employment in South Africa is highly regulated by a plethora of legislation governing, *inter alia*, unfair dismissals, minimum terms and conditions of employment, as well as workplace discrimination and employment equity[1]. South Africa's unemployment rate is approximately 24%[2] and one of the corollaries to this high unemployment rate is the marked presence in South Africa of atypical and informal modes of employment or work, which do not sit easily within the protectionist framework of labour legislation. This tension is currently being experienced most tellingly through the introduction by the ANC[3] led government ("**the Government**") of sweeping changes to employment legislation, and the fierce debate that has ensued between organised labour and business over these proposed changes. The memorandum below is primarily directed toward providing an overview of the legal developments, both proposed and already implemented, which will, and have had an impact upon the legal framework of employment in South Africa. Prior to exploring this theme of change, we have set out below a brief introduction to the current framework.

All employees, irrespective of their level of seniority or salary scale, currently enjoy protection from unfair dismissal by virtue of the provisions of the Labour Relations Act No. 66 of 1995 ("**the LRA**"). Only three grounds are recognised as constituting valid reasons for dismissal, namely, gross misconduct, incapacity (on account of poor work performance, illness or injury), and the employer's operational requirements (known colloquially as 'retrenchments'). To pass scrutiny, dismissals must be both substantively and procedurally fair, that is, a dismissal must be shown by the employer to have been for one of the three recognised grounds, and must be preceded by a fair pre-dismissal procedure. The Commission for Conciliation, Mediation and Arbitration ("**the CCMA**") is the employment tribunal established by the LRA and is mandated to conciliate and arbitrate unfair dismissal disputes. Employees who have been unfairly dismissed may be awarded compensation of up to a maximum of 12 months' remuneration[4] or may be reinstated into the employ of the employer.

Apart from regulating individual employment rights, the LRA also enshrines the constitutionally protected rights of workers to belong to a trade union and to engage in the lawful activities of their chosen trade union[5]. Although the LRA does not compel employers to bargain collectively with representative trade unions, there are a number of statutory mechanisms contained in the LRA which encourage collective bargaining, the principal of which are the organisational rights granted to trade unions which enjoy sufficient representation within a workplace. These include the right to organise within the employer's workplace, the right to require the employer to deduct subscription fees from the wages of employees and pay these over to the trade union, the right of members to elect shop stewards who may represent their interests in the workplace, and the right to compel the employer to disclose information required for the trade union to represent its members. The role that trade unions play within the South African economy, and their influence over government policy, is discussed further below.

Finally, by way of general comment, the Basic Conditions of Employment Act No. 66 of 1995 ("**the BCEA**") prescribes certain minimum terms and conditions of employment which are applicable to all employees unless varied by ministerial determination or the parties agree to more favourable terms and conditions. These minimum prescribed terms include restrictions on working hours, pay for overtime worked, leave entitlements and the like. Many of the prescribed minimum terms and conditions, such as pay for overtime and restrictions on working hours, expressly exclude employees who earn above a specified threshold, as determined by the Minister of Labour from time-to-time. Currently this threshold is set at ZAR 172,000 per annum[6]. Notably, and another facet of the complex labour and economic framework within which South African operates, is the fact that, notwithstanding the emphasis placed on the protection of workers, in the form of the LRA and the BCEA, many of the prescribed minimum terms and conditions of employment compare favourably (at least from the perspective of business) to other jurisdictions in Africa. By way of example, severance pay, as prescribed by the BCEA, is only payable to an employee who is dismissed on account of the operational requirements of the employer, and the law prescribes that severance is equal to 1 week's pay for every completed year of service. In Botswana, on the other hand, severance is payable to an employee whenever an employee's employment is terminated, whether because of resignation, death or for any other reason. In South Africa, as a further example, an employee is entitled to 15 working days' annual leave whereas in Mali the statutory minimum leave entitlement is 22 working days per year.

Trade Unions and industrial action in South Africa

Trade Unions have historically played, and continue to play an active role in shaping the Government's employment policies as well as in the arena of collective bargaining. Their strong influence on policy-making has an historical basis and is derived from the dominant role played by organised labour in the struggle against the apartheid policies of the former government. Currently, the Government is made up of a tripartite alliance between the ANC, the Congress of South African Trade Unions ("**COSATU**") and, to a lesser degree, the Communist Party. The clout exercised by some of the larger trade unions in South Africa, which are mainly located in the mining and manufacturing sectors, is evident in the 2011 'strike season' which saw a wave of strike action across the country. It is estimated that more than 24 million working days were lost in South Africa during 2011 on account of industrial action.[7] In addition, it has been reported that in 2010 South Africa lost almost double the amount of work days on account of industrial action than at the peak of labour unrest during Apartheid, an era in which rolling mass-action was prevalent.[8] It has also been noted that whereas strike action has traditionally been associated with the public sector, 2011 saw a significant increase in the number of private sector strikes.[9]

What is also of significance is the increase in conflict and violence that has become associated with strike action in the last few years. This has been widely reported on and appeared to reach a peak earlier in the year in the form of unlawful strike action which plagued the platinum industry for a period of six weeks. This particular strike commenced in January 2012 and was in response to a deadlock between the trade unions and Impala Platinum Holdings, one of the world's largest platinum producers, over wages.[10] The company dismissed 17,200 workers, which it was entitled to do because the strike action was unprotected under the LRA.[11] It was widely reported that the strike resulted in substantial damage to property, injury to both striking and non-striking employees as well as the deaths of 3 workers. The violence was reportedly sparked by conflict between two rival labour groups, the National Union of Mine Workers and an organised group of employees purportedly disenchanted with trade union management. The platinum strike is merely one, admittedly extreme, example of the increase in violence that has unfortunately become associated with strike action in South Africa. Although it is very difficult to provide an accurate assessment, it has been reported that worker absenteeism during strike action, ostensibly due to violence and intimidation, has increased four-fold in the period 2008 until 2011.[12]

Seemingly paradoxical to the increase in strike action, is the fact that trade unions in South Africa continue to lose membership on a yearly basis. The unionisation rate has declined from just under 32% (of the total workforce) to 29% in 2011.[13]

Atypical forms of employment

South African law does not distinguish between 'temporary' and 'permanent' employees, or between 'formal' and 'casual' employment[14], and all employees are entitled to protection against unfair dismissal.[15] Currently, temporary or fixed term employment is, however, recognised as a valid form of employment, and agency work is specifically recognised by the LRA. As regards the former, a fixed term employment contract terminates automatically upon the happening of an event specified in the contract of employment, or upon a date stipulated in the employment contract (i.e. there is no dismissal in these circumstances)[16]. Fixed term employees nevertheless currently enjoy limited statutory protection from unfair dismissal in that the LRA recognises, as a species of dismissal, the non-renewal of a fixed term contract of employment in circumstances in which the employee enjoyed a reasonable expectation of renewal of the contract. This statutory mechanism is primarily intended to prevent employers from placing employees on a series of fixed term contracts of employment in order to evade the statutory protections afforded permanently employed employees. As regards the latter, agency work is specifically regulated in terms of the LRA. The colloquial term used in South Africa for employers which supply labour to their clients is *"labour broker"*, which is defined, in turn, as a *"temporary employment services"* ("**TES**") in the LRA.[17] A TES means any person who, for reward, procures for or provides to a client other persons who render services to, or perform work for, the client and who are remunerated by the TES. Such employees are deemed to remain employees of the TES, although the TES and the client are jointly and severally liable if the TES, in respect of its 'employees', contravenes a collective agreement of a bargaining council, or an arbitration award governing terms and conditions of employment, or the provisions of the BCEA. Importantly, the joint and several liability does not extend to contraventions of the LRA by the client of the TES. This means that the client is at liberty to 'fire' the employee without there being any repercussion as regards the legislative protections afforded employees under the LRA. This mechanism of employment has in South Africa become the focus of fierce debate between organised labour and business. Trade unions, on the one hand, contend that labour broking tends to foster the exploitation of workers, as businesses are able to circumvent employment protections by utilising the services of labour brokers which are often disreputable, do not comply with statutory minimum terms and conditions of employment, and fail to uphold the protections afforded employees against unfair dismissal. In this three-tiered relationship (between labour broker, employee, and client), it is argued, the client is able to wield the most bargaining power and consequently the employee is rendered vulnerable to exploitation. Such is the opposition to the statutory recognition of labour broking that COSATU called for all workers in South Africa to participate in nationwide protest action[18] in March 2012, which resulted in thousands of employees participating in rallies and marches. The stance of organised labour appears to be emphatically one of out-and-out opposition to labour broking, and the concomitant call for banning of agency work. That this is the case is evident in the statement made by COSATU just prior to the commencement of the protest action referred to above: *"[we] demand a total ban of the labour brokers, a system that we have described as human trafficking and modern day slavery"*.[19]

Business contends, on the other hand, that labour broking forms a significant and important contributor to the South African economy. In support of this contention, it has been asserted that *"[agency] work is the fastest growing segment of the South African labour market, with average annual growth of 9.4% between 2000 and 2010, compared to…an average annual decline of 1.2% in permanent work"*.[20] The value of the labour broking sector in South Africa is estimated to be between ZAR 18 billion and ZAR 26 billion, and the outright banning of this mode of employment is perceived by business to potentially be catastrophic to the economy.

Impending legislative reform of labour laws

Introduction

Towards the end of 2010, the Government published a number of proposed amendments to the LRA and the BCEA[21] (collectively referred to as "**the Labour Amendment Bills**"). Their publication drew widespread criticism, albeit from opposite sides of the political spectrum, by both organised labour and business. After a year-long process of negotiation within the National Economic Development and Labour Council[22], the Labour Amendment Bills were submitted to Parliament's Portfolio Committee on Labour[23] in April 2012, notwithstanding the fact that NEDLAC failed to approve the Labour Amendment Bills prior to their submission to the Portfolio Committee due to an inability amongst members to reach agreement on key aspects of the proposed amendments. The indication from the Government is that the Labour Amendment Bills are likely to be passed by Parliament in their current form. As a general comment, it is apparent that the amendments are primarily aimed at increasing the protections afforded lower income employees, on the one hand, and providing greater security to those employees who fall within atypical or non-standard modes of employment, on the other hand. Under this section some of the key aspects of the proposed amendments as contained in the Labour Relations Amendment Bill are highlighted.

The proposed regulation of labour broking

The Labour Relations Amendment Bill proposes a number of significant amendments to the current legal position regarding labour brokers.[24] The amendments do not, *per se*, dissolve the triangular relationship between client, labour broker and employee, however, what is proposed is the effective closure of certain loopholes in the current regulation of labour broking, such that security of employment is addressed, as well as the inequality that is perceived by the Government to exist between the terms and conditions of employment of agency workers, on the one hand, and those of permanent employees, on the other hand. In the first instance, the joint and several liability of the client and the TES is expanded upon such that the employee of a TES may, in circumstances in which the TES contravenes a collective agreement, an arbitration award governing terms and conditions of employment, or the provisions of the BCEA, institute proceedings against either the TES or the client, and any award or order made against a labour broker or a client may be enforced against either. It is apparent that this enhanced liability of the client is intended to deal with the spectre of so-called 'fly by night' labour brokers and to make certain that the client plays a significant oversight role, in order to mitigate its own risk, to ensure that any TES with which it has contracted for the provision of labour is both reputable and established, and complies with its statutory or other employment obligations. The second amendment concerns the obligation placed on labour brokers to employ persons on the same terms and conditions of employment as may be applicable, by virtue of sectoral determinations or collective agreements, to permanent employees of the client with whom the employees of the TES are placed. In addition, it is proposed that employees who earn below a statutorily determined threshold and who perform services for a client for a period exceeding six months are deemed to be employed by the client (i.e. the nature of the triangular relationship is, in this instance, reversed). An employer is required to treat such employees similarly to the manner in which it treats its own employees.

Restrictions on temporary employment

Another significant amendment to the current regulation of employment concerns the treatment of fixed term contracts of employment. The Labour Relations Amendment Bill provides that an employer may only employ individuals, who earn below a stipulated earnings threshold[25], on fixed term contracts, or renewals thereof, that endure for longer than six months if the nature of the work is demonstrably of a limited duration, or if the employer is able to demonstrate a justifiable reason for fixing the duration of the contract of employment. This section provides a (closed) list of potential reasons for engaging an employee on a fixed term contract, including, for example, where the individual is required to substitute another employee who is temporarily absent, where there has been a temporary increase in the volume of work which is not expected to endure beyond 12 months, or where the individual is engaged to perform seasonal work. Any employment in contravention of this section (i.e. where the contract, or successive renewals of the contract exceed/s 6 months in the absence of any of the justifications stipulated in the section) is deemed to be employment of an indefinite duration. If we consider that temporary work is reported to comprise just over 30% of South Africa's total workforce[26] the tighter regulation of temporary or fixed term employment will have a significant impact on business.

Regulation regarding changes to terms and conditions of employment

Another significant change contained in the Labour Relations Amendment Bill concerns the employer's ability to amend terms and conditions of employment. Currently, a unilateral variation of terms and conditions of employment constitutes a breach of contract and employers are not entitled to implement such changes without the consent of the employees concerned. However, the law also does currently permit a certain level of flexibility in that an employer is entitled to invoke the retrenchment procedures contained in the LRA, and dismiss employees who refuse to countenance changes to terms and conditions of employment, where the proposed changes are operationally required, and the employer has consulted with the employees concerned on the underlying rationale for the changes. This level of flexibility was granted to employers not by the legislature but by the Supreme Court of Appeal ("**the SCA**") in 2005[27] in a decision which distinguished retrenchments in such circumstances from so-called 'lockout dismissals' which are expressly prohibited by the LRA. 'Lock-out dismissals' are dismissals the purpose of which is to compel employees to accept the employer's demand, i.e. they are 'provisional dismissals' in that the employer is effectively stating to its employees that it will rehire them subject to their agreement to new terms and conditions. The legislature has now, however, effectively rejected the SCA's decision by amending the provision in the LRA dealing with 'lock-out dismissals' such that an employer may not dismiss employees either in order to compel acceptance of a demand or because the employee refuses to accept a demand. The latter encompasses the previously permitted retrenchment of employees who refuse to agree to changes to terms and conditions. The practical significance of this legislative change remains to be seen, but it is likely that the proposed new provision will have far-reaching and negative consequences for the ability of businesses to restructure their workforces where operational requirements so dictate.

Exclusion of higher earning employees from certain protections

It has been stated above that the Labour Relations Amendment Bill proposes the introduction of exclusionary provisions similar to those contained in the BCEA, by reference to a salary threshold as determined from time-to-time. Employees earning above the threshold are exempt from the deeming provisions created in relation to temporary employment. A further, and far more radical exclusion, is that which provides that the dismissal of an employee who earns above a certain threshold is deemed to be fair if the employer gives the prescribed notice of termination (which is 3 months or any longer period as specified in the employee's contract of employment) or pays the employee *in lieu* of notice. This amendment will, however, only apply to those contracts of employment concluded before the commencement of the Labour Relations Amendment Bill, with effect from 2 years after such commencement. The exclusion will not apply to automatically unfair dismissals (discussed briefly above). The rationale for the proposed exclusion of higher-earning employees from the full protections afforded employees from unfair dismissal is set out in the Bill's Explanatory Memorandum as follows:

"*[at] the heart of the change is the disproportionate cost, complexity, and impact on an employer's operations of procedures to terminate the employment of high earning employees in circumstances where the reason for doing so may not fall clearly and neatly within the fair reasons for dismissal specified in (the LRA).*"[28]

Whether or not this provision will pass constitutional scrutiny is arguable. Constitutional rights which may be impugned by this amendment include section 9 (the equality provision), which provides that "*[everyone] is equal before the law and has the right to equal protection and benefit of the law*" and section 23 which provides that "*[everyone] has the right to fair labour practices*". Although all of the constitutional fundamental rights may, in certain circumstances, be limited by a law of general application, the Government would be required to demonstrate that the exclusion of certain levels of employees from the protections afforded by the LRA against unfair dismissal is justifiable and rationally connected to the purpose sought to be achieved by the limitation. It is debatable whether it can be successfully argued that it is more burdensome, and unfairly so, for employers to be required to comply with the provisions of the LRA in dismissing senior employees as opposed to lower level employees.

Increased regulation of strike action

The Labour Relations Amendment Bill proposes the introduction of ballots by trade unions prior to the commencement of strike action.[29] The purpose of this is to ensure that a trade union does, in fact, enjoy the majority support of its members before going out on strike. The CCMA is empowered to issue a certificate confirming that the trade union concerned has, in fact, conducted a ballot and enjoys majority support of its members before they go out on strike. COSATU has (predictably) opposed this proposed requirement on the basis that it restricts a trade union's entitlement to invoke the strike procedures of the LRA. The rationale for the proposed ballot requirement appears to be the increased presence of violence and intimidation in strike action in South Africa (discussed above) against non-striking employees, which is more likely to occur in strike action enjoying only minority support.

The transfer of contracts of employment under the LRA

General

Before the advent of constitutionalism in South Africa and the enactment of the LRA, the position at common law was that where there is a transfer of a business, the employees are required to re-contract with the new owner of the business in order to secure their on-going employment. As a result of the shortcomings in the protections offered to employees by the common law, the LRA includes a provision which provides for the transfer of contracts of employment in circumstances where there is a transfer of a business from an old employer to a new employer.[30] This provision provides that where there is a transfer of a business (defined to include a trade, undertaking or service) by one employer to another employer as a going concern, the new employer is automatically substituted in the place of the old employer in respect of all contracts of employment in existence immediately before the date of transfer; all the rights and obligations between the old employer and an employee at the time of the transfer continue in force as if they had been rights and obligations between the new employer and the employee; and anything done before the transfer by or in relation to the old employer, including the dismissal of an employee, is considered to have been done by or in relation to the new employer. The transfer also does not interrupt an employee's continuity of employment, and an employee's contract of employment continues with the new employer as if with the old employer. South African courts have by and large adopted the jurisprudence developed by the European Court of Justice in interpreting the European Union Business Transfers Directive as well as by the English Courts in interpreting the Transfer of Undertakings (Protection of Employment) Regulations, 2006. South African courts accept that there exist "...*a wide range of transactions in terms of which a business may be transferred i.e. sale, transfer, merger, takeover, donation, exchange of assets, and that section 197 need not be limited in its application to conventional transferring transactions like a sale*".[31]

Developments in the law of transfers

At the time that the Labour Amendment Bills were first published for comment in 2010, it was proposed that the provisions of the LRA dealing with transfers should be amended in order to extend their scope to various types of transactions that appear not to have been envisaged under the current section. The impetus for the proposed amendment was the judicial battle that had raged since 2007 concerning an outsourcing dispute between the South African Airlines and two trade unions. This judicial battle commenced in the Labour Court, proceeded to the Labour Appeal Court and then the Supreme Court of Appeal, and was then settled by the Constitutional Court in November 2011[32]. Because of the Constitutional Court's decision in that particular matter, the Labour Relations Amendment Bill, as placed before the Labour Portfolio Committee in April this year, no longer contains the proposed amendment to the transfer provisions, presumably since the legislature is of the view that the decision of the Constitutional Court demonstrates a satisfactory judicial interpretation of the ambit of the transfer provisions. Recent legal developments pertaining to transfers of businesses are, therefore, most pronounced in the context of outsourcing arrangements.

It has been accepted in South Africa for some years that 'first generation outsourcing' (which occurs where a principal outsources a particular service, usually a non-core function such as catering or gardening, to a third party contractor) generally triggers the application of the transfer provisions contained in the LRA, and that employees engaged in the service being outsourced will follow the service to the contractor. The difficulty that has arisen is determining whether, upon termination of the outsourcing agreement, the transfer provisions of the LRA apply to the resumption of the service by the principal (known as 'insourcing') or the appointment of a new service provider (known as 'second generation outsourcing'). The Constitutional Court's judgment has now effectively rendered these terms irrelevant to the application of the transfer provisions of the LRA. The Constitutional Court has held that the inquiry regarding the application of the transfer provisions to a particular transaction should not focus on the issue of the 'generation' of the transfer:

"[it] does not matter in principle what the 'generation' of the outsourcing is, or even whether the transaction is concerned with contracting out at all. The true inquiry is whether there has been a transfer of a business as a going concern by the old employer to the new employer. That evaluation is complex enough without it being burdened with questions about the "generation" of outsourcing."

The main thrust of the Constitutional Court's judgment, in our view, is an admonition to practitioners and businesses to pay careful attention to the underlying transaction, and the rights and obligations it creates, in order to make a proper assessment of whether the transfer provisions of the LRA may be applicable in any given set of circumstances.

The Labour Court has subsequently followed the Constitutional Court's reasoning in a judgment handed down in December 2011[33] concerning the termination of an agreement for the provision of services at various South African iron and steel production sites, and the simultaneous appointment of an American based company for the provision of similar services. It was argued by the initial service provider that this triggered the application of the LRA's transfer provisions and that, accordingly, the new service provider would be required to take over its employees upon commencement of work at the sites. The Labour Court held that on the facts, and in light of the Constitutional Court's recent judgment, the transfer provisions were applicable and, accordingly, the new service provider was required to take over all of the employees of the former service provider who were rendering the services at the various sites. Importantly, the Labour Court confirmed that there need not have been an initial transfer (i.e. at the time that the former service provider was initially engaged by the steel producer to provide the services) in order for the LRA's transfer provisions to be triggered subsequently.

Other developments in the law impacting on employment

The Companies Act

The Companies Act No. 71 of 2008 ("**the Companies Act**"), which passed into law during the course of 2011, has not only brought about vast changes to company law in South Africa but has had, and will continue to have, a significant impact on aspects of employment. Some of the key employment related issues are highlighted below:

An external profit company is required to register as such with the Companies and Intellectual Property Commission ("**the Commission**") within 20 business days after it first begins to conduct business within South Africa. Importantly, a foreign company is regarded as *"conducting business"* within South Africa for the purposes of registration with the Commission if that foreign company is a party to one or more employment contracts within South Africa. The judiciary has not yet pronounced upon the meaning of the phrase *"employment contract within [South Africa]"*, however, in the writers' view, the interpretation that is likely to be given to this phrase is that the employment contract need not necessarily have been entered into or concluded in South Africa for the provision to apply, but rather that the employment contract could have been concluded anywhere and at any time, prior to its current operation in South Africa. Accordingly, this provision of the Companies Act places an obligation on any foreign company which is party to a contract of employment that is operative in South Africa (i.e. the employee renders services to the foreign company from South Africa) to register as an external company with the Commission. Foreign companies which wish to employ individuals in South Africa but do not wish to have a 'business presence' in the country for purposes of company or tax laws or tax are, therefore, required to consider carefully the manner in which they engage individuals to work from South Africa.

The Companies Act now permits a trade union representing employees of a company to make application to the High Court to restrain the company from doing anything contrary to the Companies Act. Trade unions accordingly no longer have to go through the tedious process of making an application to court before being given the right to restrain the company as was required in terms of the previous Companies Act.

The board of directors of a company are now required to notify the trade unions representing its employees of a decision to provide financial assistance to a director or prescribed officer of the company. Trade unions and employees are also expressly recognised as *"affected persons"* for the purposes of business rescue proceedings, and are given certain protections in this regard, for instance,[34] a trade union may apply to set aside a board of directors' resolution to commence business rescue proceedings, or it may make application to a court to commence business rescue proceedings without first having to make application to the court to be provided with these rights. Trade unions must also be given access to the company's financial statements for purposes of initiating the business rescue process. In addition, trade unions are required to be given notice of any resolution to begin business rescue proceedings or of any application for business rescue. Trade unions may also participate in any business rescue proceeding, apply to set aside the appointment of a business rescue practitioner or require a practitioner to provide security. Employees are now also given preferential treatment for claims for remuneration. The Companies Act provides that any amount owing by the company to employees during business rescue proceedings is set aside as "*post commencement financing*". Such funds rank higher than secured and unsecured claims against the company and are paid second only to the practitioner's remuneration. Employees are also assured employment on the same terms and conditions as they were subject to before the business rescue proceedings, unless employment is impossible as a result of changes in the ordinary course of attrition, or the employee and the company agree on different terms and conditions.

Trade unions are entitled to qualified privilege and are immune from any civil, criminal or administrative liability in respect of a disclosure about their employers to regulatory authorities and certain company officers. It is, however, a requirement that the trade union made the disclosure in good faith and at the time of the disclosure believed that such information showed that the company, director or prescribed officer contravened certain legislation, endangered health, safety or environment or constituted or condoned unfair discrimination.

Employees may, through their trade union representative, apply to court to have a director declared delinquent or have a director placed under probation. Employees may also, through their trade union representative, demand that the company commence or continue legal proceedings or take related steps to protect the legal interests of the company. Such a demand can only be set aside by the company if it is found by the court that the demand is frivolous, vexatious or without merit. If the company does not follow the process prescribed in the Companies Act following a demand, the trade union who has made the demand may, with court approval, bring or continue legal proceedings on behalf of or in the name of the company in order to protect the legal interests of the company. In exceptional circumstances, the trade union may forego the demand process and immediately make an application to court to allow it to bring proceedings in the name of and on behalf of the company.

The Protection of Personal Information Bill

To date, the South African legislature has not promulgated any specific comprehensive data protection legislation and, accordingly, an individual's entitlement to privacy is still governed by the common law, as informed by the constitutional right to privacy[35]. The Protection of Personal Information Bill, 2009 ("**POPI**") was, however, tabled in Parliament on 25 August 2009. POPI is expected to be passed into law in the course of 2012 and will affect the way in which employers are entitled to process and hold data pertaining to their employees. POPI provides a general information protection mechanism, which will be applicable to both the public and private sector, and covers both automated and manual processing of information.[36] Should a party (including an employer) wish to process personal information, it is obliged to comply with a number of data protection principles set out in POPI, including the following:

- the processing of any personal information must be lawful, which means that there must be a lawful justification for collecting the information;

- the purpose for the processing of the personal information must be relevant, and the information must be kept up to date and accurate;

- the purpose for which the personal information is required must be communicated to the data subject and the information may not be retained longer than is strictly necessary;

- personal information may only be processed by a party that has notified the Information Protection Regulator; and

- a data subject is entitled to obtain confirmation of whether or not a body has in its possession personal information pertaining to the data subject, details regarding the nature of the information, and whether the information has been disclosed to any third party.

From an employment perspective, POPI therefore provides a number of rights to employees, *inter alia*, the right to object to the employer processing his/her personal data and the right to compel the employer to disclose what personal information it holds, or which it has disclosed to third parties, regarding the employee. An employer will also most likely be required to register with the Information Protection Regulator established in terms of POPI. Notably, POPI also prohibits the processing of "*special personal data*" unless the data-subject has given express consent to such processing. This type of data includes information concerning a data-subject's religious beliefs, race or ethnic origin, trade union membership, health or criminal history.

* * *

Endnotes

1. The main legislation governing discrimination in employment as well as affirmative action obligations is the Employment Equity Act No. 55 of 1998. A discussion of this legislation falls outside of the ambit of this memorandum.
2. As reported by Statistics South Africa in the fourth quarter of 2011.
3. The African National Congress, South Africa's single largest political party.
4. Certain types of dismissal are considered under the LRA to be 'automatically unfair' such as discriminatory dismissals, dismissals of employees who exercise their rights under the LRA to join a trade union etc. These dismissals carry a punitive compensation claim of up to 24 months' remuneration.
5. This constitutionally protected right is contained in section 23 of the Constitution of the Republic of South Africa Act No. 28 of 1996 (referred to in this memorandum as "**the Constitution**").
6. As per the Determination: Earnings Threshold issued by the Minister of Labour on 13 May 2011.
7. Adcorp Employment Index, November 2011, issued on 8 December 2011.
8. Adcorp Employment Index, November 2011.
9. Adcorp Employment Index, July 2011, issued on 11 July 2011.
10. It was also reported by Nedbank that the strike at Impala Platinum Mine's Rustenburg mine cost the company approximately ZAR 2.4 billion in lost income.
11. The LRA requires that certain procedures be followed before members of a trade union are entitled to go out on strike. Absent these procedures, the strike is unprotected. After agreement was reached between the company and the trade union 15,000 of the 17,200 employees were rehired.
12. Adcorp Employment Index, March 2012, issued on 10 April 2012.
13. Adcorp Employment Index, March 2012.
14. The provisions of the BCEA governing basic terms and conditions of employment do not, however, apply to employees who work less than 24 hours per month.
15. The test for whether or not an individual is an 'employee' is an objective one and focuses primarily on whether or not the individual is subject to supervision and control, whether he forms an integral part of the employer's organization, and the extent to which he is economically dependent upon the employer. The presence of these factors is indicative of an employment relationship irrespective of the term that may be used to characterise the relationship.
16. Dismissal of a fixed term employee prior to the expiry of the contract is subject to the same pre-dismissal procedures required to be followed by employers in relation to so-called permanent employees, and the dismissal must be substantively fair. A fixed-term contract employee can, however, only be retrenched if the contract of employment provides for premature termination on notice (since a retrenchment is a dismissal on notice).
17. For the purposes of this memorandum, the terms 'labour broker', 'agency' and 'TES' will be used interchangeably.
18. Protest Action is, subject to certain procedural requirements, recognised by the LRA which defines it as "*...the partial or complete retardation or obstruction of work, for the purpose of promoting or defending the socio-economic interests of workers...*" (section 77).
19. Press Statement issued by COSATU on 7 March 2012.
20. Adcorp Employment Index, November 2010.

21. Although the proposed changes to the BCEA are undoubtedly significant this memorandum only focuses on some of the more controversial amendments contained in the LRA.

22. NEDLAC was established in 1994 in terms of the National Economic Development and Labour Council Act No. 35 of 1994 and consists of members who are appointed by government, organised labour and business respectively, and whose functions are, *inter alia*, to consider and make recommendations to Parliament regarding any proposed labour legislation.

23. Parliament comprises a number of Portfolio Committees, each of which is mandated to address specific aspects of law and governance falling within its purview. Accordingly, the Labour Portfolio Committee is mandated to process proposed labour legislation, and to make recommendations to Parliament before any such legislation is promulgated and passed into law.

24. When the labour amendment bills were first released in 2010, the LRA's provisions pertaining to labour brokers were proposed to be deleted in their entirety which amounted, effectively to an outright ban on labour broking in South Africa. The legislative drafters have somewhat modified their approach since then.

25. The Labour Relations Amendment Bill does not stipulate the monetary amount of this threshold; it is likely to be akin to the threshold established for the purposes of the BCEA's provisions which do not apply to employees earning above the stipulated threshold.

26. Adcorp Employment Index, February 2012, issued on13 February 2012.

27. *NUMSA v Fry's Metals* (2005) 26 ILJ 689 (SCA).

28. Page 4 of the Explanatory Memorandum to the Labour Relations Amendment Bill.

29. This will also apply to lock-outs proposed to be called by employer organisations.

30. Section 197 of the LRA.

31. Todd *et al*, Business Transfers and Employment Rights in South Africa (2004, LexisNexis Butterworths), at page 25.

32. *Aviation Union of South Africa & Another v South African Airways (Pty) Ltd & Others* CCT08/11.

33. *Harsco Metals South Africa (Pty) Limited & Another v ArcelorMittal South Africa Limited & others*, handed down on 29 December 2011 (as yet unreported).

34. The aim of business rescue proceedings is either to try and keep the business solvent or to implement a plan that will allow creditors, shareholders and employees better results than those that would ensue if the company was liquidated. As creditors, shareholders and employees (whether represented by a trade union or not) are all affected by business rescue proceedings, they are, therefore, recognised by the Companies Act as "*affected persons*".

35. Section 14 of the Constitution.

36. POPI is based on European data regulations, in particular the European Union Data Protection Directive.

Claire Gaul
Tel: +27 11 530 5000 / Email: claire.gaul@webberwentzel.com
Claire is a partner and the head of the Employment and Employee Benefits Practice at Webber Wentzel. Claire graduated with the degrees BA, BA Honours (with distinction) and LLB (with distinction) from the University of the Witwatersrand, and has completed her LLM (Labour Law) through the University of Johannesburg. She has also obtained a certificate from the University of the Witwatersrand in Advanced Company Law. Claire is ranked by the 2012 edition of Legal 500 and, together with Nick Robb, has authored the employment chapters for *European Lawyer* (2011) and *Practical Law: Labour & Employee Benefits* (2011/2012).

Nicholas Robb
Tel: +27 11 530 5000 / Email: nicholas.robb@webberwentzel.com
Nick is a partner in the Employment and Employee Benefits Practice at Webber Wentzel. Nick is the President of the Gauteng Chapter of SASLAW (South African Society for Labour Law) and sits on its National Committee. He has been endorsed as a labour and employee benefits lawyer by *PLC Which Lawyer?* since 2007. In 2011 he was selected by the *International Who's Who of Management Labour and Employment Lawyers* as being among the world's leading management, labour and employment lawyers, and is also ranked by the 2011 and 2012 editions of *Legal 500*.

Webber Wentzel

10 Fricker Road, Illovo Boulevard, Johannesburg, 2196, South Africa
Tel: +27 11 530 5000 / Fax: +27 11 530 5111 / URL: http://www.webberwentzel.com

Spain

Ignacio Regojo & Juan Nasarre
Squire Sanders LLP

General labour market trends and latest/likely trends in employment litigation

By way of background, it is important to provide a brief overview of the employment situation in Spain.

Since 2008 and particularly in 2009, Spanish unemployment rates have been really unbearable. Our unemployment rate, generally speaking, is up to 24% of the working population (according to data from the first semester of 2012) and if we speak about young people, this rate reaches the scary figure of almost 50%. Even if it is true that there is a significant percentage of hidden economy and illegal employment, these official figures are really worrying.

In November 2011 the Conservative Party (*Partido Popular*) came into power in Spain. The new Government considered that there was a national need to take some action by way of employment regulations in order to stimulate our job market and our economy. This initiative resulted in the Royal Decree-Law 3/2012, of 10 February, and the subsequent Act 3/2012, of 6 July, of urgent measures to reform the employment market.

Unions have already expressed their dissatisfaction with these reforms, stating that the provisions of this new Act limit the rights which have been acquired by Spanish workers over many years. On the other hand, the Government has explained that the aim of these reforms is to obtain more security and stability for employees and more flexibility for employers.

Unfortunately the future does not look bright. The level of uncertainty as a consequence of the banking/financial crisis is high.

Taking this scenario into account, we understand that the likely trends in employment litigation will focus on **termination disputes**, especially considering the new redundancy legal framework. The legal position has been substantially clarified and now it is easier and cheaper to dismiss an employee by reason of redundancy.

In the past it has always been difficult for Spanish employers to determine with the necessary certainty whether a redundancy situation exists. In an attempt to clarify the position, the Government has now made it clear that if a business has suffered a reduction in sales for three consecutive quarters compared with the same period in the previous year, then this will constitute an "economic" reason for redundancy purposes (this is the most clear and objective reason for making somebody redundant).

On top of that, and this is also very relevant, there is no longer a requirement for the company to show that the employee's redundancy would improve the company's position. This has been done with the purpose of limiting the control of the courts over business decisions.

We understand that in view of the poor Spanish economic situation, most companies will fall within the scope of this new legal test, which will be an important source of litigation.

Another upcoming likely trend in employment litigation will be related to **tax regulations**. Prior to the reforms being introduced, it was possible for employers to pay any severance payments on a tax-free basis, provided they were made prior to any court hearing. The new wording is less clear-cut and employers should be aware that there is currently uncertainty about whether such payments can be paid tax-free, unless the fairness of the dismissal has been ruled on by a court.

We will have to wait for some rulings on this issue before we can be clear about the tax status of such payments. Meanwhile, labour litigation may increase significantly for this reason.

Key case law affecting employers' decision making over dismissal, redundancies dismissals etc.

It is important to explain that further to our employment reforms, any **collective dismissals** which take place after 12 February 2012, do not need administrative approval by the Labour Authority as before. Please note that in Spain, a collective redundancy situation will exist if an employer proposes to make the following number of redundancies in a period of 90 days: 10 workers in a company employing fewer than 100 workers; 10% of the total workforce in a company employing between 100 and 300 workers; and 30 workers in a company employing more than 300 workers. In addition, there would be a collective dismissal if a company ceases its business operations and terminates all its employees (provided that the number of employees affected is more than 5).

The role of the Labour Authority is now limited to providing follow-up and guidance on collective dismissals in order to: (i) ensure the effectiveness of the consultation period between the company and the workers´ representatives; and (ii) make suggestions to the workers' representatives.

However, any collective dismissals must be preceded by a consultation period with the workers' representatives. This consultation period is still mandatory. The aim of consulting with the workers' representatives is to avoid or reduce the number of collective redundancies and mitigate the consequences through social measures.

In addition, companies must provide workers' representatives with a memorandum explaining the reasons for the collective dismissals and documentation evidencing the reasons alleged.

In principle, we understand that under this new legal framework the risk of a dismissal being held to be null and void has been reduced. Under the previous regulations any collective dismissal without authorisation was null and void. In practice, the relevant authorisation was usually denied when the company and the workers' representatives did not reach an agreement.

Under the new regulations, redundancies will only be declared null and void where the reasons have not been evidenced properly and the consultation period has not been a real negotiation, but it is not necessary to reach an agreement with the workers' representatives.

However, having said that, we must highlight two important resolutions in this regard:

- Resolution number 415, dated 30 May 2012, issued by the Superior Employment Court of Madrid in the case CCOO Vs Talleres López Gallego SL.
- Resolution number 13, dated 23 May 2012, issued by the Superior Employment Court of Catalonia in the case Mr. Augusto Vs DOPEC SL.

Both resolutions confirmed that a failure to comply with the above mentioned formal requirements (negotiation and providing information to the workers' representatives) will determine whether a dismissal is null and void, which means that employees could be reinstated and receive back-pay for the corresponding interim wages.

Moving on to other issues, we have observed an increase in the number of dismissals arising from the **misuse of IT systems and social networks** which cause risk or prejudice to the company.

In this regard, a good and illustrative example is Resolution number 2629, dated 10 November 2011, issued by the Superior Employment Court of Andalusia in the case of Ms. Emilia vs CECOSA SUPERMARKETS.

In this case a store manager was dismissed after uploading photographs on Facebook of herself and another employee celebrating Spain's victory at the 2010 World Cup. The employees were pictured wearing Spanish football-style t-shirts, but it was also possible to see their company ID tag, including its corporate logo and colours.

The photographs were taken in the back office of the store and clearly showed the employer's safe, various documents containing confidential information, as well as the store's IT system and security alarm. To make things worse, the employees were pictured lying on the General Manager's desk surrounded by that day's takings (which should have been safely locked away in the safe) pretending to play cards and drink alcohol. The manager was promptly dismissed. The company argued that it had lost trust and confidence in her and that her actions had placed the supermarket at risk – anybody looking at the photographs could see the type and location of the safe, as well as the alarm system in place. Clearly as a manager she should have known better.

When this matter came before the Court, it held that the manager's dismissal was fair and said it was irrelevant that the store had not suffered any actual financial loss or damage. Equally, it did not matter that the employee had posted the images outside working hours and on her own equipment. Her actions in posting these photographs on a social media site had potentially damaged the store's image and placed it at risk by showing the security arrangements in place.

For Spanish employers, it is potentially fair to dismiss an employee for posting inappropriate images (or comments for that matter) on a social media site, even if it is a personal site and the posting takes place outside working hours. The key thing is to be able to demonstrate the potentially adverse impact of the employee's conduct, e.g. to reputation or security. It is always advisable to have a social media policy in place which makes it clear what employees can and cannot do when using social media inside or outside the workplace.

Recent statutory or legislative changes

As mentioned above, Spain's new Conservative Government has outlined reforms aimed at reviving the economy and promoting employment, especially amongst young people and the long-term unemployed. Described as an "extremely aggressive change", the new regulations (Royal Decree-Law 3/2012, of 10 February, and the subsequent Act 3/2012, of 6 July, of urgent measures to reform the employment market) are having, and will continue to have, a tremendous impact on the Spanish labour market.

What do the changes mean for companies doing business in Spain? We set out below 10 key points for employers to be aware of:

* Reduced severance payments: The amount of compensation that will be payable by employers for unfair dismissals has been reduced by more than a quarter from 45 days' salary per year of service to 33 days' per year of service.

* Interim wages: As a general rule if an employee was dismissed and the dismissal was found to be unfair, an employer was required to pay severance pay to the employee or reinstate him. It was also required to pay him an interim wages payment from the date of dismissal to the date of the Judge's ruling. Going forward, employees will no longer be entitled to an interim wages payment.

* Clarification on definition of "economic" grounds for redundancy purposes: As outlined above, a dismissal will be treated as by reason of redundancy if it is based on "economic, technical, organisational or production" reasons. It has always been difficult for Spanish employers to determine whether a redundancy situation exists. In an attempt to clarify the position, the Government has now made it clear that if a business has suffered a reduction in sales for three consecutive quarters compared with the same period in the previous year, then this will constitute an "economic" reason for redundancy purposes. This should make it easier for employers to make redundancies.

* Collective redundancies: The Government has removed the obligation on employers to obtain prior authorisation from the Labour Authority in a collective redundancy situation. In addition, companies with profits and more than 100 employees must pay contributions to the Spanish Treasury if they make collective redundancies involving employees aged 50 or over.

* Fixed-term contracts: With almost a third of Spain's workforce on temporary contracts, the Spanish Government is keen to boost permanent employment levels. There will be tax breaks for employers who convert fixed-term contracts into permanent contracts. Furthermore, employers will now only be able to offer fixed-term contracts for up to 24 months' duration.

* Greater flexibility to change terms and conditions of employment: Employers will have the ability to reduce salaries without obtaining employee consent in redundancy situations. The aim of this provision is to encourage employers to consider alternatives to redundancy.

* Weaker collective bargaining: Historically if an employer was unable to reach agreement on the

terms of a new collective agreement, the provisions of the old agreement would remain in force indefinitely. The Government has now said that if the parties are unable to reach agreement then the old collective agreement will only remain in force for 1 year after its expiration date. There will then be no binding collective agreement in place. This could have significant repercussions and will be welcomed by employers.

- Retirement clauses in collective agreements: Any clause in a collective agreement which provides for a mandatory retirement age of 65 is now void.

- Small employers: There will be a new type of contract to assist entrepreneurs (those with fewer than 50 employees) which contains a one-year probationary period. There will be tax and social security incentives for employers that enter into such contracts.

- Training contracts: The upper age limit for entering into a training contract will increase from 25 to 30. This is specifically designed to boost employment and the change will remain in place until unemployment rates fall below 15%.

- Leave for study purposes: Spanish employees are entitled to 20 hours' paid annual leave for educational purposes associated with their employment. They are currently allowed to carry this leave over for up to 5 years, which means that if an employee chooses to roll over his study leave, he could take all 100 hours in year 5.

- Working from home: The Government has clarified in statute an employer's rights and obligations when employing home workers.

Likely or impending reforms to employment legislation and enforcement procedures

1. Social Security Reforms that will affect **public pensions.**

It is important to point out that last year the previous Socialist Government approved reforms designed to reduce pension spending, as part of the first package of austerity measures. The key features of the reform are:

- Ordinary retirement age: This will gradually increase from 65 to 67 during a transition period of 15 years that will end in 2027. After 2027 it will be still possible to retire at 65 with a full pension if the contribution period is at least 38 years and 6 months. It will be possible to retire at 65 even if this contribution period is not reached, but an appropriate reduction will be applied.

- Early retirement age: Postponement from 61 to 63, with limited eligibility; it will only be possible after 33 contribution years rather than 30.

- Late retirement age. In order to promote a voluntary increase in the retirement age an increase in pension between 2% and 4% will be added for each year on top of the pensionable age in relation to the total period of contributions.

- Method of calculation:

  - Gradual lengthening of the period used to calculate full pension benefits from 15 to 25 years. Currently the base pension is calculated on the contributions made over the last 15 years. From 2013 to 2027 the calculation will be gradually extended to contributions over the last 25 years.

  - In order to reach the full 100% of pension the contribution base will have to be 37 years. The transition from the present 35 years contribution base will be progressive between 2013 and 2027.

The **current Spanish Government wants to toughen these regulations** even more, taking into account that pensions are currently the biggest expense on the Spanish budget. More legal reforms are likely that may affect again the retirement age and speed up the date for implementing changes, now set for 2027.

The plan includes restricting access to early and partial retirement, and faster implementation of the new retirement age, as well as different parameters for calculating pensions.

2. The Spanish Government envisages new regulations stating the grounds and procedure to be followed to implement temporary and permanent collective redundancies in public bodies.

Ignacio Regojo
Tel: +34 91 426 4804 / Email: ignacio.regojo@squiresanders.com
Ignacio Regojo is a partner based in our Madrid office. He counsels and advocates on all aspects of labour and employment law, immigration, Social Security, health and safety matters. Ignacio's expertise focuses on: contractual issues and senior executive relations including noncompetition and confidentiality covenants; severance and termination agreements; constitutional fundamental rights; discrimination, retaliation, wage and hour laws, employee privacy and employer monitoring of information technology data; and geographical and functional mobility. He also counsels clients with an international perspective on employment policies and procedures and provides direct support for a full range of corporate issues including reorganisations, TUPE, mergers and acquisitions, data protection and immigration issues.

In addition, Ignacio has extensive experience with collective bargaining agreements, worker representation election processes and union issues, grievance and arbitration procedures and strike activities. He is an experienced advocate on labour, social security and health and safety matters in Spanish labour courts and tribunals including the Spanish Supreme Court and the Spanish Constitutional Court.

Juan Nasarre
Tel: +34 91 426 4866 / Email: juan.nasarre@squiresanders.com
Juan Nasarre has practised as a lawyer, advising companies, defending them before tribunals and participating in numerous court proceedings, particularly in the labour jurisdiction. Chambers Europe 2011 wrote: "Associate Juan Nasarre is emerging as a reliable and dedicated junior lawyer with strong knowledge of employment law".

Juan covers all aspects of employment and labour law. In particular: the employment aspects of subcontracting and personal leasing; modification of working conditions; drawing up of internal policies; labour due diligence; work inspections; senior executive contracts; negotiating and drafting and collective bargaining agreements; judicial defence in dismissals and other individual proceedings (especially in matters with an international dimension or connection) as well as in collective disputes. He also advises on aspects of immigration such as the expatriation of executives or the process to obtain the corresponding work and residence authorisations in Spain.

Ranked by Chambers Europe 2012 in Band W, Juan – who was this year promoted to a Senior Associate position – is, according to clients, "reflective, accurate, and tremendously efficient".

Squire Sanders LLP

Plaza Marques de Salamanca 3-4, 28006 Madrid, Spain
Tel: +34 91 426 4840 / Fax: +34 91 435 9815 / URL: http://www.squiresanders.com

Switzerland

Balz Gross, Roger Zuber & Nadine Mayhall
Homburger

General labour market trends and latest/likely trends in employment litigation

Despite strong immigration into Switzerland of employees from EU countries for several years, the Swiss labour market remains strong and the unemployment rate even fell in 2012. There has been little pressure, therefore, to increase the protection of employees and Swiss labour law retains its liberal character; including the principle of 'freedom to terminate' employment relationships.

The Swiss financial industry has come under pressure, and the previous strong tendencies to award very high bonuses and solicit entire teams from competitors, with all ensuing legal issues from enforceability of bonus plans to non-solicitation battles, have eased a little. Still, the qualification of bonus payments remains one of the key issues in Swiss labour law, and recent precedents have provided some more certainty in this area (see below). In addition, recent legislation has added statutory requirements for bonus payments in the banking sector (see below). Important precedents have been published with regard to mass dismissals and abusive termination (see below).

Moreover, the procedural legal landscape changed fundamentally in Switzerland in 2011. On 1 January 2011, a nation-wide code on civil procedure entered into force (the Swiss Civil Procedure Code, **CPC**)[1] and replaced the 26 different cantonal codes. Simultaneously, a new unified federal Criminal Procedure Code (the **CrPC**)[2] replaced the 26 cantonal criminal procedure codes. In addition, the revised Lugano Convention,[3] governing the recognition and enforcement of judgments in certain civil and commercial matters in Europe, entered into force further facilitating the enforcement of foreign judgments rendered in a Lugano Convention contracting state. Finally, a revision of the Federal Debt Enforcement and Bankruptcy Act[4] (the **DEBA**) also entered into force on 1 January 2011, making pre- and post-judgment attachments easier.

These legislative changes have also affected employment-related proceedings; conciliation proceedings are now mandatory in all cantons, the procedure is unified giving all lawyers equal access to the court system, and the issue of arbitrability of employment-related disputes is now entirely governed by federal law (see below).

Arbitrability of disputes arising of individual employment contracts

The very idea of arbitration lies within party autonomy and flexibility. In contrast, employment law regularly intends to protect the "weaker party", *i.e.*, the employee. Not surprisingly, the conciliation of these two opposing principles has turned out to be challenging[5]. The coming into force of the CPC and recent case-law has provided some clarification on these issues, while other aspects still remain subject to controversy.

Swiss legislation applies, as a rule, to arbitral tribunals having their seat in Switzerland. Switzerland distinguishes between international and domestic arbitration. An arbitration qualifies as international if at least one of the parties to an arbitration was, when concluding the agreement to arbitrate, neither domiciled nor habitually resident in Switzerland[6]. The fact that the parties to an arbitration have changed their domicile or their residency after the conclusion of the agreement to arbitrate has no impact on this qualification.

Disputes arising out of "international" individual employment contracts may, generally, be submitted to arbitration. The arbitrability of disputes arising in "international" individual employment contracts results from the definition of arbitrability which applies to international arbitrations. Under Swiss legislation governing international arbitrations, all *pecuniary claims* may be submitted to arbitration[7].

On the other hand, disputes arising out of "domestic" employment agreements may not, *as a rule*, be subject to arbitration.

According to the provisions governing Swiss domestic arbitration, only *claims over which the parties may freely dispose* can be the object of a domestic arbitration agreement[8]. Whether a party may freely dispose over a claim has to be decided in light of the applicable *lex causae*[9]. However, the parties to a domestic arbitration dispute may not circumvent this restriction by choosing a more convenient substantive law. Contracting parties which are both domiciled in Switzerland may not choose to submit their dispute to a different substantive law than Swiss law[10].

Under Swiss employment law, the employee *may not waive claims arising from mandatory provisions of law or the mandatory provisions of a collective employment contract*, for the period of the employment relationship and for one month after its end[11].

By way of example, claims arising from mandatory provisions[12] relate to:
- the assignment and pledge of salary claims, reimbursement and advance of expenses, maturity of claims;
- overtime, holiday pay, consecutive weeks and timing of holidays, days off work, maternity leave, salary where the employer fails to accept work, or salary where the employee is prevented from working;
- employee's liability, termination of employment relationships, compensation in the event of wrongful termination, termination with immediate effect for good cause, consequences of justified termination, liability in the event of transfer of employment relationships;
- protection of the employee's personality rights in general, protection when handling personal data; and
- requirements for prohibition of competition, restrictions on prohibition of competition, extinction of prohibition of competition.

As an employee may, for the period of the employment relationship and for one month after its end, not waive such claims arising from mandatory provisions of labour law, such claims are not considered to be freely disposable. Therefore, the Swiss Federal Court held that claims arising from mandatory provisions of labour law may not be the object of a domestic arbitration agreement, if this arbitration agreement has been concluded before the above-mentioned period has elapsed[13].

This recent case leads, in a domestic context, to a bifurcation. On one hand, all claims arising of mandatory provisions have to be pursued in state courts. On the other hand, claims arising from non-mandatory provisions may be subject to arbitration.

Most importantly, claims arising for the payment (or re-payment) of a bonus are arbitrable.

In light of these restrictions, two solutions have recently been put forward.

One solution is the so-called *"opting-out"* approach. In fact, the parties to a domestic arbitration may, by making an express declaration to this effect in the arbitration agreement or a subsequent agreement, exclude the application of the CPC and instead agree that the provisions of the Twelfth Chapter of the Swiss Private International Law Act (the **PILA**)[14] apply[15]. This declaration must be made in writing or in any other form allowing it to be evidenced by text.

Some authors argue that, by opting for the applicability of the PILA instead of the CPC, the question of arbitrability will also be governed by the PILA. According to these authors, all pecuniary claims, and therefore, all disputes arising of individual employment contracts, may be submitted to arbitration[16]. However, according to certain legal opinion, the arbitrability of disputes arising of individual employment agreements should, even in such "opting out" cases, be governed by the restrictive provisions of the CPC[17]. The Swiss Federal Court has not yet decided on the issue.

The alternative would be an agreement to arbitrate which provides for an arbitral tribunal with its seat outside of the territory of Switzerland. In fact, the Swiss legislation on arbitration and, therefore, the provisions governing arbitrability are only applicable to arbitral tribunals having their seat in Switzerland[18]. In case one of the contracting parties does, in disregard of the agreement to arbitrate, file a claim with a Swiss state court, the court in question will probably have to decide on its competence. In this context, the court will have to decide, as a preliminary question, whether a valid arbitration agreement has been concluded by the parties.

Notwithstanding article V ciph. 2 lett. a of the Convention on the Recognition and Enforcement of Foreign Arbitral Awards (**New York Convention**), prevailing Swiss legal doctrine argues that the question of arbitrability is solely governed by the *lex fori*[19]. Accordingly, the validity of such an agreement to arbitrate would have to be decided applying either the PILA or the CPC. However, it may occur that a state court would leave this question unanswered and opt for applying the more restrictive provisions of the CPC based on public policy reasons[20].

Recent case law regarding abusive dismissals, waiver of claims, mandatory salary or bonus payments and consultation requirements

Abusive dismissals

Swiss law is governed by the principle that both employer and employee have the right to give notice of termination for any reason ("freedom of termination of employment relationships"). Hence, employers neither have to rely on a particular justification for a termination, nor do they have to follow a specific procedure. However, the employer cannot give any notices during protection periods. Such protection exists while the employee is on military or civil service or a foreign aid project, while the employee is totally or partially incapacitated to work due to sickness or accident (the latter protection period is limited to between 30 and 180 days, depending on the years of service), or during pregnancy and 16 weeks following childbirth. Moreover, employees can rely on additional protection in cases of mass dismissals or if notice has been given in connection with a gender-related issue or dispute.

Furthermore, the dismissal must not be abusive. Such abuse exists, for example, if notice of termination is given because the employee raises a *bona fide* claim arising out of the employment agreement, because the employee exercises a constitutional right, because notice is only given to prevent a claim arising out of the contract from coming into existence, or because notice is given for a reason that is inherent to the personality of the other party (race, origin, nationality, etc.). An abusive dismissal will be effective, but the employee is entitled to financial compensation of up to an amount equal to six monthly salaries.

The intention of the law with respect to abusive dismissals was to protect employees from notices which were obviously not in line with the principle of good faith. Case-law published in the last few years, however, tends to restrict the employers' right to give notice. While many of these decisions will only need to be considered under specific circumstances (*e.g.* terminations shortly before the employee reaches the retirement age or in connection with [alleged] bullying situations), a Swiss Federal Court decision rendered on 25 August 2011[21] might have an impact on a considerable number of dismissals. The factual background of the case was the following: a human resources manager had various disputes with her superior, *e.g.* regarding expenses and responsibilities. She informed her employer that these disputes resulted in a complete lack of trust and that she was, therefore, no longer prepared to continue to work with her superior. Based on this refusal to work with her superior, and after discussions with all individuals involved, the employee was terminated.

The Swiss Federal Court held that a termination is abusive if the employer caused the situation that triggered the notice. In the present case, tasks and responsibilities were not clearly assigned between the employee and her superior. This shortcoming was the source of most disputes. Given that the employer was responsible for this lack of clear organisational rules, the Swiss Federal Court stated that it was at least partly responsible for the situation that resulted in the termination. While the employer tried to resolve the conflict between the employee and her manger before notice was given, the source of the problem (*i.e.* the lack of clear organisational rules) had never been duly addressed. Therefore, the termination was considered to be abusive and the employee was found to be entitled to financial compensation.

Discrepancies and lack of trust between employees and superiors that cannot be resolved within a reasonable time might call for a dismissal. Employers need to be aware that they run the risk that a notice given will be qualified as abusive if their own faults have, at least, partly contributed to the conflict. Depending on the facts of the case, employers can take steps to reduce this risk.

An unconditional salary payment might constitute a waiver of the employer's claims

The Swiss Federal Court held in a judgment of 5 September 2011[22] that the unconditional payment of a salary can constitute a waiver of any employer's claims.

A drunk-driving employee caused two accidents with a company car. Thereafter, the parties agreed in an annex to the employment agreement that the employee would abstain from consuming alcohol. In addition, the employer reserved its right to claim damages for any costs resulting out of the accidents. Six months later, the employee was dismissed for cause. In the written notice, the employer referred to the executed annex and reserved once more its right to claim damages. The salary until the termination date was paid to the employee the following week. After the employee filed a claim for compensation for unjustified dismissal for cause, the employer declared that any compensation would be set-off with its damages claim.

The Swiss Federal Court held that the damage claim would only be time-barred after ten years. However, according to the principle of good faith, the unconditional payment of the final salary after the termination of the employment can be considered as a waiver of any known (financial) claim against the employee. In the case under consideration, the notice letter contained a reservation with respect to certain claims. Despite this reservation, the Swiss Federal Court considered the unconditional salary payment a few days later as an implicit waiver of these claims. Given that such a waiver is irrevocable, the employer's counsel's letter sent out one month later stating that damages would be claimed, should the employee challenge the termination, could not have any impact on the legal situation.

Precedent with respect to many areas of law state that creditors are under no duty to enforce their claims immediately. Unless a claim is time-barred, it can be asserted anytime and in most, aside from exceptional cases debtors are unable to establish an "implied" waiver. However, previous case law suggested that a different standard applies in employment law and that the unconditional payment of the final salary might constitute a waiver of certain employer's claims. The recent Swiss Federal Court decision went one step further: even if the claim was expressly reserved a few days before and one month after the salary was paid, this payment was considered as unconditional and therefore qualified as a waiver of the previously reserved claim. The reasoning in the judgment suggests that even salary payments made during an ongoing employment relationship might – subject to certain conditions – result in a waiver of any known (financial) claim against the employee.

Unfortunately, the judgment does not fully take into account the fact that payroll is often handled by specialised staff or even external providers. Hence, in practice, the payment of salaries is an automatic process and does not have to reflect any intention of the company. Thus, it is questionable that such payment should override the content of a letter sent out a few days before. However, considering the recent decision, employers are well advised to expressly reserve their claim directly on each and any payslip.

Mass dismissals: consultation proceedings

Employers must consult with the employees before a final decision is taken on dismissals if the dismissal is considered a "mass dismissal", i.e. if more than 10 to 30 employees (depending on the headcount of the business) are terminated within 30 days. During consultation, the employer shall give the employees the possibility to make suggestions on how to avoid the dismissals or to limit the number of dismissals or to alleviate their consequences.

In order to initiate the consultation proceedings, the employer has to inform the employees in writing of the reasons for the mass dismissal, the number of employees to be dismissed, the number of persons usually employed and the time-period within which the notices of termination are to be given. Further, the employer has to provide – on its own initiative or on request – all pertinent information.

A Swiss Federal Court decision of 11 March 2011[23] provides some guidance as to what information is considered to be pertinent and how such information shall be given. During consultation proceedings, employees requested the employer to provide answers in writing to a considerable number of questions. They claimed that the employer breached its duties with late and partly incomplete answers.

The Swiss Federal Court held that information is "pertinent", if it is required in order to put the employees in a position to submit additional or improved proposals that have realistic prospects to be implemented and that, in fact, might result in a reduction of the number of dismissals or will alleviate their consequences. However, the consultation process does not require that all information be provided when it might, in theory, only be potentially helpful to draft additional proposals. Moreover, the court stated that information given orally might be more appropriate under certain circumstances, because employees can ensure with follow-up questions that incomplete information is further detailed.

While the claim of the employees was dismissed, the reasoning of the judgement makes clear that the employer is under a duty to provide considerable additional information during the consultation process on request by the employees. Employers that do not have such information available at short notice might have to extend the consultation period. If the final decision on the mass dismissal is taken before all requests for pertinent information are dealt with, the terminations will be considered to be abusive and the employees are entitled to financial compensation.

<u>Enforceability of provisions of employee incentive schemes</u>

Swiss statutory labour law has no specific rules for employee incentive schemes (employee stock option plans, cash plans, bonus schemes, etc.). Rather, all such benefits must be qualified as one of several forms of compensation under Swiss law. Benefits awarded under employee incentive schemes regularly qualify as either *salary* or *gratification*.

The distinction between salary and gratification is crucial in Swiss labour law. While the payment or clawback of a gratification may depend on various conditions, clauses which limit the right to salary are generally unenforceable. For example, incentive schemes often provide that the employee forfeits awards and loses the right to benefits during notice period if the employee has given notice of termination of the employment relationship. The enforceability of such provisions depends on whether the respective benefits are qualified as salary or as gratification under Swiss law.[24]

The qualification of a benefit as either salary or gratification will firstly depend on the agreement of both the employer and the employee. In addition to the wording of the employment agreement and of special incentive plans or bonus schemes, the communication of the employer when granting the yearly benefit is considered important.

However, even if the agreement between the parties provides that the benefit is not mandatory and the grant of payments remains in the full discretion of the employer, the benefit may still be qualified as salary.

This is the case if the benefit and its amount actually does not depend on the employer's discretion, but exclusively on objective factors, *e.g.*, if the amount of the benefit is guaranteed or fixed or if it can be calculated based on targets or a formula[25].

Moreover, the Swiss Federal Court held that only benefits that are of "secondary nature" or "secondary importance" as compared to the total compensation can be considered gratification. Excessive payments are re-qualified as salary.[26] Finally, even if the "discretionary" amounts are below this threshold, and even if the employer expressly stated that the payments are discretionary, the employee might have a right to payment of the benefit should the employer's reservation after several years have become pure rhetoric without actual meaning.

Regrettably, despite various published precedents, there is little settled law regarding the above-mentioned issues. In particular, the courts have not defined a specific ratio which would determine the acceptable amount for a benefit bonus to still qualify as gratification. After all, it follows from the jurisprudence that the higher the base salary, the higher the allowed percentage of the benefit. But if the value of the benefit regularly exceeds the base salary, the allowed ratio between the benefit to the base salary might not be respected. On the other hand, even a very high bonus can be deemed gratification if the (excessive) payment is non-recurring.[27] Finally, the existing line of precedents does not clarify whether excessive benefits would be split in a part salary and a part gratification, so that at least a partial forfeiture of benefits upon termination is possible.[28]

Two recent decisions, both relating to claims brought by senior bank employees, (the Swiss Federal Court decision of 15 May 2012[29] and the Zurich High Court decision of 14 September 2011)[30] have shed a little light on the present status of the law. In summary, both decisions have confirmed a relatively employer-friendly line of precedents.

The Zurich High Court had to decide a case in which a bank employee had received bonuses that were considerably higher than the base salary over several years. The Court first confirmed that it would apply the (vague) criteria of the Swiss Federal Court despite the lower court's criticism of the Federal Court's precedents. Furthermore, the High Court clarified that benefits that had too high a value compared to total compensation, in order to be qualified as gratification, would only partially be re-qualified as salary, i.e. that only the "excess" part would be considered as salary, the other gratification. The court found that, generally, gratification payments should not be higher than 50% of the total compensation. For the part of the bonus payments that was within that range, the court confirmed that the payment could be made conditional on the lack of any notice to terminate the employment relationship.

In its decision of 15 May 2012, the Swiss Federal Court first confirmed its long-standing jurisprudence according to which the payment of "gratification" becomes mandatory if it was paid for three consecutive years, unless the employer has made a respective reservation. In the case under consideration, the senior bank employee had received bonus payments during a period of nine years, but always (apart from once) made a reservation that the payments were voluntary. To the surprise of various employee lawyers, the Federal Court decided that the reservations of the employer were sufficient to prevent the creation of a right to the bonus payments, and that a right to the bonus would only be created if the bonus had been paid for ten years or more.

Secondly, the Swiss Federal Court confirmed that benefits could only be qualified as gratification if they had a secondary importance. In this case, the Federal Court first noted that the employee had received a salary that was clearly above average (CHF 200,000 to CHF 300,000), and that the relationship of bonus payments to total compensation had varied from 30% to 63%, but that on average they had been 44% and, therefore, not lost their secondary nature. Accordingly, the payments were qualified as gratification and not mandatory.

Recent legislative changes: Variable remuneration and System-Relevant Banks

On 1 March 2012, art.10a of the Swiss Federal Law of 8 November 1934 on Banks and Savings Banks (**Banking Act, BA**) entered into force. According to this provision, system-relevant banks have to adopt provisions in their remuneration schemes stating that the legal right to variable remuneration may be curtailed in case state support is granted to the bank.

In this context, the question may arise whether such provisions, once adopted, are enforceable or whether mandatory principles of labour law contradict the banking legislation. In particular, certain forms of variable compensation could be considered *salary* within the meaning of Swiss labour law and, therefore, mandatory so that no curtailment is possible. In addition, it may not be possible to curtail awards that have already been granted in the past.

There are no precedents dealing with this question. If the courts rule that article 10a BA prevails over mandatory rules of Swiss labour law, such provisions will be enforceable. On the other hand, in case the courts consider the validity of such provisions in light of the mandatory rules of Swiss labour law, such provisions may (partly) not be enforceable.

In any event, the system-relevant banks have to include in their variable compensation schemes provisions that incorporate the new rules of the BA.

* * *

Endnotes

1. Swiss Civil Procedure Code of 19 December 2008, SR Number 272. For an English translation without legal force, *see*: http://www.admin.ch/ch/e/rs/c272.html.
2. Swiss Criminal Procedure Code of 5 October 2007, SR Number 312.0. For an English translation without legal force, *see*: http://www.admin.ch/ch/e/rs/c312_0.html.
3. Convention on the Jurisdiction and the Recognition and Enforcement of Judgments in Civil and Commercial Matters of 30 October 2007, SR Number 0.275.12. For an English version, *see*: http://www.rhf.admin.ch/rhf/de/home/zivil/recht/sr0-275-12.html.
4. Federal Debt Enforcement and Bankruptcy Act of 11 April 1889, SR Number 281.1.
5. In detail ISABELLE WILDHABER | ALEXANDRA JOHNSON WILCKE, Die Schiedsfähigkeit von individualarbeitsrechtlichen Streitigkeiten in der Binnenschiedsgerichtsbarkeit, in: *Zeitschrift für Arbeitsrecht und Arbeitslosenversicherung* (ARV) 2010 p.150 ss.
6. Article 176 para.1 of the Swiss Federal Act on International Private Law (**PILA**) of 18 December 1987. Decision of the Swiss Federal Court (**DFT**) 136 III 467 cons.4.2.
7. Article 177 para.1 PILA.
8. Article 354 of the Swiss Civil Procedure Code (**CPC**).
9. FELIX DASSER, in: Oberhammer (ed.), *Kurzkommentar zur schweizerischen Zivilprozessordnung, Basel 2010*, Art.354 N 6.
10. DASSER, l.c., Art.381 N 7.
11. Article 341, Swiss Code of Obligations (**CO**).
12. Article 361 s. CO.
13. DFT 136 III 467.
14. Swiss Private International Law Act of 18 December 1987, SR Number 291.
15. Article 353 para.2 CPC.
16. BSK OR I-PORTMANN, Vor Art.319 ff. N 96 and N 99.
17. THOMAS KOLLER | NORBERT SENNHAUSER, Die arbeitsrechtliche Rechtsprechung des Bundesgerichts im Jahr 2010, in: *Zeitschrift des bernischen Juristenvereins* (**ZBJV**) 148/2012 pp.405 ss.; MARC ANDRÉ MAUERHOFER, Gültigkeit statutarischer Schieds- und Gerichtsstandsklauseln, in: *Gesellschafts- und Kapitalmarktrecht (GesKR) 2011*, pp.20 ss.
18. *Cf.* Article 353 para.1 CPC, and Article 176 para.1 PILA.
19. *Cf.* CHRISTIAN JOSI, Die Anerkennung und Vollstreckung der Schiedssprüche in der Schweiz, Diss. Bern 2005, p.91, with further references.
20. *Cf.* in a different context Cantonal Court of Zug, 16 August 2006, in: *Gerichts- und Verwaltungspraxis des Kantons Zug* (**GVP**) *2006*, pp.179 ss. *Cf.* to public policy with regard to international individual employment contracts DFT 136 III 392.
21. Swiss Federal Court's Decision 8C_594/2010, 25 August 2011.
22. Swiss Federal Court's Decision 4A_351/2011, 5 September 2011.
23. Swiss Federal Court's Decision 4A_483/2010, 11 March 2011, publ. in the official gazette DFT 137 III 162.
24. Swiss Federal Court's Decision 4A_509/2008, 3 February 2009, cons.5.1; 4C.426/2005, 28 February 2006, cons. 5.2.
25. Long-standing practice of the Swiss Federal Court, *cf.* see decisions in DTF 131 III 615 cons. 5.2; 109 II 448 cons. 5c and recent Swiss Federal Court's Decisions 4A_509/2008, 3 February 2009, cons. 4.1; 4A_115/2007, 13 July 2007, cons. 4.3.3, publ. in ARV 2007 p. 249 ss.
26. See decision of the Swiss Federal Court in DTF 131 III 615 cons. 5.2.
27. So the Swiss Federal Court in DTF 131 III 615 cons. 5.2; 129 III 276 cons. 2.1; decisions of the Swiss Federal Court 4A_115/2007 and 4A_511/2008.
28. The Swiss Federal Court has touched on this question by stating that a high bonus (compared with the base salary) will at least partly be deemed to be (variable) salary (DTF 129 III 276 cons. 2.1). Later decisions have not made this distinction.
29. Swiss Federal Court Decision 4A_26/2012, 15 May 2012.
30. Zurich High Court Decision LA100002, on a Zurich Labour Court Decision AN080738 of 18 December 2009.

Balz Gross
Tel: +41 43 222 16 39 / Email: balz.gross@homburger.ch
Balz Gross is the Deputy Head of Homburger's Litigation | Arbitration practice and Head of the employment law group. He has extensive experience regarding all aspects of international arbitration and complex litigation. Recommended in Chambers (2011 etc. "leading litigator and arbitration counsel" 2010).

Roger Zuber
Tel: +41 43 222 10 00 / Email: roger.zuber@homburger.ch
Roger Zuber's practice focuses on domestic and international litigation and arbitration. Furthermore, he has extensive experience in rendering advice on employment law and he frequently represents clients in related court proceedings.

Nadine Mayhall
Tel: +41 43 222 10 00 / Email: nadine.mayhall@homburger.ch
Nadine Mayhall's practice focuses on domestic and international litigation and arbitration. She is also a member of Homburger's Employment Law working group.

Homburger

Prime Tower, Hardstrasse 201, CH-8005 Zurich, Switzerland
Tel: +41 43 222 10 00 / Fax: +41 43 222 15 00 / URL: http://www.homburger.ch

Tanzania

Dr Wilbert Kapinga
Mkono & Co

Introduction

Tanzania overhauled its employment and labour laws in 2004 when it enacted the Employment and Labour Relations Act, Act No. 6 of 2004 ("the Employment Act") and the Labour Institutions Act, Act No. 7 of 2004 ("Labour Institutions Act"). Whereas the Employment Act provides for labour standards, rights and duties, the Labour Institutions Act constitutes the governmental organs charged with the task of administering the labour laws. Subsequently, in 2007 several pieces of subsidiary legislation were promulgated to facilitate the enforcement of labour rights and standards stipulated in the Employment Act. One of the most significant of these is the Employment and Labour Relations (Code of Good Practice) Rules, G.N. No. 42 of 2007. It is noteworthy that the new labour laws enumerated above borrow heavily from the employment and labour laws which are currently in force in the Republic of South Africa. Indeed, the new laws further enact employment and labour standards which, by and large, conform to the labour standards set by the International Labour Organization.

Fundamental rights and protection

As a general rule, the law prohibits the employment of children who are under the age of 18 years. Where the employer entertains doubt as to whether a potential employee is of majority age, the law requires the employer to investigate the issue of age prior to hiring. An employer commits a criminal offence where the employer recruits a minor. The only exception to the above prohibition of child labour is where there are special circumstances that require a child of the age not below 14 years to work in order to earn livelihood. In these circumstances, the child should be assigned light work which shall not prejudice the child's education or vocational training.

The Employment Act further prohibits forced labour. Indeed, a criminal offence is committed where an employer exacts forced labour from a person. Nevertheless, the Act provides five exceptions where a person may be compelled to work despite his unwillingness, for instance, providing compulsory labour under the National Defence Act, 1966 for work of a military character.

The new labour laws further prohibit discrimination in the workplace, of any kind, by the employer, trade union or employers' association. The breach of this prohibition amounts to a criminal offence. It is instructive that where discrimination is alleged in any proceedings, the Respondent employer, trade union or employers' association is legally required to disprove the same.

Under the new labour regime, every employee has the right to form or join a trade union and participate in its lawful activities. However, a senior management employee is barred from joining a trade union that represents non-senior management employees of the employer. On another note, every employer is entitled to form or join an employers' association and participate in its lawful activities.

Employment standards

The Employment Act comprehensively regulates the hours of work of an employee. The ordinary days of work are set at six days in a week. Further, the ordinary hours of work are set at 45 hours in a week, and 9 hours in a work day, inclusive of a 1 hour meal break per work day. An employee can be required to work for overtime hours only where the parties have concluded an agreement to that effect. In any event, the law provides a ceiling of 12 working hours per day inclusive of ordinary and overtime working hours.

The Employment Act further enacts detailed guidelines for the calculation of wages of an employee who is entitled to hourly, daily, weekly and monthly wage rates. The payment of remuneration to an employee must be in the form of money; not in kind. As a general rule, an employer is not entitled to make any deductions from an employee's remuneration.

The exception thereto is where the deduction is permitted by written law, collective agreement, wage determination, court order or arbitration award. Where the deduction is not based on any of the above grounds, the employee must agree in writing to such deductions from his remuneration. Indeed, the legal restriction on deductions from remuneration has been contentious, especially where the employer unilaterally deducts from the remuneration a sum of money to recover loans and advance payments made to an employee. The labour tribunals and the courts of law have been consistent that in the absence of a written agreement between the parties or court order sanctioning the deduction, such deduction is unlawful.

An employee is entitled to annual leave of not less than 28 consecutive days during one leave cycle. One leave cycle is constituted by a period of 12 months' consecutive employment. The 28 days' leave is inclusive of any public holiday which may fall within the period of the leave. During the annual leave, the employee is entitled to payment of his full remuneration in spite of his absence from work.

In Tanzania, an employee is entitled to sick leave for at least 126 days during one leave cycle. The employee is entitled to full wages during the first 63 days of the sick leave. For the second 63 days, the ailing employee is entitled to half wages. An employer is not obliged to pay an employee wages during sick leave if the employee does not produce a medical certificate issued by a medical practitioner. It is further noted that no wages are payable to an ailing employee if the employee is entitled to paid sick leave under any other law, fund or collective agreement.

It is further noted that a female employee is entitled to paid maternity leave of not less than 84 days during one leave cycle. The maternity leave period would be 100 days if the employee gave birth to more than one child. Most curiously, the employee is entitled to an additional 84 days' paid maternity leave within the same leave cycle if the child dies within a year of birth. The law further puts a ceiling of 4 maternity leave terms which an employee is entitled to take. Where the employee is breastfeeding, the employer is obliged to allow her time off, not exceeding two hours, to feed the child during working hours.

The labour reforms have factored in the concerns of working male parents as well. During each leave cycle, a male employee is entitled to 3 days of paid paternity leave. The only conditions stipulated are that the employee must be the father of the newly born child and that the leave must be taken within the first seven days of the birth of the child.

The Employment Act further provides for what we may refer to as "compassionate leave". An employee is entitled to 4 days' paid leave in the event of death or sickness of the employee's child. Upon the death of the employee's spouse, parent, grandparent, grandchild or sibling, the employee is nevertheless entitled to 4 days' paid leave.

Strikes and lockouts

Under the Employment Act, every employee has the right to strike in respect of a dispute of interest. Equally, every employer is entitled to lockout in respect of a dispute of interest. A dispute of interest refers to a labour dispute which does not arise from the application, interpretation or implementation of an agreement with an employee, collective agreement, the Employment Act or any other written law administered by the Minister responsible for labour. It follows that for labour rights which are already provided for in a written agreement or labour laws, the right to strike or lockout is unavailable.

The law provides an elaborate procedure to be followed before an employee engages in a lawful strike. As already noted above, the dispute must be a dispute of interest. The first step is that the dispute must first be referred to the Labour Commission for Mediation and Arbitration ("CMA") for mediation. The CMA is a quasi-judicial organ which undertakes mediation and arbitration of disputes in labour dispute proceedings. During mediation proceedings, decisions are arrived at by mutual consent of both parties. If the CMA mediation fails and the strike has been called by a trade union, the second step is that the trade union must conduct a ballot. For the strike to be sustainable, a majority of the trade union members who voted must support the strike. Finally, the employees are required to issue to the employer a 48-hour notice of their intention to strike before commencing lawful strike.

It is significant to underscore that the Employment Act further stipulates the procedure for lawful lockouts. Firstly, an employer who intends to engage in lockouts is required to refer the dispute to the CMA for mediation. If the dispute remains unresolved at the conclusion of mediation proceedings, the next step is for the employer or employer's association to issue to the employees or trade union a 48 hours notice of intention to lockout before commencing lockouts.

We are of the view that the staggered procedure, not to mention the intervening mediation proceedings, for lawful lockouts and strike action, gives the parties an opportunity to resolve their differences amicably. The stepped procedure further allows the employer to take remedial measures with a view to mitigating his losses when the intended strike commences.

Dispute resolution

All labour disputes must first be referred to the CMA for mediation. The mediator is required to resolve the dispute through mediation inside 30 days unless the parties agree to a longer period. If mediation fails, either party may further refer the labour complaint to a CMA arbitrator; or in the case of a dispute of interest, to the High Court, Labour Division (hereinafter "the Labour Court"). Both the arbitrator and the Labour Court are required to take evidence, hear both parties' legal submissions before rendering a decision on the merits of the case.

The Labour Court has been consistent in enforcing the rule that all labour disputes must first be referred to the CMA for arbitration. In the case of Hector Sequeiraa v. Serengeti Breweries Ltd, High Court of Tanzania, Labour Division, Labour Complaint No. 20 of 2009, the Labour Court dismissed as "incompetent" a labour complaint which was filed directly in the Court without first pursuing mandatory CMA mediation. Indeed, the significance of mediation cannot be ignored. There is an increasing trend by employers to settle labour disputes during CMA mediation especially where the employer's case is apparently weaker.

Where a party is aggrieved by the award of the CMA arbitrator, he is entitled to apply to the Labour Court for revision of the award. Such an application is sustainable only where the revision application reveals issues relating to jurisdiction, material irregularity, error material to the merits of the case. Further appeal against the decision of the Labour Court lies in the Court of Appeal of Tanzania.

Conclusion

In sum, we are of the view that the new labour regime obtaining in Tanzania is commendable for introducing mediation proceedings to resolve disputes. Where the parties are acting in good faith, mediation has proved to be a valuable tool in amicable settlement of disputes, thereby saving time and resources of the parties. The employment standards are further useful in setting the minimum labour rights, which both the employer and employee cannot downgrade by contract. Nevertheless, the stepped procedure for engaging in strikes and lockouts is meant to weed out surprise industrial action which may be detrimental to the employer's investment and the livelihood of employees.

Dr Wilbert Kapinga
Tel: +255 22 211 8789/8790/8791/4664 / Email: wilbert.kapinga@mkono.com
Dr Wilbert Kapinga is specialised in corporate law, finance law, banking, privatisation, telecommunications and competition law and has over 10 years' experience of transactions and projects in these areas. He is ranked Top Band (4 stars) specialising in Mergers and Acquisitions in the Chambers and Partners: the World's Leading Lawyers 2000-2001, and in the Chambers and Partners: The World's Leading Lawyers 2001-2002. Since the 2002-2003 Chambers & Partners, he is in Band 1 and still occupies the number 1 position as a leading individual in corporate law. He has been at the centre of advising several local and international banks on loan facilities, bond issuances and other type of securitisations. He has also been involved in a wide range of regulatory matters for petroleum and electric utilities and other facilities built through private finance initiatives.

Mkono & Co

8th Floor, Exim Tower, Ghana Avenue, P.O. Box 4369, Dar es Salaam, Tanzania
Tel: +255 22 211 8789/8790/8791/4664 / Fax: +255 22 211 3247/6635 / URL: http://www.mkono.com

Turkey

Gönenç Gürkaynak & Ayşın Obruk
ELIG, Attorneys-at-Law

General labour market trends and latest/likely trends in employment litigation

Mobbing is a fairly new subject, the number and claims for which are likely to increase. The relevant concept is not yet stipulated in Labour Law number 4857 ("Labour Law") or in relevant legislation. This being the case, it is evaluated through the decisions of the Turkish High Court of Appeals ("High Court of Appeals"). *As per* the relevant decisions, mobbing is defined as the systematic derogatory conduct, threat or violence realised against employees by their seniors, co-workers or juniors, at the workplace. Within this scope, the employees are protected against both their employers and co-workers.

The High Court of Appeals seeks consistency in the acts/events which comprise mobbing and any strong indication of its existence. Each case is examined individually to determine whether acts/events which comprise mobbing were, indeed, of a continuing nature and whether mobbing really took place.

In case an employee succeeds in proving that continuing psychological pressure against him/her did indeed take place through "strong indication", the employee will be able to terminate the employment agreement for cause and request the employer to pay: (i) the salary for the term when she/he was employed; (ii) severance pay, in case the employment term was over a year; (iii) pay for work on holidays, if any; (iv) overtime pay, if any; (v) pay for unused annual leave, if any; and (vi) premiums, bonuses, etc., if any. The employees may use e-mail correspondence or witness statements to demonstrate to the court "strong indication" of mobbing.

In light of the above, although in cases of resignation, no severance pay is paid to the employee; in those cases where an employee succeeds in proving that she/he resigned because of mobbing, she/he would most probably be entitled to severance pay since the relevant termination would be deemed to be executed by the employee for cause.

Key case law affecting employers' decision making over dismissal, redundancies dismissals etc.

The guidelines surrounding the admissibility of an employer's decision to dismiss vary on the ground on which the dismissal is based. The general outline of those guidelines is explained below and is also illustrated with several instances borne from the precedents of the High Court of Appeals, which, through its decisions, comprise the case-law of the Turkish legal system.

Reasons which are considered valid grounds to dismiss an employee are: (i) any act which disrupts the harmony and smooth operation of the workplace; or (ii) lack of performance in carrying out of his/her duties.

Before executing a dismissal based on the conduct of an employee, the employer is expected by law to: (i) analyse the situation which causes dissatisfaction following the employee's relevant conduct; (ii) request the relevant employee's defence regarding his/her actions; (iii) make an objective evaluation by taking into account the employee's defence and the circumstances of the case revealed by the enquiry; and (iv) serve a written warning to the employee, should it be deemed necessary, which also informs the employee that if such an act is to be repeated, the employer may resort to terminating the employment agreement. Only if the employee continues with such an act, even after the aforementioned written warning, the employer may then resort to termination. On that note, the mentioned act shall be deemed to have an effect so as to disrupt the harmony and smooth operation of the work place. Below, derived from various precedents, are illustrations of examples of actions which are accepted by the High Court of Appeals in that context to constitute grounds for dismissal:

Incurring pecuniary damage to the employer; performing his/her duties in a manner which causes grievance in the workplace; asking for a loan from a colleague on the condition that it harms the work relation; provoking his/her colleagues against the employer; engaging in long and personal phone calls which halt the smooth flow of work etc.

In addition to the employer's compliance to the process explained above, the Labour Law obliges the employer to serve the employee with a termination notice which explicitly states the reason for the dismissal decision of the employer. In the management of the abovementioned process, the High Court of Appeals fundamentally requires the employer to be moderate and take reasonable measures in face of the employee's actions.

Provided that the employee shows unsatisfactory performance with respect to the standards and expectations of the employer, the employer is entitled to terminate the employee's employment agreement. Nevertheless, the High Court of Appeals presents strict guidelines in order to avoid the misuse of power by the employer. In other words, the employer is bound by certain criteria and duties set out by the High Court of Appeals in its precedents. Below are illustrated examples, derived from various precedents, of insufficient performance which are accepted by the High Court of Appeals in that context:

Performing less efficiently than other employees who undertake the same or similar work; demonstrating a lower performance than expected by his/her qualifications; losing focus on the job at hand; getting sick leave frequently; not to be keen on the job; unable to learn and improve his/her capabilities; incapable of adapting to the workplace's environment etc.

On that note, the High Court of Appeals also asserts that the insufficiency has to be determined objectively. That is to say, the employer has to exclude any prejudice and/or personal preferences when determining and deciding on the insufficient performance of an employee. When the insufficiency of an employee is first detected, the employer has to make sure that the relevant employee undergoes a certain performance evaluation system (a performance improvement plan would qualify as such a performance evaluation system), in line with the principle of termination being considered as the last resort. Such a performance evaluation system has to include the determination of personal objectives, the measurement of the relevant employee's performance in the light of these objectives and informing the relevant employee of the result. Should the employee's performance be determined as insufficient after applying the aforementioned system, the employer shall: (i) ask the employee to provide written defence regarding his/her performance; and (ii) serve a written warning to the employee, should it be deemed necessary, which also informs the employee that if his/her performance does not show any progress, the termination of the employment agreement may take place. The High Court of Appeals requires the employer to execute its dismissal decisions as a last resort and prior to termination, the employer is to consider assigning the employee to some other position which may be deemed more suitable for the employee's skills and knowledge.

In cases of dismissal for cause, the High Court of Appeals establishes the following examples as cause in its precedents:

Deceiving the employer by claiming to have qualifications which he/she does not actually possess; insisting on not doing the tasks which are instructed by the employer; abusing the employer's trust, stealing, disclosing employer's trade secrets; sexually harassing another employee; insulting the employer or its family, making false and demeaning allegations about the employer, etc.

In that sense, the employer shall be careful to be in a position to be able to prove the existence of the abovementioned cases. The High Court of Appeals underlines the fact that the burden of proof is on the employer with respect to proving such claims to be true.

The High Court of Appeals' admissibility guidelines on redundancy dismissals are as follows: (i) the employer shall resort to dismissal only if the circumstances which affect the employment conditions make redundancy dismissals inevitable; (ii) the employer shall make an operational decision regarding the redundancy; (iii) such a decision shall be executed in a consistent manner; and (iv) the employer shall not act arbitrarily in making the decision that leads to the redundancy. Should those conditions be met, the employer's operational decision is not subject to judicial review. Furthermore, the employer shall not get involved in any practices which contradict with the operational decision. The High Court of Appeals adopts the *"dismissal to be considered as last resort"* principle in those cases as well and obliges the employer to evaluate any other position that the employee may be assigned to, instead of resorting to termination. The following are cases in which the High Court of Appeals deem to be the cause of redundancy in the workplace:

Decrease in sales opportunities or demand; energy shortcomings; economic crisis; recession in the market; shortcomings in raw materials; implementation of new technology; closing of certain divisions in the work place; annulment of certain jobs; etc.

With the most prominent and well-established precedents of the High Court of Appeals, a more definitive and elaborate guideline and roadmap are set out for the employers to follow and consider prior to making any decision as to the dismissals or redundancy dismissals.

Recent statutory or legislative changes

The latest change in legislation which had a great impact on employment relations is the new Turkish Law of Obligations number 6098, which came into force at the beginning of July 2012, i.e., July 1st, 2012 ("Law of Obligations"). The Law of Obligations is the most general law to apply to all contractual relations, including employment relations. In case the Labour Law does not contain a specific provision regarding a specific subject matter, the provisions of the Law of Obligations shall apply. One of the most prominent effects the Law of Obligations had on employment relations are on release letters.

With respect to the Labour law, a release is often granted by the employee regarding one or many receivables which she/he is entitled to collect from the employer.

Before the Law of Obligations came into effect, there was no specific provision under Turkish legislation which regulated release. This being the case, Turkish legal opinion and precedents of the High Court of Appeals accepted the existence of these without doubt. Release was defined as an agreement between two parties through which the creditor waived his/her receivables, released the debtor and the debtor showed consent to the creditor's act. The consent of the debtor for such a relation to be established did not necessarily have to be explicit; it could also be implicit. As for the formal requirements of a release; a release would only be valid where it was in writing. Nevertheless, such a requirement was not a validity requirement; it was solely a proof requirement. That is to say, even if the release were to be made orally, it would still be deemed valid. However, the party, which tried to rely on the relevant release, could not prove the existence of an oral release if the counter-party were to claim that no such release exists. Thus, it was recommended that the release be made in writing.

Listed below are precedents developed by the High Court of Appeals which had a great impact on the handling of release letters in employment law and which were consequently reflected within the Law of Obligations too:

1. The precedents of the High Court of Appeals suggested what the release letters should contain explicitly for the creditors to release debtors. General remarks stating that one party does not have any receivables to collect from the counter-party were and are deemed invalid by the High Court of Appeals. Accordingly, the items for which the creditor releases the debtor should be specifically mentioned within the release letter. In practice, most of the release letters which are in use by employers mention explicitly that the employees release the employers with respect to their severance pay, payment in lieu of notice, unused paid annual leave, etc. Such release letters are deemed valid by the High Court of Appeals.

2. Release letters, which contain an amount as to the items listed within, are deemed to be official

documents that prove that the relevant payments are indeed made. This is to say the explicit statement of each item for which the creditor releases the debtor and which specifies the amount due for each item, vests in the relevant document the quality of a receipt. It should be noted that the High Court of Appeals established the need to specify each item explicitly, for which the creditor releases the debtor, as a formal requirement for validity. Showing the amount of the relevant items, on the other hand, does not affect the validity of a release letter, it only vests in the relevant document the quality of a receipt with respect to the amount mentioned therein. In case it is found that the amounts mentioned within a release letter are less than what they ought to be, the amount exceeding the amount mentioned in the relevant release letter should be paid to the employee.

3.   In case the release letters contain a remark so as to state that the employee waives his/her right to resort to judicial proceedings, such a remark will not be deemed valid.

4.   Standarised release letters, the blanks of which are filled in later, are not deemed valid by the High Court of Appeals. This is to ensure that the principle of protection of the employee is preserved. An average employee might be led to think that it is appropriate to sign the relevant document since it is a standard text, used probably several times and signed by many. Having thought so, the relevant employee will not question much the content of what she/he is signing. Thus, each release letter must be tailored to meet the facts and circumstances of the case.

5.   The most important precedent which directly went into the wording of the Law of Obligations was regarding the date on which the release letters were signed by the employee. In practice, it was noted that most of the employers obtain release letters from employees prior to termination of the employment agreements; in fact, even at the beginning of the employment. The High Court of Appeals found it not to be possible for a document, in which the employee states that she/he received his/her employment rights before she/he was paid them, to be deemed valid.

In light of the above, Article 420 of the Law of Obligations introduced the conditions of a release letter for the first time within Turkish legislation. Accordingly: (i) a release letter should be in writing; (ii) a term of at least one month should exist between the date of termination of an agreement and the release date; (iii) the amount and the subject of the release should be explicitly regulated; and (iv) the payment should be made in full and via bank account. *As per* the Law of Obligations, those release letters which do not comply with the aforementioned conditions, are definitely invalid.

What is regulated within the Law of Obligations has combined principles that were already adopted through doctrine and the precedents of the High Court of Appeals, and it, taking one additional step, extended the term to take place between termination and release, to at least one month. The ideal situation envisaged by the Law of Obligations is that the agreement is terminated first, then a payment will be made through a bank, and then the release letter is signed at least a month after the date on which the agreement was terminated.

One important amendment adopted by the Law of Obligations is with regard to non-compete obligations, which could be imposed on the employees. *As per* both the previous Law of Obligations and the current Law of Obligations, the non-compete obligation to be imposed on the employee shall be so that the economic independence of the employee is not hindered. This was/is achieved through imposing reasonable limitations as to the place, term and subject on the non-compete obligation. The relevant amendment is regarding the term of the said obligation. Previously, there was no explicit provision of law on the matter and the precedents of the High Court of Appeals provided guidance on the issue. *As per* the Law of Obligations, the term is limited to two years, subject to exceptions.

Another change is the Law on Employment Health and Safety ("Health and Safety Law") number 6331.

The purpose of the Health and Safety Law is to regulate employers' and employees' assignments, authorities, responsibilities, rights and obligations in order to provide labour safety and health at the workplace and to improve present health and safety conditions. The Health and Safety Law shall apply to all businesses and workplaces belonging to the public and private sector, to the employers of these workplaces and to all employees including employer's representatives, apprentices and interns, irrespective of the subject matter of their activities.

The most important regulation within the Health and Safety Law is that the employer will have to assign a workplace doctor and other healthcare personnel for all the places of work, in order to avoid occupational risks. *As per* this provision, the previous legislation which obliges the employer to assign a workplace doctor in cases where the number of employees is 50 and above is abolished and the workplace doctor becomes compulsory for all workplaces.

Furthermore, *as per* Article 8 of the Health and Safety Law, the employer is obliged to assign an expert in labour safety, who has: (i) a class (A) certificate for the workplace which is classified as very dangerous; (ii) at least a class (B) certificate for the workplace which is classified as dangerous; (iii) at least a class (C) certificate for the workplace which is classified as less dangerous; and (iv) a workplace doctor and other healthcare personnel for all the workplaces regardless of which danger classification they fall under, in order to avoid occupational risks and to provide labour health and safety services involving the workplace in order to protect employees from these risks. Those workplaces which do not employ personnel with these characteristics can fulfil the whole or a part of this service by receiving services from common health and security units.

The assignments and authorities, operating rules and procedures and qualifications of the workplace doctor and labour safety expert will be determined through the regulation issued by the relevant ministry following the publication of law.

Another new instrument which was introduced by the Health and Safety Law is the Board of Labour Health and Safety. Under the Health and Safety Law, for workplaces employing 50 and more employees, where work is carried out continuously for longer than six months, the employer is obligated to establish a Board of Labour Health and Safety and to implement the decisions taken by the Board of Labour Health and Safety in accordance with legislation on labour health and safety. The composition, assignments and authorities, operating rules and procedures of the Board of Labour Health and Safety are determined through a regulation issued by the relevant ministry.

The Health and Safety Law also sets forth administrative penalties including an administrative fine and suspension of business. Article 25 reads: *"In case a matter which may endanger the life of employees is determined in the workplace buildings and extensions, working methods and procedures or equipment of a workplace by labour inspector authorized for inspection with respect to labour health and safety, the operation is suspended until this danger is eliminated. The decision for suspension of business may include a part of the workplace or the whole. The suspended business shall not be carried on until the matter endangering the life of employees is eliminated"*. Article 26, which stipulates the administrative fines and their enforcement, set forth various administrative fines between TL 200 – TL 50,000.

As per Article 38 of the Health and Safety Law, the date of entry into force varies between workplaces according to the number of their employees.

Likely or impending reforms to employment legislation and enforcement procedures

The Turkish government is currently working on a new regulation pertaining to severance pay. The said regulation involves major amendments compared to the current regulation as to that matter. The most prominent changes presented with this new regulation are as follows:

- The form of payment of the severance pay will be changed. The severance pay will be paid by a retirement company (which is selected by the employee for his/her social premiums to be deposited to) upon request of the employee.

- *As per* the new regulation, the severance pay will be paid as 4% of the employee's gross salary to the retirement company's relevant account, while the current regulation suggests that the employee's one month of gross salary shall be paid for each year of seniority.

- The employees who resigned or left work due to any other reason will also be entitled to the severance pay. The current regulation does not oblige the payment of severance pay to employees who have resigned or left work for any reason other than being dismissed without cause or without valid reason by the employer.

- The new regulation also suggests that the employees of any seniority will be entitled to the severance pay while the current regulation stipulates that the employee should have at least one year of seniority in order to be entitled to the payment of severance pay.

- The conditions for the request of severance pay have also changed. The employee shall have 15 years of insurance period and premium payment *in lieu* of 3,600 days in order to be able to demand the payment of severance pay. Nevertheless, the employee may still be entitled to such payment in case he/she will use that money to invest in the purchase of a house. The current litigation does not involve such an exception for payment.

- The new regulation suggests that the statute of limitations for the request of severance pay will be 10 years as of the date on which the employee is deemed entitled to request such payment.

- The said regulation has not yet passed the parliament reading, hence it is subject to further amendments which will be held in the legislation commission as to that regulation.

Gönenç Gürkaynak
Tel: +90 212 327 1724 / Email: gonenc.gurkaynak@elig.com
Gönenç Gürkaynak holds an LL.M. degree from Harvard Law School, and he is qualified in Istanbul, New York and England & Wales (currently a non-practising Solicitor). Mr. Gürkaynak heads the regulatory & compliance department of ELIG, together with the litigation practice group. Mr. Gürkaynak has represented numerous multinational companies and large Turkish entities before Civil Courts, Courts of Appeal, Administrative Courts and the High State Court on hundreds of disputes, in addition to coordinating various out-of-court settlements, mediations and dispute resolution processes. Prior to joining ELIG as a partner in 2004, he worked in Istanbul, New York, Brussels and again in the Istanbul offices of White & Case LLP for more than eight years.

Ayşın Obruk
Tel: +90 212 327 1724 / Email: aysin.obruk@elig.com
Followed by her graduation from Marmara University School of Law in 2005, Ayşın Obruk started to practise civil law by handling various high-profile litigation cases as a member of the Istanbul Bar Association. During her LL.M. studies in Business Law in Istanbul Bilgi University School of Law, Institute of Social Sciences, she attended civil law courses at the University of Ghent in Belgium for a semester in 2007. As a senior associate, she mainly focused on legal counseling for a wide range of international and Turkish clients in labour law matters along with litigation services and has a diverse legal expertise and practice in assistance for the draft of employment contracts, handling day-to-day employment law matters of clients, counselling on termination procedures and providing assistance in every step of the way. She is also specialised as a litigator in intellectual property law, media law and commercial law matters. She is fluent in English.

ELIG, Attorneys-at-Law

Çitlenbik Sokak No: 12, Yıldız Mahallesi, Beşiktaş 34349, İstanbul, Turkey
Tel: +90 212 327 1724 / Fax: +90 212 327 1725 / URL: http://www.elig.com

United Arab Emirates

Samir Kantaria
Al Tamimi & Company

Overview

Generally speaking, employment relationships in the United Arab Emirates ("**UAE**") are regulated by the UAE Federal Law No. 8 of 1980, Regulating Labour Relations, as amended ("**Labour Law**"), together with regulations promulgated under that law. The Labour Law applies to all employees working in the UAE, whether national or non-national, with the exception of certain categories of people (including, for example, domestic servants, agricultural workers, members of the armed forces, individuals employed by the Federal Government, individuals employed by companies in the Dubai International Financial Centre, etc.).

Employees working in the Dubai International Financial Centre ("**DIFC**") are subject to the DIFC Employment Law No. 4 of 2005 ("**DIFC Employment Law**"). The legislative regime in the DIFC (save for certain laws, such as criminal and immigration) is independent to the UAE. The DIFC has its own laws and regulations which govern commerce within the DIFC, supported by its own independent English language common law court system to interpret its laws and adjudicate DIFC-related civil and commercial cases.

The UAE faces relatively unique challenges, in that its population and workforce are predominantly made up of expatriates (for example, figures released last year indicated that 93% of the private sector workforce was made up of expatriates). The UAE must therefore balance the need for access to jobs and training for its local population and the retention of expatriates, particularly in the light of the recent changes provoked by the economic climate.

Largely in response to this challenge, the UAE authorities introduced a positive discrimination policy of "Emiratisation", which sought to increase the number of UAE nationals in the private sector by providing recruitment targets of UAE national employees for employers. The Emiratisation quotas were set at a minimum of 2% of the workforce for most employers (where a company has at least 50 employees), with the exception of the banking and insurance sectors, where the quotas were set at 4% and 5% respectively, and increased year-on-year. Additionally, in 2009, new regulations were issued in 2009, which limited the circumstances in which UAE nationals' employment could be terminated by an employer.

The Arab Spring has also had an effect, with a number of foreign and multinational investors reviewing their investment strategies into those affected countries, such as Bahrain. The effect in the UAE has largely been positive, with a number of foreign employers relocating a large number of their staff (and families) to the UAE, cancelling planned expansions and refocusing the expansion on their UAE/DIFC operations and with certain organisations resolving to shut down operations in affected countries and shifting entire operations to the UAE/DIFC.

Key Developments

It is possible to characterise the recent key developments in the law as addressing certain areas which, as identified above, result from the UAE's unique position. These broadly fall into the following categories: (a) the management of the movement of workers; (b) the protection of UAE nationals; and (c) developing practices that ensure that the UAE is in line with international standards for workers. Each of these is dealt with in turn.

Management of the movement of workers

Labour Bans

Prior to January 2011, the Ministry of Labour imposed an automatic 6-month ban on all expatriates leaving their employer. This applied to all employees falling within their jurisdiction (i.e. this would not affect employees based within one of the free zones, or the DIFC). The ban could only be lifted for those individuals with more than one year's service by way of a "no objection certificate" given by the former employer and/or payment of a fee (depending upon length of service).

However, during the economic downturn of 2009/2010, the automatic ban affected employees who had been made redundant by their employer, and it can be assumed that this, in turn, resulted in the loss of certain skilled workers with a local knowledge from the UAE.

From January 2011, the practice has been amended and, in accordance with a Ministerial resolution, the automatic ban will not be imposed in certain circumstances, having regard to issues such as length of service, level of expertise, and reason for dismissal, including whether the termination is due to a business reorganisation. It is worth noting that there are no transfer regulations in the UAE and, accordingly, on any "transfer" of employment from one employer to another, the employment with the first employer is treated as having been terminated and the employee enters into a new employment contract with the second employer.

In addition, in practice, the Ministry of Labour have relaxed the enforcement of the employment ban provisions even further, so that, at present, employees are free to move between employers (subject to any post-termination restrictions or other issues raised before the Ministry of Labour). However, the Ministerial resolution remains in place and could be enforced in the future.

Internal work permits

In order to work in the UAE, an expatriate must obtain a residency visa and work permit. If the employee works within a free zone, their residency visa and ID card (work permit) is obtained via the relevant free zone (for example, DIFC). Where the individual is employed by a private entity outside of the free zones, the residency visa and work permit will be obtained via the UAE Department of Naturalization and Residency ("DNR") and Ministry of Labour respectively. UAE nationals are also required to obtain a work permit from the relevant authority.

The use of work permits is a further method by which the relevant authorities are able to manage the movement of workers. From January 2011, the Ministry of Labour introduced five new work permits, which are applicable in cases where the relevant individual already has a residence visa (or, in the case of a UAE national, is entitled to reside in the UAE). These permits are for a work transfer, temporary work, part-time work, cases where individuals are sponsored by family members and for juveniles. One of the aims of the temporary work permit is to allow expatriates to obtain employment from another employer, pending the outcome of any ongoing litigation with their former employer (with whom they retain their visa). The part-time work permit is open for use by both expatriates and UAE nationals, although it is likely that one of the aims of the permit is to encourage UAE national females into the workforce. As with all permits, these are only issued upon the approval of the Ministry of Labour and therefore they are tightly controlled. The use of the part-time permit remains in doubt, in light of the fact that the UAE Labour Law does not make any provision for part-time work and therefore minimum provisions applicable to full-time employment (such as annual leave and sickness absence entitlement) will continue to apply without amendment to part-time employees.

Retirement

As noted above, all employees must have approval to work, by way of a work permit or ID card from the relevant authority. Prior to January 2011, employees falling under the Ministry of Labour jurisdiction were required to obtain express approval for the continuation of their work status once they reached the age of 60 years. The age limit after which express approval must be obtained has been increased to 65 years (although the "retirement age" for the purposes of UAE national pension entitlement remains at 60 years).

Notwithstanding the work permit requirements noted above, it should be borne in mind that there is no concept of "retirement" in the UAE Labour Law (or the DIFC Employment Law) and therefore any termination of employment due to a company retirement scheme is nevertheless subject to the usual termination provisions contained in the law.

The Protection of UAE nationals

Legislation seeking to protect UAE nationals addresses two main issues, namely, access to jobs, and protection from dismissal.

As set out in the Overview, the UAE authorities operate a policy of "Emiratisation", which seeks to encourage private sector employers falling under the Ministry of Labour jurisdiction to maintain minimum levels of UAE nationals in their workforce. Whilst, prior to January 2011, the Emiratisation policy was relatively indiscriminate, focusing purely on the number of UAE nationals in the workforce, a Ministry of Labour resolution which came into force in January 2011 now addresses the requirement for UAE nationals to fall within the white collar labour force and in particular, UAE nationals should make up 3% of the top three professional categories in an employer's workforce. The professional categories have to date been based upon educational qualifications, although there is a move towards reclassifying these, based upon professional experience.

Firms which maintain the required level of UAE nationals at the professional categories, and also comply with certain other Ministry of Labour requirements, are categorised as "First Class" companies, out of three possible categories (of which the "Second Class" category is further divided into three sub-groups). The Second Class categorisation also focuses on employee diversity, and seeks to limit the percentage of the workforce made up of one of three nationalities (Indian, Pakistani, and Bangladeshi). The category into which a company falls will determine the amount of fees and bank guarantees that the company will be required to pay to the Ministry of Labour, as part of the normal administrative requirements when obtaining Ministerial consent for the employment of staff.

UAE nationals have also enjoyed protection from dismissal, since 2009, when a Ministerial resolution was introduced which limited the circumstances in which a UAE national may be dismissed. The resolution provides that the termination of UAE nationals in the private sector is unlawful if the employer does not first notify the Ministry of Labour of the proposed dismissal (and at least 30 days before the termination date). The Ministry of Labour will investigate whether the employment is being terminated for a legally valid reason. If the Ministry of Labour decides the termination is not for a legally valid reason, the employer is given 15 days to resolve the situation. In accordance with the resolution, the termination will not be valid where: (a) the employment is being terminated for a reason other than one of ten specified reasons for cause listed in the UAE Labour Law (in practice, the ten reasons listed in the law are very narrowly interpreted); (b) a non-national is undertaking the same role (in other words, the non-national should be dismissed first); or (c) where the UAE national has not received all end of service benefits due to them.

Development of employment standards and employee protection

Although it remains the case that collective bargaining and strike action remain illegal in the UAE, there have been a number of recent developments intended to give protection to employees, particularly blue-collar workers who may lack the ability to challenge unfair practices. Recent key developments are as follows:

- In 2009, the Wage Protection System ("WPS") was introduced and came into effect in 2010. This applies to all employees falling within the Ministry of Labour jurisdiction. Employers are required to pay employees' salaries in UAE dirhams through the WPS. This is intended to ensure that employees are paid the correct salary amounts, and that the salaries are paid on time.
- In September 2009, the Ministry of Labour introduced the "Manual of the General Criteria for Workers Accommodation" which regulates labour camp accommodation, and specifies matters such as building materials, covers water systems, sewerage, air-conditioning, lighting systems, elevators, emergency exits, fire extinguisher systems, and indoor air quality. At least 35% of the total space must be allocated for entertainment, parking, yards, walkways and green spaces. Each accommodation complex should have its own mini market and playgrounds.
- "Manpower supply companies" are organisations which supply temporary labour and provide

recruitment services. These are strictly regulated by the Ministry of Labour and a Ministerial resolution in 2010 revised the criteria for the provision of licences to labour supply entities. The key requirement in order to apply for a licence is that the owner (whether an individual or an entity) must be a UAE national. Subject to satisfaction of the relevant criteria, the company's trade licence will specify that it is licensed for "On Demand Labour Supply" activities. Upon the provision of such licence, a company is permitted to provide temporary employment services. The resolution was issued in response to complaints that certain employees recruited by manpower supply companies offshore were badly treated or misled over employment opportunities. Although the resolution only regulates UAE-based manpower supply companies, in January 2011, the Ministry of Labour organised a workshop (held in Dubai) in co-operation with the International Labour Organisation (ILO), International Organisation for Migration (IOM) and the office for the Higher Commission on Human Rights. At the workshop, the federal Government called on nations that supply labour to the UAE to strengthen their laws regulating recruitment agencies in order to better collaborate with UAE authorities for the protection of workers.

- In January 2011 the Ministry of Labour issued a new resolution to regulate the operation of recruitment agencies in the UAE. According to the resolution, agencies are now obliged to return any recruitment fees paid by a worker – whether in the UAE or abroad. Under the law, it is the employer's responsibility to pay agency fees.

- As noted above, the classification of companies includes a "third class" category. This category includes those companies who receive a certain number of fines or "penalty points" issued by the Ministry of Labour for breach of Ministerial resolutions, as well as companies undertaking more serious activities, such as human trafficking.

- Although the DIFC Employment Law contains anti-discrimination protection, the UAE Labour Law only contains positive discrimination provisions. However, the Twofour54 Abu Dhabi Media Free Zone introduced anti-discrimination provisions in its employment regulations in 2011, which state that the free zone aims to create an environment within the free zone where employment and advancement is based on merit and an employee is not treated less favourably by reason of gender, marital status, race, religion or disability. The regulations also impose an obligation on companies operating in the free zone to be guided by the principle of non-discrimination when employing employees.

- The DIFC Court offers employees an informal forum in which to bring employment claims, being the Small Claims Tribunal. In 2011, the SCT extended its jurisdiction to all employment claims which equal or are less than AED200,000, and in addition, it is possible for the SCT to hear all employment claims (regardless of size of the amount of the claim), upon consent by both parties.

- The DIFC also introduced a *pro bono* scheme, the first of its kind in the Middle East, with the aim of offering access to justice for all, and to ensure that all parties to a dispute are on an equal footing.

Looking Forward

In light of recent socio-economic and political developments in the region, it is likely that the UAE will remain one of the prime destinations for expatriates but at the same time the UAE government will be keen to continue to ensure that its nationals are protected adequately. After a relatively busy year in 2011 on the legislative front, it is envisaged that the authorities will consolidate the changes implemented.

We expect that the Arab Spring will continue to have a positive effect in the UAE with more foreign investment earmarked for the region being channelled into the UAE but at the same time it is likely that focus will fall on the issue of jobs for UAE nationals. There has been some discussion on implementing new schemes to encourage Emiratisation, for example by partnering with the private sector to train and employ UAE nationals for a minimum period in return for subsidies provided by the government.

Pensions for expatriate employees are expected to be high on the agenda for 2012 following widely reported talks between the World Bank and the UAE. Currently expatriate employees are only entitled to statutory end of service gratuity (in the form of a lump sum payment) at the end of service which is calculated by reference to their period of service with employers in the UAE/DIFC. This is seen as one of the key requirements to make employment in the UAE more attractive to expatriates and encourage individuals with specialised expertise to remain in the UAE for longer.

Along with the possible changes in the UAE legislation, the DIFC is also likely to implement amendments to the DIFC Employment Law. A consultation paper on proposed amendments to the DIFC Employment Law was launched in December 2011 with the consultation period ending on 14 January 2012. The proposed amendments are being viewed as an attempt to address some of the inconsistencies in and provide clarity on certain aspects of the law.

Samir Kantaria
Tel: +971 4 3641 641 / Email: s.kantaria@tamimi.com
Samir Kantaria is a partner at Al Tamimi & Company and heads the firm's employment practice. Samir has over 10 years of experience in the UAE and his practice covers the full range of employment law issues, contentious and non-contentious. Samir leads the largest team of specialist employment lawyers in the Middle East region and his experience includes regularly advising major blue chip, multinational and semi-governmental companies in relation to their day-to-day employment queries. He combines technical expertise with business acumen and project management skills, and is known for giving pragmatic and commercial advice.

Al Tamimi & Company

DIFC, Building 4 East, 6th Floor, Sheikh Zayed Road, P.O.Box 9275, Dubai – UAE
Tel: +971 4 3641 641 / Fax: +971 4 3641 777 / URL: http://www.tamimi.com

United Kingdom

Charles Wynn-Evans & Georgina Rowley
Dechert LLP

Introduction

This chapter summarises some of the key areas in which employment law in the United Kingdom has developed over the past year or so. The difficult economic situation faced in the United Kingdom since 2008 has contributed, in some respects, to the changing employment law environment. It is not surprising that litigation over issues such as redundancies, bonuses and unlawful discrimination should increase in difficult economic times and lead to more issues of principle being tested before the appeal courts. Many of the important cases decided in recent times address those sorts of issues.

The Coalition Government has also embarked on a programme of reform as part of its strategy to deal with the economic crisis, and which not only seeks to reduce the perceived burden on business imposed by the operation of the employment tribunal system, but is also examining whether legislation should be enacted to address concerns about excessive executive remuneration. Wider reform has also been enacted in terms of expansive anti-bribery legislation and, in order to comply with EU law requirements, the introduction of specific legislative protection for agency workers.

This chapter is divided into four sections. The first addresses the trends in employment litigation over the last year. The second discusses some of the most significant recent changes to the UK's legislative framework. The third reports on various important case law developments. The final section addresses some of the reforms to the United Kingdom employment law which are being implemented or are under consideration.

Litigation statistics

The statistics for litigation in the employment tribunals (the forum in which most statutory employment law disputes are adjudicated at first instance in the United Kingdom) for 2010-2011 demonstrate a number of developments.

There was an 8% fall in claims received when compared with 2010 but a 9% rise in the number of cases disposed of. The number of "single" claims brought by just one claimant received has fallen by 15% and the number of "multiple" claims brought fell by 4%.

The number of unfair dismissal and redundancy pay claims fell slightly. However, claims under the Part Time Workers (Prevention of Less Favourable Treatment) Regulations increased almost threefold and claims of unlawful age discrimination rose by approximately 32%.

The median award of compensation in unfair dismissal claims was £4,591 and for the various types of discrimination claim in the range of £5,000-£6,500, save for age discrimination where the median award was £12,697. The highest award for unfair dismissal was £181,754 (which, being more than the statutory cap which applies in most cases, is likely to have been the award in a case of whistle-blowing or health and safety where there is no limit on compensation). The highest award for discrimination was £289,167 (sex) compared with £729,347 (disability) in 2009-2010.

Legislation

Increase in compensation limits

The maximum compensation that the employment tribunal can award for unfair dismissal (save in exceptional cases) and the basis upon which statutory redundancy payments are calculated increased from 1 February 2012. A week's pay (for the purposes of calculating the basic award in unfair dismissal cases and statutory redundancy payment entitlements) is now capped at £430 (the previous limit was £400). The basic award is calculated by applying a formula based on age, length of service and a week's pay. As a result of this increase in a week's pay, the maximum total basic award is now capped at £12,900. The maximum compensatory award for unfair dismissal (save in the prescribed exceptional cases) is now capped at £72,300 (the previous limit was £68,400). As a result of these increases, the maximum amount which a successful claimant for unfair dismissal can recover (i.e. the basic and compensatory awards) is now capped at £85,200.

Agency Workers Regulations 2010

The Agency Workers Regulations came into force on 1 October 2011 and apply to workers offered temporary work through an employment agency. The objective of the European Temporary Agency Workers Directive 2008 (which is imported into UK law by the 2010 Regulations) is to harmonise certain basic working and employment conditions for temporary workers supplied through employment agencies such that they are in no worse position than if they had been recruited directly by the end user organisation for which they carry out work (the "hirer").

Under the 2010 Regulations, temporary agency workers now enjoy the same basic working and employment conditions as if they had been employed directly by the hirer to perform the same or a similar role. This right will accrue after the agency worker has worked for the hirer for 12 weeks. These basic work conditions are pay, working time, night work, rest periods, rest breaks and annual leave.

In addition, temporary agency workers now enjoy the right to access information about a hirer's comparable permanent employment vacancies and the use of a hirer's facilities and amenities. These rights will apply immediately from the outset of a temporary assignment.

Abolition of the default retirement age

The statutory ability to retire employees at the "default retirement age" of 65 was an exception to the age discrimination legislation implemented in 2006, which provides that employees should not be treated less favourably because of their age unless the treatment can be objectively justified.

Following the abolition of the default retirement age on 6 April 2011, employers are no longer able to instigate retirement at the default retirement age as of right. They now have two options available to them – to cease compulsorily to retire employees or to adopt a compulsory retirement age for part or all of the workforce.

Given the uncertainty associated with justifying a compulsory retirement age, the majority of employers are likely to abolish compulsory retirement. This will undoubtedly require a change of mindset such that older workers are managed according to the same principles as others. Dismissals will only be fair if effected for one of the five potentially fair reasons (capability, conduct, redundancy, illegality or some other substantial reason) coupled with a fair procedure. Employees also need to be aware of the risks of an employee who is terminated near to what would previously have been retirement age and may, in any event, argue that the decision to terminate his or her employment is unlawful age discrimination, the compensation for which is unlimited.

The abolition of the default retirement age does not close the door entirely to employers introducing or maintaining a compulsory retirement age for all, or part, of the workforce. Since compulsory retirement is age related, to maintain compulsory retirement risks age discrimination claims unless in the particular circumstances the compulsory retirement age adopted by the employer can be justified. To avoid successful claims of unlawful age discrimination, employers will need to be able to objectively justify a compulsory retirement age by showing that it is a proportionate means of achieving a legitimate aim.

Termination payments

The Income Tax (Pay As You Earn) (Amendment) Regulations 2011 now require a post-termination payment that is made to a departed employee to be taxed using the 0T tax code (which utilises the 20%, 40% and 50% rates) rather than only the 20% basic tax rate previously used.

Paternity leave

The Additional Paternity Leave Regulations 2010 and the Additional Statutory Paternity Pay (General) Regulations 2010 came into force in 2010 and extend paternity leave for employees who are expecting a baby or matched for adoption by up to an additional 26 weeks.

Bribery Act 2010

The UK Bribery Act came into force on 1 July 2011. It sets a new gold standard in anti-corruption legislation and has broad jurisdictional reach. It can apply even where no UK persons are involved, and where the act in question takes place outside the UK. It is also more extensive than the US Foreign and Corrupt Practices Act in that:

- it outlaws commercial bribery as well as the bribery of foreign public officials;
- no corrupt intent is required for an offence of bribing a foreign official;
- it applies to the receipt and solicitation of bribes, as well as to the giving, offering and promising of bribes;
- it applies to domestic acts of bribery as well as bribery overseas;
- it outlaws facilitation payments;
- it creates a new corporate offence of failing to prevent bribery; and
- organisations can be held liable for actions of third parties acting on their behalf – whether or not they were aware of any misconduct.

The corporate offence exposes companies and partnerships to criminal liability. There is only one possible defence – to show that the organisation has "adequate procedures" in place.

Therefore, an awareness of these offences and an appreciation of their operation is important for commercial organisations, individual executives and employees alike, as is the introduction of appropriate policies and training.

Key case law affecting employers' decision making over dismissals, redundancies dismissals etc.

In addition to these legislative changes, there have been a number of interesting cases on various aspects of employment protection in the UK. A selection is as follows.

Consistent treatment – the employer's knowledge

In Orr v Milton Keynes Council, in relation to all unfair dismissal claims, it was held that an employer cannot be deemed to know all the facts known to its employees when deciding whether a dismissal is reasonable. Provided that a fair and thorough investigation is carried out, only those facts known to the decision-maker at the time are relevant in determining whether the dismissal was unfair.

Overseas employees

In British Airways plc v MAK, it was held that the employment tribunal had jurisdiction to hear race and age discrimination complaints bought by employees who were resident in Hong Kong but who performed their duties as cabin crew on flights between Hong Kong and London. The Court of Appeal found that the employment tribunal had been entitled to find that these relevant staff did their work partly in Great Britain and, therefore, were to be regarded as employed at an establishment in Great Britain. This enabled them to bring claims under the discrimination legislation as it applied prior to the introduction of the Equality Act 2010.

Redundancy selection and discrimination

In Eversheds Legal Services Ltd v De Belin, an employer inflated the score of a female colleague who was on maternity leave in a redundancy selection exercise by way of giving her the notional maximum score in respect of the relevant criterion which was a measurement applied to a period when the female employee was absent on maternity leave. A male colleague who was assessed by reference to his actual score in relation to that criterion successfully claimed unlawful sex discrimination. It was held that pregnant employees and those on maternity leave should only be treated more favourably than male colleagues to the extent that it is reasonably necessary in order to remove any disadvantage suffered by the woman as a consequence of her pregnancy and/or maternity leave. The employer could have used historic data relating to prior periods of time to compare actual performance rather than deem the pregnant employee to have achieved the maximum score in respect of the period when she was on maternity leave.

Self-employed contracts

In Autoclenz v Belcher, the Supreme Court, in assessing whether sub-contractors who performed valet services were genuinely self employed or were "workers" for the purposes of UK employment protection legislation, held that it was open to a tribunal to disregard written terms in the relevant contracts if this does not reflect the actual legal obligations of the parties. Despite the fact that the contractual terms of the relevant car valeters provided that they were engaged on a sub-contract basis, they could provide substitutes and were not obliged to provide their services on any particular occasions, the tribunal was entitled to hold that they were workers and that the relevant contractual provisions with regard to substitutes, were not genuine.

Apportioning discrimination compensation

In London Borough of Hackney v Sivanandan, the Employment Appeal Tribunal ("EAT") held that the Employment Tribunal is not entitled to apportion liability between respondents to a claim of unlawful discrimination. Any award is "joint and several" as against all respondents. An employee respondent in a discrimination case could in theory, therefore, be liable for all the relevant compensation awarded.

Career-long discrimination comparison

In Wardle v Credit Agricole Corporate & Investment Bank, the Court of Appeal held that in most cases, loss of earnings in a discrimination claim should only be assessed up to the point where the employee is likely to secure an equivalent job. "Career-long" compensation should only be awarded when there is no real prospect of the employee ever obtaining an equivalent job.

References

In McKie v Swindon College, an ex-employer was held to be liable for negligent mis-statement in respect of a former employee as a result of an email sent to his subsequent employer which led to his dismissal but which was inaccurate and produced carelessly. Even though the communication was some years after the end of the relevant employment, it did communicate information about the previous employment and, therefore, led to the ex-employer having a duty of care to the ex-employee. Damages could, therefore, be recovered for the loss caused by the ex-employer's negligent mis-statement.

In Jackson v Liverpool City Council, the Court of Appeal held that an employer was not in breach of duty when it provided a reference about an ex-employee which referred to allegations which had been made against the former employee in question but had made clear that these allegations had not been investigated. The reference was true, accurate and fair.

Reasonably refusing an offer of suitable alternative employment

It is an established principle of employment law that the dismissal of an employee for redundancy will be unfair if the employer fails to carry out a reasonable search for suitable alternative employment. Separately, under section 141(2) of the Employment Rights Act 1996, provided that certain conditions regarding the offer are satisfied, an employee who unreasonably refuses an offer of suitable alternative employment will not be entitled to a redundancy payment.

In Readman v Devon Primary Care Trust, the EAT held that it was possible for an employee to reasonably refuse a suitable offer of alternative employment, and therefore still be entitled to receive a redundancy payment, even where the employment tribunal had correctly concluded that a reasonable employee would have accepted the employer's offer.

The EAT held that the offer constituted an offer of suitable alternative employment and held that the correct test was whether the employee in question, taking into account their personal circumstances, had acted reasonably in refusing the offer or, in other words, whether the employee had sound and justifiable reasons for turning down the offer. In the EAT's opinion, the claimant's reason for turning down the offer, namely that she had worked in a community setting for 23 years and had no desire to return to a hospital setting, constituted a sound and justifiable reason even though a reasonable employee would have accepted the offer, and accordingly it held that she was entitled to receive a redundancy payment.

Consulting with employees about whom to include in a redundancy pool

To avoid unfairly dismissing an employee whose position has become redundant, employers must show that the dismissal is genuinely on the grounds of redundancy and that it has acted reasonably in all the circumstances in treating redundancy as a sufficient reason for dismissing the employee.

The case of Fulcrum Pharma (Europe) Ltd v Bonassera and another provides a helpful reminder of the importance of consulting with affected employees about whom to include in a redundancy pool. The employer's HR team comprised two employees: the claimant, who was the HR manager, and a more junior HR executive. The employer decided that there was a diminished need for the HR manager's role and made the claimant redundant. The claimant complained and told the employer that she thought the HR executive should also have been placed at risk of redundancy, but the employer refused to alter its decision. The employment tribunal held that the claimant had been unfairly dismissed and the EAT agreed. According to the EAT, the employer was in error in automatically determining that because the manager's role had to go, the pool should only contain one employee, without any further or meaningful consultation as to the size of the pool. The EAT held that when considering whether subordinate employees should be included in a pool, employers should consider the factors set out by the EAT in 2004 in Lionel Leventhal Ltd v North, namely:
- whether or not there is a vacancy;
- how different the two jobs are;
- the difference in remuneration between them;
- the relative length of service of the two employees;
- the qualifications of the employee in danger of redundancy; and
- other factors which may apply in a particular case.

The EAT also added that as a starting point it may be appropriate to determine during the consultation process whether a more senior employee would be prepared to consider a more junior role at a reduced salary. It appears that it will not be enough for the employer to consider this issue internally – the employer must actually raise this issue with the employee.

Harassment – the perceptions and feelings of the complainant

In Thomas Sanderson Blinds v English, the EAT held that the employment tribunal had applied the correct test when considering whether an employee had suffered harassment by taking into account the employee's own perceptions and feelings to determine whether the unwanted conduct in question had the effect of violating his dignity or creating an intimidating, hostile, degrading, humiliating or offensive environment. The Equality Act 2010 defines harassment as unwanted conduct related to any protected characteristic which has the purpose or effect of violating a person's dignity or creating an intimidating, hostile, degrading, humiliating or offensive environment for them. In deciding whether the conduct has this effect, the legislation explicitly provides that the employment tribunal must consider the perception of the alleged victim, the circumstances of the case and whether it is reasonable for the conduct to have that effect.

Mr English, who is heterosexual, complained that he had suffered homophobic banter and innuendo from his colleagues because he had attended a boarding school and lived in Brighton. He brought a claim of harassment on the grounds of sexual orientation under the legislation introduced in 2003, which is now set out in the Equality Act 2010. As a preliminary issue, the Court of Appeal held that Mr English was protected by the sexual orientation legislation even though he was not gay and his tormentors knew that he was not gay.

At the subsequent substantive hearing, the employment tribunal held that his claim of harassment was only made out in respect of an article written about him in an internal magazine in August 2005. This was held to be a "tipping point" which exceeded what Mr English considered to have been an acceptable level of personal attack and insult. The employment tribunal rejected all other claims of harassment relating to previous conduct on the basis that Mr English had himself engaged in banter and written similarly offensive articles "riddled with sexist and ageist innuendo" in the internal magazine, he was good friends with his tormentors and he had not complained before the article was written. The employment tribunal, therefore, concluded that all but one aspect of the conduct complained of did not have the effect of creating an intimidating, hostile, degrading, humiliating or offensive environment. However, the article in the magazine was found to meet the test for harassment. Nonetheless, the claim was out of time.

On appeal, the EAT upheld the employment tribunal's decision as the employment tribunal had correctly applied the test, i.e. whether the claimant felt or perceived their dignity to have been violated or an adverse environment to have been created; and whether it was reasonable for them to do so. For example, if the employment tribunal considered that the claimant was unreasonably prone to take offence, then, even if he did genuinely feel his dignity to have been violated, there would be no harassment. The employment tribunal must also have regard to all the relevant circumstances, including the context of the conduct in question. It was entirely proper for the tribunal to take into account Mr English's own offensive behaviour and the fact that he was friendly with his tormentors in reaching its decision that the conduct directed at him did not have the effect of violating his dignity or creating an adverse environment.

This case should not be seen as relaxing the test of what constitutes unlawful harassment or legitimising offensive banter, which may in any event provoke complaints and claims from those who are affected, even if they are not the direct targets of the comments in question. It does, however, emphasise the need to address the context of the events complained of to determine if they truly constitute harassment.

Bonuses

One particularly litigious area in UK employment law in recent years has been executive bonuses. Much of the recent case law in this area has focused not on discretionary bonuses, where claims have become more difficult following the principle established in the <u>Keen v Commerzbank</u> case that a claimant needed to show an overwhelming case that a discretionary bonus award was irrational; rather, recent disputes have focused more on the interpretation and operation of specific contractual bonus arrangements. The current difficult economic climate has not discouraged claimants from pursuing such claims and the courts can be seen in the recent cases to have held employers to their commitments.

In <u>Khatri v Cooperative Centrale Raiffesen-Borerenleenbank</u>, a dispute arose over whether the employer had the unilateral right to change an employee's bonus arrangement when the bonus formula in question reserved to the employer the right to review or remove the bonus at any time. The court held that the provision could not reasonably be interpreted to permit the employer to change the bonus arrangement during a particular bonus year – more explicit wording would be necessary for that to have been the case. Moreover, the employee was not found to have accepted the change imposed upon him simply by continuing to work – for example, he had not accepted the new terms in the manner requested of signing and returning a letter.

In <u>Anar and others v Dresdner Kleinwort</u>, the employer had announced a guaranteed Euro 400m bonus pool at a staff meeting and had subsequently confirmed its existence on a number of occasions. At a later stage, staff were notified of what was provisionally awarded to them in letters which reserved to the employer the right to make adjustments to reflect any material deviations from forecast earnings and revenue. The dispute arose when the employer sought to reduce the payment to reflect such deviations. At first instance, the High Court found that the employer's announcements were mere statements of intention rather than being legally binding given the informality of the communications and lack of specificity about awards. However, the Court of Appeal disagreed – the announcement might have been informal but was not casual. The issue was dealt with as a summary judgment matter so the claims remain ongoing and are yet (at the time of writing) to be determined.

In <u>GX Networks Limited v Greenland</u>, the employer had the right to cap an executive's bonus payment "by exception only" and sought to do so when the bonus produced dramatically higher payments than it had wished to pay out. The court found that the employer had failed to adjust the executive's targets when it was entitled to have done and that to seek to cap the bonus retrospectively was not contractually permissible. In a scheme encouraging effort and success, an unusual degree of success was not seen as an exceptional circumstance entitling the employer to cap the executive's bonus.

Likely or impending reforms to employment legislation and enforcement procedures

All change for tribunals?

Looking forward, 2012 promises to be a year of considerable upheaval in terms of the operation of the employment tribunals (the forum in which most statutory employment claims are adjudicated), as well as substantive employment law reform. The objective of the proposed and possible reforms is to reduce the burden of regulation on business.

Proposed reforms, most of which are expected to come into force in April 2012, include:
- witness statements being taken as read unless the tribunal otherwise decided;
- increasing the limit on the costs which a tribunal can award against a party without a formal court assessment in respect of an unsuccessful claim which was misconceived or conducted inappropriately (the test remaining somewhat restrictive) from £10,000 to £20,000;
- extending the qualifying period needed to be able to claim unfair dismissal from one to two years; and
- unfair dismissal cases being heard by an employment judge sitting alone rather than by a panel of three comprising an employment judge and two lay members.

Other reforms are also on the way:
- the Government is consulting about the level of, and arrangements for, charging fees for the lodging and subsequent hearing of claims with the employment tribunal;
- it is also considering introducing a concept of "protected conversations" entitling an employer to have an "off the record" discussion with an employee about certain specific topics such as, for example, poor performance or succession planning. The detail of any such proposal is awaited; and
- reform is being considered to the UK's collective redundancy consultation regime in terms of whether the obligation to consult with appropriate employee representatives should be reduced from 90 days to 30, 45 or 60 days where 100 or more redundancies are proposed – the obligation is 30 days where between 20 and 99 redundancies are proposed at one establishment in a 90-day period.

New executive pay proposals outlined by the UK Government

In September 2011, the UK Department for Business Innovation & Skills ("BIS") issued a consultation paper on executive pay for quoted companies. The paper's premise was that whilst executive remuneration is an important part of promoting growth (as long as it is well structured and provides rewards for executives that contribute to long-term success), in the past decade the link between remuneration and performance has not been clear. The paper put forward various measures to strengthen the link between pay and performance with the purpose of stimulating debate and gathering evidence. BIS sought responses in particular on the subjects of remuneration reports, the role of shareholders, the structure of remuneration and remuneration committee composition.

A summary of responses to the paper was published in January 2012. The general consensus of respondents was that the remuneration landscape should be improved; however, there were mixed views on the best methods to achieve such an improvement. Over half of the respondents wanted remuneration packages to be simplified. The majority were against shareholders being given a binding vote on remuneration reports as a whole; however, some suggested that a binding vote on a future-looking part of a report might be more practical. The majority also opposed having shareholders or employees on remuneration committees as they would not have the breadth of knowledge and overview of the company that board members have.

On 23 January 2012, Vince Cable, the Secretary of State for BIS, announced the UK Government's latest proposal on executive pay. Four main areas were identified: transparency; shareholder involvement; diversity of boards and remuneration committees; and best practice. Mr Cable also gave a more detailed speech to the Social Market Foundation on 24 January 2012.

The UK Government intends to introduce secondary legislation in 2012 which will require companies to publish more informative remuneration reports. The remuneration report will be divided into one section setting out the future policy on executive pay, and a second setting out the implementation of pay policy in the previous year. In relation to future policy, an explanation will be required as to why specific benchmarks have been used, how employee earnings have been taken into account and how employees have been consulted. Particular attention was drawn to the Information and Consultation of Employees Regulations 2004 which allow employees in large companies to request a consultation on certain issues. The use of this mechanism was encouraged. As for the previous year's policy, a single figure for each director's total pay will be required and an explanation of how company performance and pay awards are related. Companies will need to produce a distribution statement comparing executive pay to dividends, business investment, taxation and staffing costs. The UK Government has also been addressing employee representation on boards and pay ratios (between CEOs and average employees). Whilst worker participation is seen as a good idea for many companies, it would be difficult for a large number of FTSE companies, whose employees are predominantly overseas. Mr Cable welcomed worker participation but by a non-prescriptive route. Similarly, in relation to pay ratios, Mr Cable explained that these should not be mandated or prescribed due to the discrepancy between companies that have large numbers of unskilled workers and those that outsource their unskilled labour, which would produce meaningless figures with respect to ratios.

The UK Government plans to hold a consultation on specific proposals to give shareholders a binding vote on certain issues, including future pay policy, director notice periods if longer than a year and exit payments comprising more than one year's salary. The consultation will also consider the percentage of shareholder support required to pass proposals and, in particular, whether the threshold should be increased to 75%.

It was stated that diverse remuneration committees are needed in order to reform executive pay and that the best way to achieve this is through diversification of boards. Mr Cable suggested more appointments of public servants, lawyers, academics and those who have not previously been directors. It was noted that approximately 6% of remuneration committee members in the FTSE 350 are also executives of other companies and that the Government would look at mechanisms to limit this potential conflict of interest. The UK Government will also request that the Financial Reporting Council (the UK's independent regulator responsible for promoting high quality corporate governance) amends the UK Corporate Governance Code so that all large public companies are required to adopt clawbacks that give them the ability to recoup pay when performance has not lived up to expectations.

As the fourth part of the UK Government's plans, Mr Cable encouraged companies and shareholders to take responsibility for changes to executive pay going forward. A new project to be launched by the chair of the High Pay Commission was also mentioned which will monitor "the state of pay at the top".

Reaction to the proposals has, predictably, been mixed. Some commentators say that reform will leave the UK with the toughest rules on executive pay in the world, whereas others defend high executive pay arguing that it is necessary to foster competitiveness and to retain executives when a company is performing badly and in need of talented direction. It is clear that proposals such as these will ignite debate between those who are uncomfortable with the vast increases in executive pay and the differential between executive and average pay (particularly in the midst of economic difficulty) and those who believe that excessive guidance and restrictive rules will hamper the effective running of their business in a climate where business needs encouragement to grow. For now, we await the finer detail of the proposals as they are fully consulted on and become legislation.

Charles Wynn-Evans
Tel: +44 20 7184 7545 / Email: charles.wynn-evans@dechert.com
Charles Wynn-Evans leads Dechert's London employment practice. His work covers all aspects of contentious and non-contentious employment law, including downsizings, discrimination issues, industrial action, boardroom disputes, restrictive covenants, severance negotiations, tax issues and all kinds of employment-related litigation in the Employment Tribunal and High Court. Charles trained with the firm and was admitted as a solicitor in 1992. He has been a partner at Dechert since 1997. He writes regularly on employment law issues for journals such as *People Management, Personnel Today, Industrial Law Journal* and *Employment Law Journal* and is the author of *Blackstone's Guide to the New Transfer of Undertakings Legislation* (Oxford University Press, 2006). He is an accredited CEDR Mediator and a member of the Employment Law Committees of both The Law Society of England and Wales and the City of London Law Society. He is a fee-paid (part-time) employment judge assigned to the Birmingham region.

Georgina Rowley
Tel: +44 20 7184 7800 / Email: georgina.rowley@dechert.com
Georgina Rowley deals with a wide range of employment related disputes including litigation in the Employment Tribunal, County Court and High Court. She also advises in relation to appeals to the Employment Appeal Tribunal and Court of Appeal. Georgina also advises on contractual issues, terminations, TUPE, trade union matters, outsourcing and secondment arrangements and large-scale redundancy exercises. Georgina trained with Dechert and was admitted as a solicitor in 2004. She is a member of the Employment Lawyers Association. Georgina regularly speaks at seminars, delivers in-house training to clients and authors updates and articles.

Dechert LLP

160 Queen Victoria Street, London EC4V 4QQ, United Kingdom
Tel: +44 20 7184 7000 / Fax: +44 20 7184 7001 / URL: http://www.dechert.com

USA

Peter R. Bulmer, Francis P. Alvarez & Philip B. Rosen
Jackson Lewis LLP

Overview

The relationship between employers and employees is far less regulated in the U.S. than in many other countries. In general, the government has enacted laws to set minimum wage and working conditions, and to prohibit discrimination against specific groups or categories of persons; otherwise, employers and employees are free to negotiate the terms and conditions of employment. The general rule throughout the U.S. is that employment is "at-will" – meaning either the employer or the employee can terminate the employment relationship at any time and for any lawful reason.

The U.S. does not have one set of employment and labour laws that uniformly applies in all 50 states and every municipality within each state. Instead, the federal government enacts certain laws that provide minimum protections, which pertain to employers engaged in interstate commerce. State governments are free to enact laws that apply within their state and provide protections beyond those afforded by the federal law. Moreover, municipalities may enact local laws that give yet more protection to employees. Thus, when assessing the U.S. employment and labour law landscape, one starts with the federal law, then checks the particular state to determine if it has related laws, and finally a check is done of the local municipality to determine whether any local law applies. In addition to the laws enacted by the federal, state, or municipal legislatures, it is important to determine if the common law – the law developed by judicial decisions over time – restricts the employer's right to take the action contemplated.

Below we provide an overview of the principal areas of the law affecting the relationship between employers and employees in the U.S. We note that, in the U.S., reference to "labour" law generally means those laws governing the rights of workers to form unions for the purpose of negotiating terms and conditions of employment, as well as the rights of the employer *vis-á-vis* the union which represents some or all of the employer's workers. Reference to "employment" law generally refers to the gamut of laws other than "labour" laws.

Employment Contracts

Employment contracts are not required in the U.S. And if an employer enters into an employment contract with an employee, there are no required terms. The vast majority of employees in the U.S. do not have written contracts and are employed "at-will", meaning they can quit or be terminated without advance notice.

It is common, however, to provide written offers of employment for management employees, and care must be taken to ensure that the language of the offer letter does not create more contractual rights than the employer intends to provide. Some states now require employers to provide written notification to employees of the terms of their employment (though not as extensively as in many European Union countries). For example, in New York, employers must notify employees in writing (a) at the time of their hire, of (i) rate or pay, and (ii) if the employee is eligible for overtime pay and, if so, the rate of overtime pay, and (b) the employer's policies on sick leave, vacation, personal leave, holidays and work hours.

Highly-skilled and/or highly-compensated employees and executives are often employed pursuant to a written agreement. These contracts can cover any terms the parties have agreed to, and most often include at least the position, pay, benefits, and any restrictions on the employer's right to terminate the employee at-will (*e.g.*, some form of "cause" requirement that is defined in the agreement as authorising termination). Very often these employment agreements also contain post-employment restrictions against the employee's working for a competitor, soliciting clients and other employees, and using or disclosing the employer's confidential and proprietary information. It is important to note that employers may not remove the minimum protections afforded by applicable laws, even if the employee is willing to contract away those rights (*e.g.*, the minimum wage and overtime requirements cannot be waived by the employee).

Termination of Employment

Because the U.S. generally adheres to the "at-will" employment doctrine, an employer may terminate an employee at any time, and for any reason – as long as the reason is not unlawful. Put another way, there generally are only three restrictions on an employer's right to terminate an employee. First, the termination must not violate any contractual restriction in any agreement between the employer and the employee. Second, the termination must not violate a statute (federal, state, or local). Third, the termination must not be deemed in violation of a "public policy".

The contractual restriction can be found in an express contract or an implied one. The express contract typically is found in a written agreement between the employer and employee. Implied contracts may arise where a court deems that a promise was made – even if the employer did not think it was making a binding promise (such as when supervisors make certain promises, or where general policy statements are written in such a way as to rise to the level of a promise) – and the employee relied on that promise.

By far the most common restrictions are those arising from a particular statute. For example, the non-discrimination statutes discussed below prohibit terminating employees based on, for example, their race or sex.

The most amorphous restriction is that which arises from a "public policy". Such public policies most often arise under the common law (*i.e.*, judicial decisions) of a particular state. In general, such "public policies" are intended to prevent an employer from terminating an employee in retaliation for the employee's having engaged in some conduct that promotes an important interest of the citizens of that particular state. For example, it is unlawful to terminate an employee for having exercised his or her rights under the state's workers' compensation law (the law that compensates employees for on-the-job injuries). Many states use this public policy exception to the at-will employment doctrine to protect "whistleblowers" from retaliation for reporting illegal conduct. Thus, prior to terminating an employee based on conduct that is not directly related to performance on the job, the employment counsel should be consulted.

Anti-Discrimination Laws

It is illegal under the federal civil rights laws for U.S. employers to discriminate against an individual on account of his or her race, colour, religion, sex (including pregnancy), national origin, age (40 or older), disability or genetic information. This includes discrimination in the context of hiring and firing decisions, as well as with respect to an employee's "compensation, terms, conditions, or privileges of employment". It is also illegal under U.S. law to discriminate or "retaliate" against an employee because he or she complained about discrimination, filed a charge of discrimination, or participated in an employment discrimination investigation or lawsuit. Most employers with at least 15 employees are covered by this body of federal law, as are most labour unions and employment agencies.

There generally are two different types of prohibited discrimination under the civil rights laws – "disparate treatment" and "disparate impact". While the former involves deliberate or "intentional" conduct, the latter applies to facially-neutral employment practices that disproportionately or "unintentionally" discriminate against protected groups. Harassment, including most notably sexual harassment, is also prohibited under U.S. law. In some limited instances, federal law also requires employers to make "reasonable accommodations" as part of the statutory and regulatory schemes prohibiting disability or religious discrimination, provided that these reasonable accommodations do not pose an "undue hardship" on the employer.

State and local laws mirroring the federal civil rights statutes are common and often extend their coverage to a larger group of protected characteristics, adding, for instance, protected categories such as marital status, sexual orientation, sexual identity, and familial status. State and local laws often apply to employers with workforces of fewer than 15 employees.

U.S. employees who believe they have been discriminated against in violation of the law must file a charge of discrimination with the Equal Employment Opportunity Commission (EEOC), the agency charged with enforcing the federal civil rights laws, or the relevant local agency before bringing a lawsuit against the employer in court. The agency will then investigate and find that there either is or is not "reasonable cause". If there is reasonable cause, the agency will attempt to reach a voluntary settlement with the employer and may even file a lawsuit in federal court on the employee's behalf. If the agency does not find reasonable cause – or cannot settle the case and decides not to file a lawsuit – the employee can sue the employer in court on his or her own.

If the court finds that an employee was terminated unlawfully, he or she may be entitled to some or all of the following remedies: 1) reinstatement to former position; 2) monetary damages for wages and benefits lost as a result of the termination; 3) monetary damages for any emotional or physical distress suffered as a result of the employer's actions; 4) punitive damages intended to punish an employer for egregious violations of the law; and 5) attorneys' fees.

Leaves of Absence (Disability, Family, etc.)

Disability and leave management sits at the intersection of various federal and state laws, including the Americans with Disabilities Act (ADA), Family and Medical Leave Act (FMLA), Genetic Information Nondiscrimination Act (GINA), Pregnancy Discrimination Act (PDA), Age Discrimination in Employment Act (ADEA), and their state counterparts. Given this complex array of legal mandates, disability and leave management is a constant source of frustration for U.S. employers. In addition to the routine employment decisions involving injured or ill employees or individuals with family caregiving responsibilities, one particular area of confusion for employers is determining how much leave an employee is legally entitled to take and in what form. To make this issue even more challenging, the agency charged with enforcing the ADA, the EEOC, has been very critical of common employer leave practices, such as fixed leave and no-fault attendance policies that establish uniform limits and standards for workers.

The discussion below provides an overview of some of the legal requirements in this area of the law and highlights critical issues for employers.

A. The Americans with Disabilities Act

The ADA is a federal law that prohibits discrimination against a "qualified individual with a disability", meaning a disabled individual who can perform the essential functions of his or her job either with or without a reasonable accommodation. The ADA defines "disability" as a physical or mental impairment that substantially limits one or more major life activities, a record of such an impairment, or being regarded as having such an impairment.

Employers are obligated to provide disabled employees with "reasonable accommodations" under the ADA so long as doing so does not pose an "undue hardship". "Reasonable accommodation" may include "job restructuring, part-time or modified work schedules, reassignment to a vacant position... appropriate adjustment or modifications of examinations, training materials or policies". The ADA also includes "job protected leave" as a potential "reasonable accommodation" for disabled workers but offers no guidance on how much leave must be provided. Employers must engage in an "interactive process" to determine whether a reasonable accommodation is available for employees with disabilities.

The ADA Amendments Act (ADAAA), which took effect in January 2009, makes it significantly easier for a plaintiff to establish that he or she is disabled under the ADA. In addition, the ADAAA makes clear that "[a]n impairment that is episodic or in remission is a disability if it would substantially limit a major life activity when active". What this all means is that a number of conditions that would not be considered disabilities prior to enactment of the ADAAA now fall under the ADA's definition of disability and require employers to provide reasonable accommodations.

B. The Family and Medical Leave Act

The FMLA is a federal law that provides up to 12 weeks of unpaid leave in a 12-month period for the birth, adoption, or foster care of a child, to care for a child, spouse, or parent with a serious health problem, for the employee's own serious health condition that renders the employee unable to perform the functions of his or her job, or for any qualifying exigency arising out of the fact that one of a number of certain enumerated relatives of the employee is a covered military member on active duty (or has been notified of an impending call or order to active duty) in support of a contingency operation. In addition, eligible employees are entitled to 26 work weeks of leave in a single 12-month period to care for a covered service member with a serious injury or illness if the employee is the spouse, son, daughter, parent, or next of kin of the service member. The statute also requires that group health benefits be maintained during any FMLA-qualifying leave and has a number of requirements with respect to medical certifications and other paperwork.

The FMLA permits employees to take leave intermittently if medically necessary. That means that if it were medically necessary for a full-time eligible employee to take FMLA leave in one-day increments, the employee could take off 60 days per year. If it were medically necessary for the employee to take off for smaller increments of time, he or she could be absent numerous times per week, on average, and still have the job security provided by the FMLA.

Whereas the FMLA protects the job security of an employee who is unable to perform the essential functions of his or her position, the ADA requires that the employee be able to perform the essential functions of the position with or without reasonable accommodation. Despite this difference, the EEOC maintains that individuals covered by the ADA may be entitled to more than 12 weeks of unpaid leave as a reasonable accommodation.

C. The Genetic Information Non-Discrimination Act

GINA prohibits health insurers and employers from discriminating against individuals because of their genetic composition and makes it illegal for employers to request that employees undergo genetic testing or provide family medical information, except in limited circumstances. Unlike the ADA, GINA does not prohibit discrimination based on the actual presence of a genetic disorder. However, GINA places restrictions on the types of questions an employer can ask an employee about his or her family's medical history, as well as how the employer must store information it receives regarding an employee's genetic information. One of the ramifications of GINA is that it makes efforts to manage employee disabilities proactively and prevent illness through voluntary wellness programmes more complicated. Employers must now have employees sign authorisations before providing family medical histories and provide notices directing doctors not to provide genetic information while conducting routine medical evaluations.

D. Military Service

The federal Uniformed Services Employment and Reemployment Rights Act (USERRA) provides certain employment protections to U.S. military personnel. Many states have enacted laws similar to USERRA that afford additional protections. Thus, before making decisions that might affect the employment of military personnel, USERRA and the particular state's law should be considered.

Wage-Hour and Working Conditions Laws

A. Federal Wage-Hour Law

The main federal law governing wages and hours of employment in the U.S. is the Fair Labor Standards Act (FLSA). The FLSA regulates minimum wages, maximum hours, child labour, and record-keeping. Specifically, the FLSA currently requires that most covered employees receive at least $7.25 per hour for their work, as well as an hourly wage premium of at least 50 per cent for work in excess of 40 hours in a workweek. The FLSA also limits the types of work that employees between 14 and 17 years of age may perform and requires that employers maintain a variety of records.

In the FLSA, Congress delegated to the Secretary of Labor the authority to issue interpretations of many of the terms contained in the statute. Since the 1930s, the Secretary, through the Administrator of the Wage and Hour Division of the U.S. Department of Labor, has issued extensive regulations, opinion letters, and other guidance documents providing greater explanation of the FLSA's terms. There are certain terms that apply only to government employees or to specific types of government employees, such as alternative overtime standards for police officers and fire fighters.

Coverage

The FLSA applies to workers in one of two ways: individual coverage; and enterprise coverage. Individual coverage extends the reach of the FLSA to employees who are personally engaged in commerce or the production of goods for commerce, regardless of the size or nature of their employer's operations. This means that cashiers or clerks who take credit card payments or use the telephones or the U.S. mail will likely be subject to the FLSA's terms even if their employer is otherwise a small, local business.

The second way that the FLSA applies to workers is through enterprise coverage. Businesses that are engaged in commerce or the production of goods for commerce and that have an annual revenue of at least $500,000 are deemed covered enterprises such that all of their employees are subject to the FLSA.

Occasionally, disputes arise regarding whether a worker or a business is subject to the FLSA. Among other things, certain types of non-profit entities, as well as purely local businesses with annual revenues above $500,000 per year, contend that they are not covered. The courts resolve these disputes by looking closely at the facts of each case.

Exemptions

Much of the focus of wage and hour counselling and litigation in the U.S. concerns whether workers fall within one of the numerous exemptions to the FLSA's requirements. Some of these exemptions excuse compliance with both the minimum wage and the overtime requirement. These exemptions include, among others:

- executive, administrative, and professional employees;
- outside salespersons;
- employees of seasonal amusement or recreational establishments;
- employees in certain computer-related occupations;
- seamen on vessels flying non-U.S. flags; and
- certain employees providing companionship services to individuals unable to care for themselves.

Other exemptions eliminate the need to pay the overtime premium but not the minimum wage. These exemptions include, among others:

- long-haul truckers and other employees subject to the Motor Carrier Act;
- certain employees of rail and air carriers;
- taxicab drivers;
- certain agricultural employees;
- employees of motion picture theatres; and
- certain commissioned employees of retail establishments.

B. State and Local Wage-Hour Law

As a general matter, the FLSA does not displace state or local regulation of wages and hours of work. As a result, an employer in the U.S. must comply with both the FLSA and the wage and hour law of any state in which it has employees. Many states have set their minimum wage at a level above the FLSA's rate. With regard to exemptions, many states either have no overtime law or adopt the FLSA exemptions. Other states have important differences in their overtime exemption schemes. California, for example, approaches exemptions in a manner very different from federal law.

Beyond minimum wage and overtime, the states often have requirements addressing a variety of topics including:

- timing of wage payments, including wages upon termination of employment;
- permissible deductions from wages;
- contents of wage statements; and
- child labour.

In addition, certain cities, such as San Francisco, California, have living wage ordinances specifying wage requirements for work performed within their territory.

C. Occupational Safety and Health

The Occupational Safety and Health Administration (OSHA) is the federal agency tasked with promulgating and enforcing workplace safety and health rules under the Occupational Safety and Health Act of 1970. An employer must follow the specific safety and health requirements put forward by the agency, as well as ensure its workplace is free from serious, recognised hazards.

OSHA has been aggressively enforcing its workplace standards. OSHA enforcement is at historically high levels, as measured by several indicators (*e.g.*, numbers of inspections, significant cases, and willful violations issued). It has numerous National and Special enforcement "Emphasis Programs", which target certain industries and hazards for inspection activity. This active enforcement is expected to continue over the next several years.

OSHA has also been developing new rules, but most are not expected to be finalised for several years. In 2012, OSHA did complete an update to its Hazard Communication standard, harmonising its "right-to-know" rule with the Globally Harmonized System for the Classification and Labeling of Chemicals.

Privacy Laws

The privacy of personal communications and security of personal information continue to generate significant legislative and enforcement activity, particularly in the areas of social media and health care.

For example, the states of Maryland and Illinois became the first U.S. state to prohibit employers from demanding passwords to employee/applicant online accounts such as Facebook. To date, California, New York, and others states have proposed similar bans.

Reviewing the public social media sites of employees/applicants remains generally permissible, but poses some risks. For example, the Genetic Information Nondiscrimination Act prohibits collecting "genetic information", including family medical history. Reviewing an applicant's posts about her spouse's cancer treatments, for example, or the applicant's own disability, could get the employer into trouble.

The global recession has also given reason to keep private an employee's credit history to avoid a barrier to employment. Eight states now limit use of credit history/information in hiring/employment: California; Connecticut; Hawaii; Illinois; Maryland; Oregon; Vermont; and Washington.

Another significant development in this area is enforcement activity following data breaches affecting personal information. In one recent matter, a health care agency agreed to pay $1.7 million to settle a government action under the Health Insurance Portability and Accountability Act (HIPAA) following the loss of a flash drive containing patient information. This and other activity emphasises businesses' need to safeguard employee and consumer personal information.

"Whistleblower" Anti-Retaliation Laws

The U.S. has a long legislative history of encouraging and protecting whistleblowers from adverse action, particularly with respect to their employment. Developing federal and state laws not only provide protection for employees, but in some instances, also provide rewards to whistleblowers and penalties for those who retaliate against them.

During the American Civil War, the U.S. firmly entrenched the role of whistleblowers in society and business with the passage of the False Claims Act. The False Claims Act remains significant today as it actively enlists private citizens to combat fraud against the government through the potential for financial rewards for information regarding fraudulent activity. The False Claims Act typically involves healthcare, military, or other federal government spending and prohibits a person or entity from knowingly presenting a fraudulent claim for payment or approval to the government, or from knowingly making, using or causing to be made a false record or statement to have a fraudulent claim paid or approved. An important provision, called "*qui tam*", allows private citizens to sue on behalf of the government and provides successful whistleblowers 15 to 30 percent of the government's monetary recovery from information the individual provided.

In recent years, a number of federal and state whistleblower statutes have been enacted, often in response to corporate scandals. For example, the Sarbanes-Oxley Act (SOX) was adopted in response to concerns about the financial reporting of publicly traded companies. Under SOX, employers are prohibited from retaliating against whistleblowers who provide evidence or information of fraud or violations of U.S. Securities and Exchange Commission (SEC) rules and regulations by publicly traded companies. Criminal sanctions may also be imposed against employers for SOX violations, and aggrieved whistleblowers may be entitled to significant damages, including reinstatement to their previous position.

In 2010, the U.S. Congress passed the Dodd-Frank Act, substantially expanding the government's authority to provide compensation to individuals who provide information concerning violations of federal securities laws that result in sanctions of over $1 million. Such awards can be 10 to 30 percent of the sanctions collected.

Many states have their own whistleblower statutes, such as the New Jersey Conscientious Employee Protection Act and the California False Claims Act. Such statutes typically provide remedies to employees who can demonstrate they engaged in protected activity that was known to their employer and suffered an adverse employment action as a result. In addition to statutory whistleblower protections, employees may also have a remedy for retaliatory discharge under common law, depending on the state.

Employers can proactively address the challenges created by whistleblower protections through Codes of Conduct, reporting mechanisms for suspected fraud, and procedures for thoroughly and effectively investigating complaints and preventing retaliation. Due consideration must be paid to conflicting legal obligations, such as the anonymous reporting mechanisms required by SOX and Dodd-Frank and the prohibition against anonymous reporting under certain European laws.

Labour Law

Recent government initiatives have created new labour relations challenges for U.S. employers and may make it easier for unions to organise workers. To what extent these changes will alter U.S. labour policy and how they will affect the decline in union membership rates over the past few decades may depend, to some extent, on the results of the 2012 presidential election.

As of 2011 (the latest statistic available), only 6.9 percent of the American private workforce was represented by a union. (The number becomes 11.8 percent when public employees are added.) The discussion below provides an overview of U.S. labour law and highlights some key developments. All employers should develop a strategic, integrated labour relations programme that takes into account its culture, business goals, and the labour relations landscape of all countries in which it operates.

A. The National Labor Relations Act

Enacted by Congress in 1935, the National Labor Relations Act (NLRA) gives employees the right to "self-organiz[e], to form, join, or assist labor organization, to bargain collectively through representatives of their own choosing, and to engage in other concerted activities for the purpose of collective bargaining or other mutual aid or protection, and the right to refrain from any or all of such activities….". Among other things, this means employees are protected by federal law in raising work-related complaints, and engaging in bargaining, strikes, picketing, union organising, and other "protected concerted activities". The NLRA also gives employers the right to express their views about union organising and bargaining so long as they do not interfere with, restrain, or coerce employees with respect to their exercise of rights protected by the Act. Such infringements on employees' rights constitute "unfair labour practices" under the Act; so, too, do certain union actions identified in the NLRA. The legal parameters for employer communications should be reviewed with counsel to ensure compliance.

Employers doing business in the U.S. should take note of the following attributes of U.S. labour law under the NLRA, which are significantly different from the law in other jurisdictions.

- Unless voluntarily recognised by an employer, labour unions generally gain the right to represent employees only after (1) a third of the employees first sign an "authorisation" card, and then (2) a majority of the employees vote in favour of the union in a secret ballot election. If elected, the union becomes the exclusive bargaining representative of all employees in the bargaining unit.

- Supervisors and managers are not covered by the NLRA, and, thus, do not have the legal right to form or be represented by a labour union.
- Employee participation groups can be problematic under the NLRA.

B. The National Labor Relations Board

The National Labor Relations Board (NLRB) is the federal agency responsible for administering and enforcing the NLRA. This is primarily accomplished through the adjudication of unfair labour practice charges (*i.e.,* determining what employer and union actions are and are not permissible under the law). The Board is also responsible for overseeing union elections and issuing bargaining orders, and has the authority to impose penalties on employers and unions. In addition, under the NLRA, the NLRB has the authority "to make, amend, and rescind...such rules and regulations as may be necessary to carry out the provisions" of the Act.

Though not required by law, by tradition, the political party of the current president typically enjoys a three-person majority of the five-member Board when it comes time to replace a Board member whose term is expiring. The president is also responsible for selecting the individual who serves as NLRB General Counsel. The General Counsel has significant power, including the sole authority to reverse any decision from regional NLRB offices dismissing unfair labour practice charges and the ultimate say in deciding whether or not to prosecute unfair labour practice charges.

Recent NLRB Initiatives

Recent NLRB decisions dealing with "protected concerted activity" expand employee rights and may call into question certain employer policies. These decisions affect unionised and non-unionised employers alike; they have been particularly significant in publicising an alternative for employees not represented by a union to contest employer policies and practices. Therefore, all workplace policies must be carefully reviewed. Some examples include the following:

- In *D.R. Horton, Inc. and Michael Cuda*, 357 NLRB 184 (Jan. 3, 2012), the Board held that requiring employees to agree to a class action waiver as a term and condition of employment violates the NLRA. (The NLRB decision does not restrict an employer's right to require arbitration of individual claims as long as the employee retains the right to pursue/join a collective/class action in a judicial forum.)
- The NLRB is taking a hard look at company social media policies, as employee communication through social media often involves "protected concerted activity".
- The NLRB has found that a number of common employer policies can constitute unfair labour practices, including, for example:

  - The Board has ruled that, if not carefully worded, broad, generic policies prohibiting "harassment" of co-workers may be "reasonably interpreted" as improperly prohibiting employees from partaking in protected concerted activity in violation of the NLRA.

  - The Board has held that some policies which prohibit employees from speaking to the media without prior authorisation are unlawful because they "chill" employees' statutory right to publicise their grievances.

In another decision entitled *Specialty Healthcare*, the Board significantly modified its approach to bargaining unit issues – effectively enabling unions to choose much smaller and more strategic units. As a result, employers could have multiple bargaining units, multiple unions, and multiple bargaining contracts.

Employee Benefits Laws

In the U.S., private employers commonly provide pension benefits and health and welfare benefits to their employees. In heavily unionised industries, these benefits are often provided pursuant to a collective bargaining agreement with contributions being made to a multi-employer plan associated with the union.

Pension benefits are not mandated, whereas beginning in 2014, employers with 50 or more full-time employees will be required to provide minimum health benefits or pay a penalty.

Pension plans and health and welfare plans are generally governed under two complementary sources of federal law: the Internal Revenue Code (the Tax Code); and the Employee Retirement Income Security Act (ERISA). The Tax Code sets forth the requirements to preserve favourable tax treatment for the employer (via tax deductions) and the employees (via determining when or if the benefits are to be treated as taxable income). The Tax Code includes various coverage and nondiscrimination rules intended to limit how much an employee benefit plan can favour highly compensated and key employees.

ERISA protects the rights of plan participants via rules relating to reporting and disclosure, claims and appeals, participation, vesting, benefit accrual, and plan funding, as well as other administrative activities. ERISA also provides the responsibilities of plan fiduciaries and limits the remedies available to plan participants (no consequential or punitive damages or other tort remedies). All state laws that relate to pension or welfare benefit plans are preempted by ERISA. However, ERISA does not preempt state laws relating to compensation, payroll practices, or insurance.

Deferred compensation plans for executives (which includes various arrangements beyond just salary and bonus deferrals) should be designed to either comply with, or meet an exception for, Section 409A of the Tax Code which generally governs the election, timing, and form of such payments. The consequences for failing to comply with Section 409A are borne by the employee (generally, current taxation, 20 percent excise tax, and interest).

Buying/Selling a Business, Plant Closings, & Layoffs

There are a number of labour, employment, and benefits-related issues that arise under U.S. law in the context of mergers, acquisitions, and other business transactions. It is best to consider these issues as part of the strategic decision whether to buy (or sell) a company, as well as when negotiating the purchase/sale agreement, completing due diligence review, and in planning the post-transaction transition.

As a general matter, in a stock purchase, the buyer typically inherits all of the seller's commitments to its employees, including its liability for any labour and employment violations, collective bargaining agreements, and benefits obligations. Even in an asset sale, however, the buyer may be considered a "successor" to the seller under certain circumstances, and thus held to many of the seller's obligations. For example, a business that provides essentially the same services to the same customers and continues with the same employees doing the same jobs under the same working conditions and supervision is more likely to be considered a successor.

In the labour context, the buyer could be bound by the seller's union bargaining obligation and/or the specific collective bargaining agreements. Such obligations might restrict a purchaser's ability to establish initial terms and conditions of employment based on the structure of the transaction, or other statements or actions by the purchaser. The purchaser also may be responsible for pending unfair labour practice charges against the seller.

In the employment context, the buyer in a transaction could be bound by the seller's existing oral or written employment, stay, golden parachute, and other agreements. U.S. courts have required successor employers to defend employment discrimination complaints and related litigation, as well as wage and hour lawsuits filed against the predecessor. Buyers also could be held responsible for their predecessors' health and safety-related issues, as well as non-compliance with immigration requirements, particularly when a company gains employees through a stock purchase and relies upon the predecessor's immigration paperwork.

Similarly, in the benefits context, buyers in a stock purchase could be bound by the seller's pension, profit-sharing, health and welfare, termination, and other benefit programmes. This could also result in potential liability for underfunded defined benefit pension plans and withdrawal liability when purchasing a company that participates in a multi-employer pension plan.

With this in mind, it is important to plan ahead and review existing labour, employment, and benefits commitments when making strategic determinations regarding the structure of a corporate transaction.

A Note on Plant Closings and Layoffs

When dealing with plant closings and/or mass layoffs (including those resulting from corporate transactions), employers must consider such issues as the business reason for the closure/layoff and whether planned terminations will have a disproportionate effect on a particular category of workers within a protected classification. Under the disparate impact theory of employment discrimination, an employee may challenge an employer's policy or practice that appears neutral on its face but disproportionately affects a protected group in application. After making initial termination decisions, therefore, employers should conduct a "disparate impact analysis". If a disparate impact exists on the basis of gender, race, or another characteristic protected under the U.S. laws, an employer should evaluate whether selection can be justified by business necessity, or in the case of older workers, by reasonable factors other than age. If not, an employer will be able to consider alternative selections before announcement in order to minimise potential liability.

Employers should also keep in mind that the Worker Adjustment and Retraining Notification Act (WARN) and similar state/local statutory schemes require covered employers to provide notice in advance of covered plant closings and mass layoffs to the affected workers or their representatives, as well as other entities specified in the statute. The Act's advance notification obligations also may be triggered simply by transferring employees from one payroll to another. Some states and cities have similar local advance notice requirements. There also are benefits considerations (such as employee right to benefits continuation) under the Consolidated Omnibus Budget Reconciliation Act (COBRA). Therefore, advance planning on key issues becomes important.

Trends and the Year Ahead

A. Anti-Discrimination Laws

The EEOC received a record number of private sector discrimination charges in FY 2011, the most frequent of which alleged race discrimination, retaliation, and sex discrimination. In addition to these administrative charges, the EEOC has been pursuing cases involving potential "systemic discrimination", which the EEOC defines as "a pattern or practice, policy, or class case where the alleged discrimination has a broad impact on an industry, profession, company or geographic area". Some examples of recent cases involve pre-employment background checks that the EEOC believes have a disproportionate impact on protected groups and inflexible leave policies that the EEOC maintains discriminate against certain disabled employees. Discrimination claims will continue to be a major concern for U.S. employers, particularly in light of the EEOC's systemic discrimination initiative and other large-scale class actions involving allegations of systemic discrimination.

B. Leaves of Absence

The EEOC has been aggressively pursuing employer leave policies that automatically terminate employees after exhausting all available leave provided by law or company policy. In the EEOC's view, such individuals may still be "qualified individuals with disabilities" entitled to additional leave time as an ADA reasonable accommodation. In many cases, the EEOC's challenges come with allegations of systemic discrimination against a class of individuals and have resulted in settlements in the millions of dollars. Contemporaneous with this targeted enforcement effort, employees are filing ADA charges with the EEOC at a record pace. In 2011, there was an almost 36 per cent increase from the previous year in monetary relief obtained by the EEOC on behalf of individuals who filed disability discrimination charges with the agency. At the same time, the recent amendments to the ADA make it easier for plaintiffs to sue employers in court, as many more physical and mental conditions are now considered disabilities under the law. Within this legal framework, U.S. employers must routinely evaluate their leave management protocols and individually assess all requests for leave.

C. Wage-Hour and Working Conditions Laws

On the regulatory front, the main initiative from the U.S. Department of Labor's Wage and Hour Division is the rulemaking proceeding intended to limit substantially the scope of the companionship services exemption, which currently exempts from the overtime and minimum wage provisions of the FLSA home healthcare workers paid not by patients or their families but instead by third parties such as insurers or healthcare plans. There are currently efforts in Congress underway to block this rulemaking and to preserve the current scope of the exemption.

With regard to enforcement, the U.S. Department of Labor is currently focusing heavily on independent contractor misclassification, prevailing wages on federal government contracts, off-the-clock work in car washes, and wage practices generally in the residential construction industry, janitorial companies, healthcare facilities, and hotels and motels.

D. Privacy Laws

Managing data and keeping it private and secure will continue to be critical challenges for companies in the decades ahead. For example, the coordination of various international privacy standards, such as the EU Privacy Directives and the APEC Privacy Framework, with local and industry standards, such as under HIPAA and state law mandates, will need to be addressed as businesses continue to grow internationally. The explosion of social media, biometrics, and other technologies, and the more effective utilisation of data analytics, will undoubtedly raise issues for companies not only concerning their customers and their competition, but also in connection with attracting, encouraging, managing, and retaining productive workforces. Indeed, global businesses need to be mindful of these developments, while also being sensitive to the local customs and practices concerning privacy rights and expectations.

E. Labour Law

The NLRB approved two new rules in 2011 that, if upheld by the courts, could make it easier for unions to organise workers.

First, the NLRB's Notice posting rule would require private sector employers – both those with and without unions – to post an official government Notice advising employees of their legal rights under the NLRA, including the right to unionise and/or engage in strikes, picketing and other protected concerted activity. The Notice also provides instructions for employees on how they can file charges against an employer and offers contact information for the NLRB. The Board's authority to issue such a ruling is currently subject to debate in federal court. If the Court rules that the NLRB has authority to require the Notice posting, employers will have to post the Notice where other employment notices are customarily posted, as well as on a company's "intranet or internet site if the employer customarily communicates with its employees about personnel rules or policies by such means". If upheld, a legal compliance programme is recommended.

Second, at the end of 2011, the NLRB published a final rule amending its union election process. The "quickie election" rule, which was scheduled to take effect on April 30, 2012, would significantly change the NLRB election process and limit an employer's opportunities to challenge the process before an election is held. The rule would also shorten the time period before an election, thus limiting an employer's opportunity to communicate with its employees over key issues before a vote is taken. A federal court in Washington, D.C. recently invalidated the Board rule because only two members of the Board, instead of the three needed to make up a Board quorum, participated in the final vote to pass it. While the court decision is being challenged, the Board also can re-issue the rule by voting on it now. Therefore, employers should be ready in case the rule is upheld on appeal or re-issued.

Regardless of whether these two rules take effect in 2012 or beyond, the current Board is taking an aggressive stance on many employer policies. Therefore, key executive and management education training is important to ensure compliance. To what extent this trend continues depends in part on which political party prevails in the 2012 election, as the next president will have the power to influence the composition of the Board when individual members' terms expire.

Peter R. Bulmer
Tel: +1 312 787 4949 / Email: BulmerP@jacksonlewis.com

Peter R. Bulmer is a Partner in the Chicago, Illinois office of Jackson Lewis LLP. Mr Bulmer represents management nationwide in all facets of employment and labour law. He counsels management on employment matters and preventive measures to avoid litigation and, where litigation cannot be avoided, he defends employers before state and federal administrative agencies and courts. He also represents employers in prosecuting and defending claims of unlawful competition.

Mr Bulmer has been named one of Illinois' "Super Lawyers," a distinction accorded no more than 5% of Illinois lawyers, and has been selected for inclusion in Best Lawyers in America. He is also Martindale-Hubbell AV Preeminent rated ("highest level of professional excellence").

Francis P. Alvarez
Tel: +1 914 328 0404 / Email: AlvarezF@jacksonlewis.com

Francis P. (Frank) Alvarez is a Partner in the White Plains, New York office of Jackson Lewis. Mr Alvarez is the national coordinator of Jackson Lewis' Disability, Leave and Health Management Practice Group, which assists employers in meeting the legal and practical challenges posed by federal and state laws protecting injured and ill employees. Counselling hundreds of employers each year, Mr Alvarez spearheads the firm's effort to provide imaginative and creative solutions to the complex array of workplace disability and health management issues faced by both large and small companies. In the Jackson Lewis tradition, Mr Alvarez counsels clients with the goal of either avoiding litigation entirely or improving outcomes before administrative agencies, courts and juries.

Philip B. Rosen
Tel: +1 212 545 4001 / Email: RosenP@jacksonlewis.com

Philip B. Rosen is a Partner in the New York office of Jackson Lewis LLP and leads the firm's Labor Practice Group. He joined the Firm in 1979 and served as Managing Partner of the New York City office from 1989 to 2009. He is also a member of the firm's Management Committee. Mr Rosen lectures extensively, conducts management training, and advises clients with respect to legislative and regulatory initiatives, corporate strategies, business ethics, reorganisations and reductions-in-force, purchase/sale transactions, sexual harassment and other workplace conduct rules, compliance with the Americans With Disabilities Act, wrongful discharge and other workplace litigation, corporate campaigns and union organising matters, collective bargaining, arbitration and National Labor Relations Board proceedings.

Jackson Lewis LLP

150 North Michigan Avenue, Suite 2500, Chicago, IL 60601, USA
Tel: +1 312 787 4949 / Fax: +1 312 787 4995 / URL: http://www.jacksonlewis.com

Venezuela

Juan Carlos Varela
Littler Mendelson

General Summary of the Labour Regulations in Venezuela

The following summary comprises the main labour provisions under the Organic Labour Law ("OLL") and other Venezuelan labour and social laws.

I. Labour benefits and rights provided under Venezuelan Labour Laws

Minimum wage

Salaries and/or wages are freely negotiable between the employers and employees as a general labour principle. However, the OLL establishes that salaries and wages may not be set under the minimum wage level determined by the corresponding authority. The minimum wage is periodically adjusted by the government. The current minimum wage is Bs. 1,780.44 per month, effective from May 1st, 2012. On September 1st, 2012 it will be increased to Bs. 2,047.51 per month.

Vacation and vacation bonus

According to the OLL, the employees are entitled to enjoy fifteen (15) working days of paid vacations upon the completion of one (1) uninterrupted year of service, plus one (1) additional working day for each subsequent uninterrupted year of service, up to fifteen (15) additional working days.

Additionally, employees are entitled to receive payment, when enjoying vacations, of a vacation bonus equivalent to fifteen (15) days' salary upon completion of the first uninterrupted year of service, plus one (1) additional day of salary for each subsequent year of service, up to a maximum of thirty (30) days of salary.

Vacation payments must be made upon the basis of the normal salary, which is the salary earned by the employee on a regular and permanent basis.

Profit sharing

The OLL establishes a duty to employers of distributing among their employees fifteen per cent (15%) of their annual net income. Within the limits mentioned below, employers must distribute said percentage of net profits, determined on the basis of their income tax return.

Employees are entitled to receive the annual profit sharing payment (*utilidades*) in an amount of not less than fifteen (15) days of salary and not more than four (4) months' salary.

This benefit must be paid within two (2) months following the end of the company's fiscal year. It is mandatory to make an advance payment of this benefit equivalent to at least fifteen (15) days' salary, before December 15th of each year. Profit sharing is paid in direct proportion to the number of full months of service rendered and based on the salary earned by each employee during the given fiscal year.

Paid holidays and mandatory weekly rest

According to the OLL, the following dates are considered as holidays: Sundays, January 1st, Maundy Thursday and Good Friday, May 1st, December 24th, 25th and 31st; the dates listed in the Law of National Holidays, including April 19th, June 24th, July 5th, July 24th and October 12th; and those days declared holidays by either the National Government, or the State or Municipal authorities, up to a maximum of three (3) days per year.

It is a Constitutional right that the employees enjoy weekly rest days. The holidays and the obligatory weekly rest days are compensated by the payment of one (1) day's salary. When a monthly fixed salary has been agreed upon, the payment of holidays and rest days are already included in the salary.

When an employee works on his/her mandatory weekly rest day, the employer must pay the work performed with a surcharge of fifty percent (50%). Should the work be performed for four (4) or more hours, the employer must pay a complete day of salary, and if it is for less than four (4) hours, a half day salary payment must be made. When working during the mandatory weekly rest day, a compensatory rest day must be given within the following week.

Overtime

The daily workday is limited to eight (8) hours, and the weekly work hours must not exceed forty (40) hours. The night workday is limited to seven (7) hours daily and to thirty-five (35) hours in a week. Work performed during night hours (from 7pm to 5am) must be compensated with a surcharge of thirty per cent (30%) over the day's work payment.

Overtime work is compensated with a fifty percent (50%) surcharge. No employee may work more than ten (10) hours of overtime weekly, or more than one hundred (100) hours in a year. In unforeseeable and urgent circumstances, overtime may be worked without the prior permission of the Labour Inspector, provided that notice is given to the Labour Inspector on the following working day explaining the reasons for the overtime work performed.

Paid maternity and paternity leave

Women are entitled to maternity leave of six (6) weeks prior to giving birth and twenty (20) weeks thereafter. The post-natal leave can be extended in case of illness. Employees may not be dismissed without cause during the entire pregnancy and until two (2) years after giving birth (both the father and the mother).

Initial education centre for employees' children

Employers with more than 20 employees are required to provide day-care service for their employees' children from three to up to six (6) years of age. To comply with this requirement, employers may choose among: (i) providing a day-care centre for its employees' children directly or through a non-profit civil association established by the employer; (ii) establishing a joint child-care centre with one (1) or more employers operating in the same area either directly or through a non-profit civil association; or (iii) paying the cost of an approved private or public day-care centre located near the residence of the employees, with a maximum tuition and monthly fee of forty percent (40%) of the minimum wage. Payments are made directly to the institution providing child care and are not deemed part of the employee's salary.

Food

According to the Feeding Law for Employees, employers are obliged to provide healthy food during the workday, during vacation, leaves of absence, and any absence not attributable to the employee.

This benefit may be granted through coupons or electronic debt cards, in which case the value of the benefit may not be less than 0.25 Tax Units nor exceed 0.50 Tax Units per day worked. This benefit is not deemed part of the employee's salary.

Health and safety

The employer must provide a safe environment for work. Failure to comply with obligations set forth in the Organic Law on Prevention, Conditions and Environment of Work ("LOPCYMAT") may subject the employer to severe penalties and the employer's representative to criminal liability.

LOPCYMAT also establishes penalties to employers who do not assure that employees enjoy their vacation, take their daily rest, or breach the provisions related to maximum duration of daily work shifts and night surcharges. These situations are considered as very serious infractions and employers may be subject to fines of between 76 and to 100 Tax Units (currently, from Bs. 5,776.00 to Bs. 7,600.00) *per* affected employee.

II. Severance payment

According to Article 142 of the OLL, severance payment is equivalent to thirty (30) days of salary per year of service or a fraction higher than six (6) months. To that amount, the employer can deduct the amount received by the employee during the employment relationship as advances to the severance.

During the employment relationship, the employee is entitled to receive fifteen (15) days of salary each quarter. This payment must be calculated based upon the salary earned by the employee in the corresponding month (at the end of the quarter). The employee may elect whether this seniority payment is deposited in an individual trust, on the employer's books or in a public fund.

In addition, starting from the second year of service, the employer must pay two (2) days' salary for each year up to a maximum of thirty (30) additional days.

Employees may request advances of up to seventy five percent (75%) of the amount credited or deposited to meet obligations arising from: (i) the construction, purchase, improvement or repair of his family residence; (ii) the cancellation of mortgages or any other loan on the family residence; (iii) educational expenses for himself, his spouse, his children, or common-law spouse; and (iv) medical and hospitalisation expenses of any of the people listed in the preceding item.

System applicable in the case of an unjustified dismissal

Should employment end because of an unjustified dismissal, the employee is entitled to receive an additional amount equivalent to the severance payment explained above.

The labour law contains a series of provisions designed to promote employment stability. Therefore, as a matter of general policy, dismissed workers have the right to petition for reinstatement in special "Labour Stability Courts". These courts are empowered to order the reinstatement of a worker if they deem that the worker's dismissal has been unjustified.

The employer cannot dismiss the employee without cause unless the employee accepts the payment of the indemnity for unfair dismissal.

Bar against dismissal

There is a special bar against dismissals (*inamovilidad*) for all employees with the exception of the management employees. Employees protected by *inamovilidad* cannot be dismissed without a justified cause. In order to dismiss these employees with cause, employers must previously obtain an authorisation from the Labour Inspector, for which purposes an administrative procedure must be filed.

There are other reasons under which employees are protected by the *inamovilidad*, such as: pregnant women (during pregnancy and two years after giving birth); fathers of a child (during pregnancy and two years after giving birth); and members of the board of Unions, Health and Safety Committee Members, constitution of Health and Safety Committee, among others.

III. Mandatory employer's contributions and withholding obligations

Social Security contributions

Both employers and employees must contribute monthly to the Venezuelan Social Security Institute ("IVSS"). The employer is required to withhold and pay the employee's contributions. All contributions are computed as a percentage of the employee's normal salary up to a maximum of five (5) minimum monthly salaries.

Employees are obliged to contribute 4% of their salary, and employers between 9% and 11%, according to the occupational risk the law assigns to the employer's business. Companies must register with the IVSS within three (3) working days of beginning activities and must also register all their employees within three (3) working days after their hiring.

According to LOPCYMAT, these contributions shall remain in force until the National Treasury of the Social Security System is created. After its creation, employer's contributions will vary from 0.75% to 10% of employees' salaries, depending on the risk and classification of the employer's business, to be determined by the Regulations to the LOPCYMAT.

Employment

Contributions to IVSS for Employment Regime (previously named *Paro Forzoso)* are also calculated based upon the employee's monthly salary. Employers must contribute an amount equal to 2% of the employee's normal salary and must withhold the employee's contribution, which is 0.5%. The maximum taxable base for these purposes is ten (10) minimum monthly salaries.

Housing and Habitat Regime

Employers' contributions to housing funds (previously named *Politica Habitacional)* are equivalent to 2% of the employee's broad salary and the employee's contribution (which must be withheld by employer) is equivalent to 1% of their salary. There is no cap to this contribution.

INCES contributions

Employers with more than five (5) employees must contribute to the National Institute of Training and Socialist Education ("INCES") with 2% of the normal salary paid to their personnel. Employees' contributions are 0.5% of the profit sharing received, which must be withheld by employer.

Employers with fifteen (15) or more employees are also obliged to employ and train INCES apprentices between fourteen (14) and seventeen (17) years of age.

Juan Carlos Varela
Tel: +58 212 610 5450 / Email: JCVarela@littler.com
Mr. Varela is the Office Managing Shareholder of Littler's Caracas, Venezuela office. He also spends time in Miami in supporting the interests of clients in Venezuela and the entire Latin America region. He focuses his practice on traditional labour and employment matters in the Latin American region. Prior joining Littler he was in charge of the Latin American practice in Squire Sanders & Dempsey. He was also a partner at Baker & McKenzie.

He is actively involved in the firm's International Employment and Labour Law practice group. He was noted for his labour expertise in the most recent editions of LatinLawyer 250, Chambers Latin America and The Best Lawyers in Venezuela.

Mr. Varela also advises on employment planning and structuring of employee compensation packages, rewards and merits. He designs and implements employment structures for expatriates and conducts labour audits in different countries.

In addition, Mr. Varela assists in the determination of labour benefits for termination of employment, counsels in mass layoff processes and represents employers in labour trials and labour administrative claims.

Mr. Varela is a labour law professor at the Universidad Católica Andrés Bello. He has written numerous articles on labour-related issues and is regarded as one of the best labour lawyers in Venezuela.

Littler Mendelson

Avenida Blandin, Centro San Ignacio, Torre Kepler, Piso 9, Ofic 9-2, La Castellana, Caracas 1060, Venezuela
Tel: +58 212 610 5450 / Fax: +58 212 951 4182 / URL: http://www.littler.com